15 minute Painting

EFFORTLESS WATERCOLOR

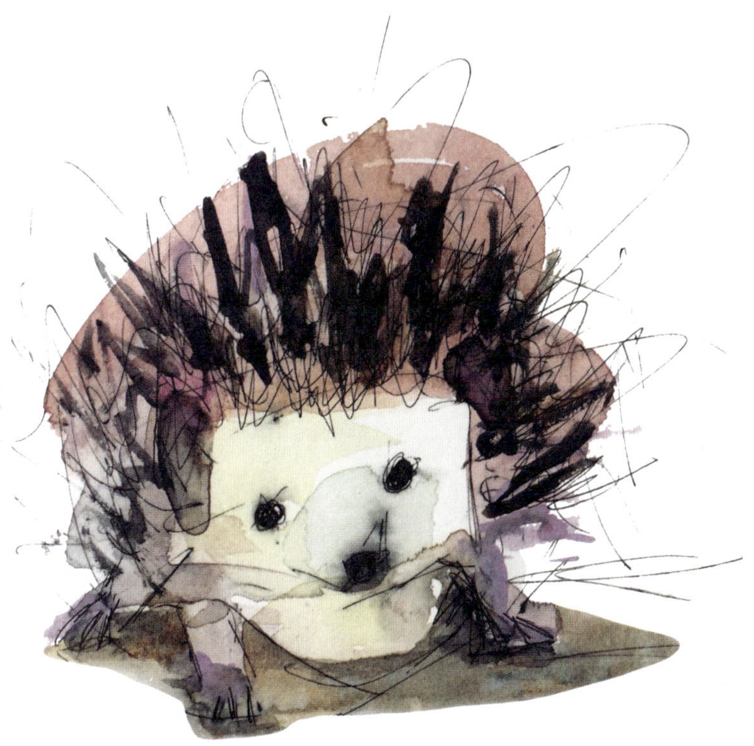

Angela Moulton

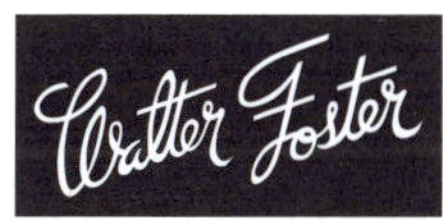

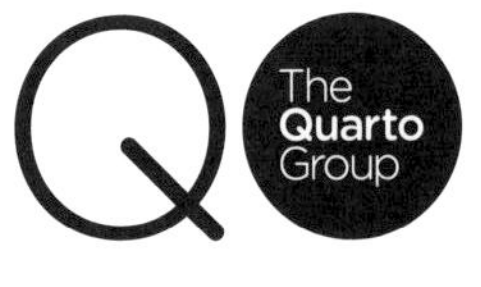

Brimming with creative inspiration, how-to projects, and useful information to enrich your everyday life, quarto.com is a favorite destination for those pursuing their interests and passions.

First published in 2022 by Walter Foster Publishing, an imprint of The Quarto Group.
100 Cummings Center, Suite 265D, Beverly, MA 01915, USA.
T (978) 282-9590 **F** (978) 283-2742 **www.quarto.com • www.walterfoster.com**

Walter Foster Publishing titles are also available at discount for retail, wholesale, promotional, and bulk purchase. For details, contact the Special Sales Manager by email at specialsales@quarto.com or by mail at The Quarto Group, Attn: Special Sales Manager, 100 Cummings Center, Suite 265D, Beverly, MA 01915, USA.

ISBN: 978-1-60058-924-9

Digital edition published in 2022
eISBN: 978-1-60058-925-6

Printed in China
10 9 8 7 6 5 4 3 2 1

TABLE OF CONTENTS

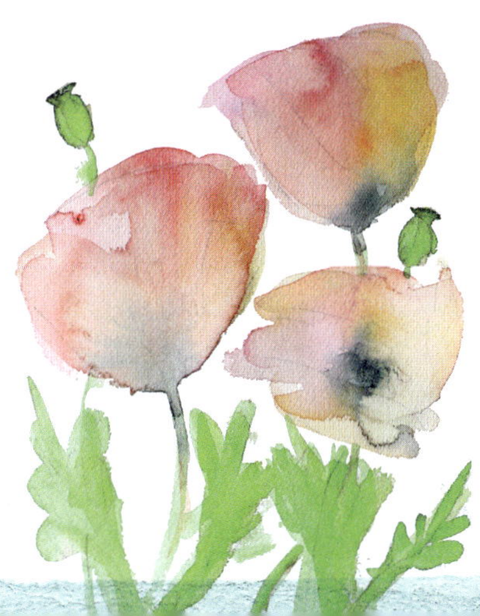

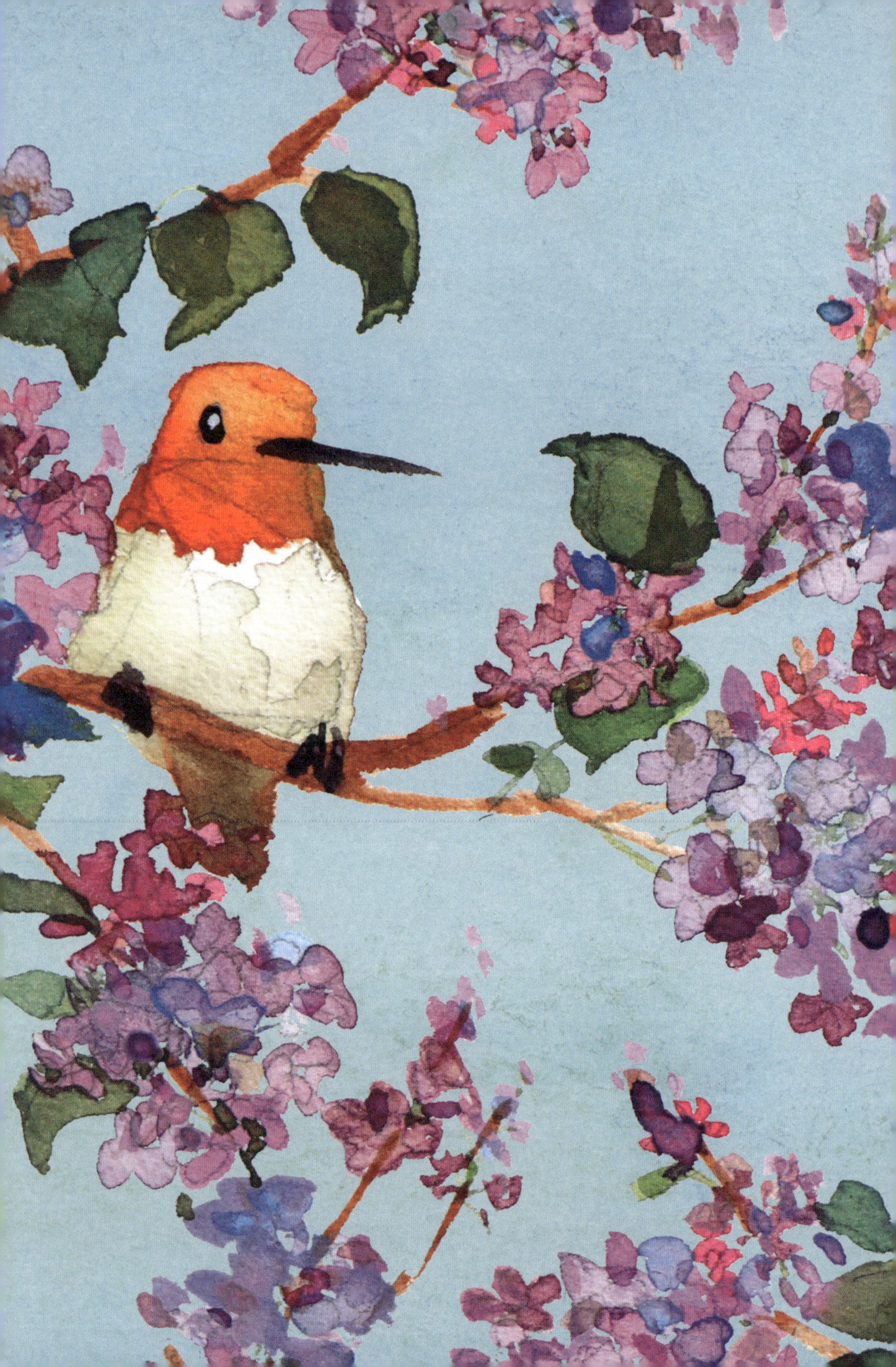

Getting Started

While many people may feel inspired to paint with watercolor, the challenge is finding the time to make it happen. This book will help you get started using approachable projects that can be completed in just 15 minutes. Of course, you may take more time, but you should be able to complete each project in one sitting.

But remember, there are no hard and fast rules. You are in charge. You are in control. Sometimes all one needs is a little nudge. And now, you are off and running!

Tools & Materials

One of the keys to quick painting is to have your supplies gathered and ready to go before you begin. Organization and cleanliness are important for a pleasant and joyful experience. The following pages include some tips for creating the perfect environment for effortless watercolor painting.

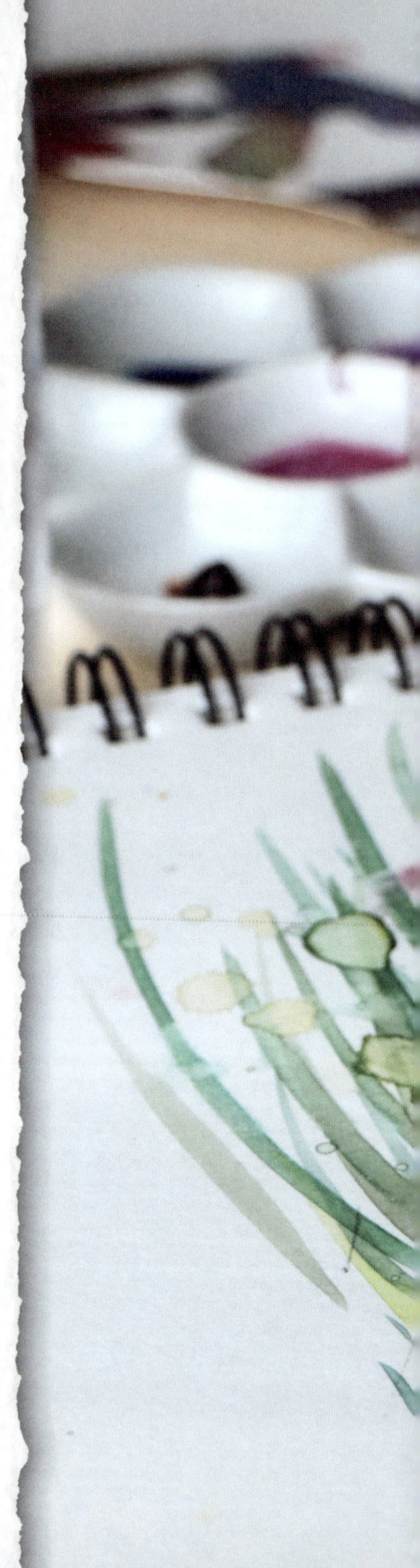

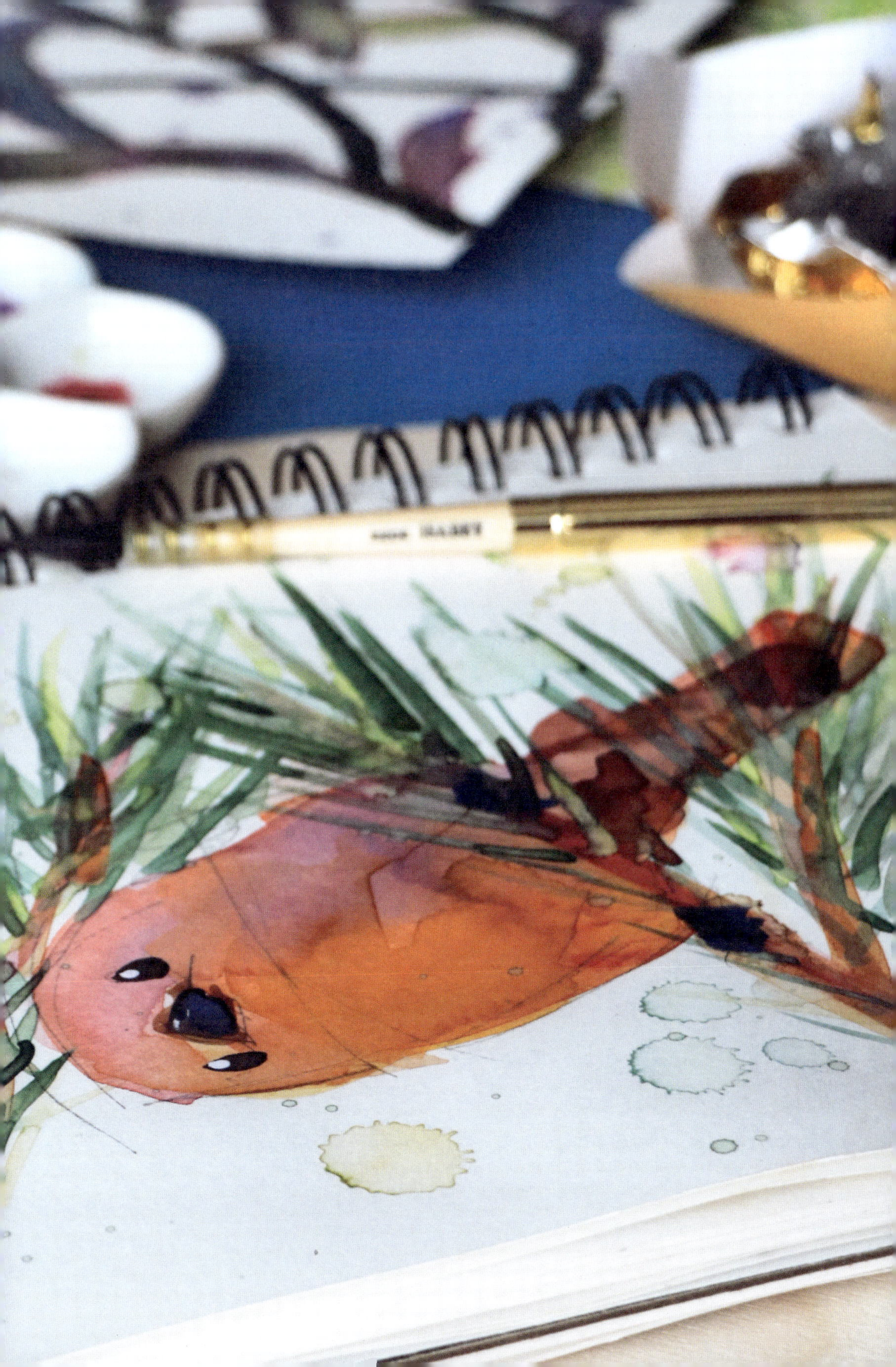

SURFACES

In this book, the projects are painted on watercolor paper. There are other options, such as watercolor panels and stretched canvas; however, we will concentrate on using watercolor paper. Watercolor papers come in different weights, sizes, and textures. They also come in different formats, such as sketchbooks, blocks, or loose sheets and rolls.

Paper weight is usually measured in pounds. The heavier the weight, the thicker the paper. A heavier paper is a good choice when using lots of washes of paint. Thinner or lighter-weight papers are usually the smoothest papers. They are more likely to buckle and ripple with large amounts of water. Thinner papers may need to be taped down or stretched.

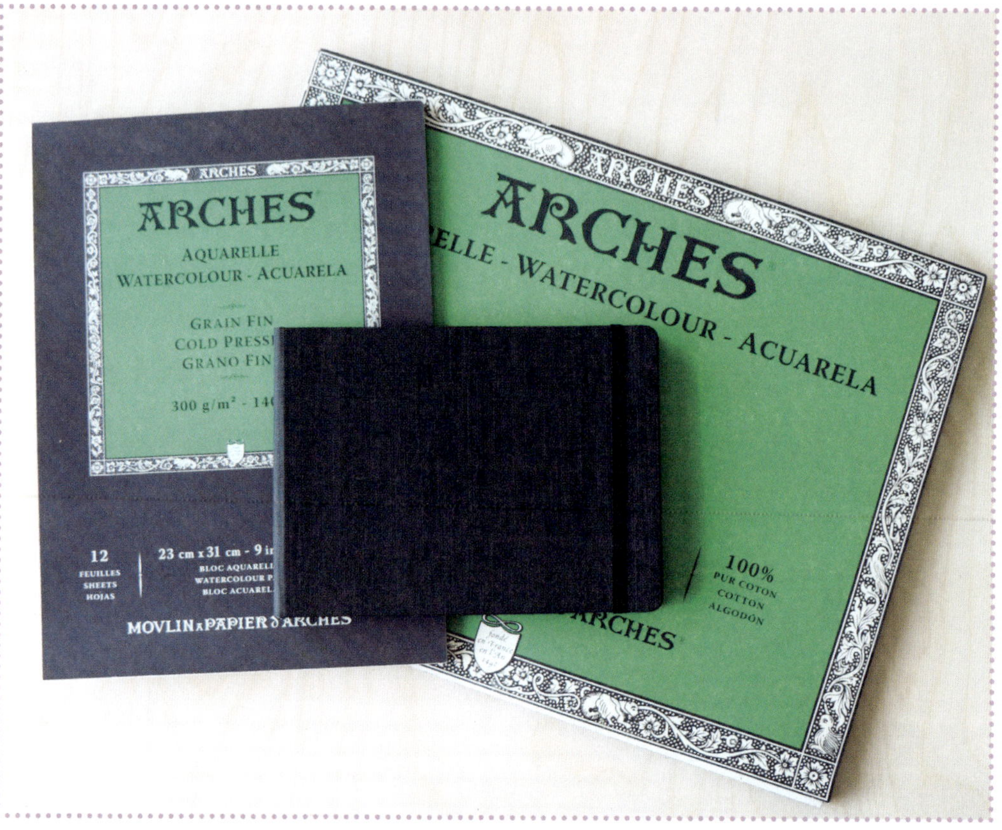

WATERCOLOR BLOCKS

Watercolor blocks are pads that are bound on all four sides, which prevents the paper from buckling. Once the painting is dry, insert a flat palette knife under the top sheet of paper and gently slide along the edges to remove it from the block.

SKETCHBOOKS & PADS

A watercolor sketchbook is portable and great for painting on-the-go. Because the paper is not taped or fastened on the edges, the paper can only take small amounts of paint. Otherwise, the pages may ripple or curl at the edges.

Watercolor pads are similar to sketchbooks as they are fastened at one end. Like a sketchbook, smaller-sized pads are great for traveling or outdoor painting.

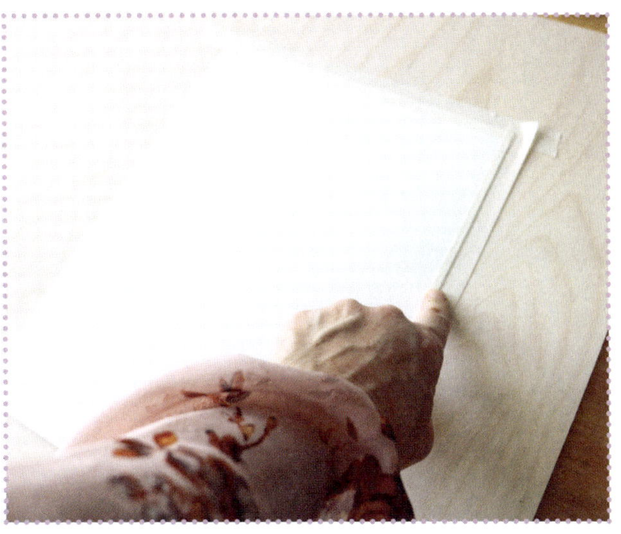

Use your finger to remove air bubbles and prevent seepage.

WATERCOLOR PAPER

Loose watercolor paper sheets should be taped down to prevent rippling. I use a maple plywood board as my support. Maple and birch plywood are great because they can absorb large quantities of water without warping. You can use washi tape, masking tape, or paper kraft tape to attach the paper to your support.

Some other support options are watercolor panels, rolls, and canvas. If you want to explore more options for painting surfaces, these are great places to start.

Tape along all four sides to secure the paper to the watercolor board.

PAPER TEXTURE

Watercolor paper comes in different textures. The size and type of artwork, as well as the amount of washes of paint, should determine what kind of paper to use.

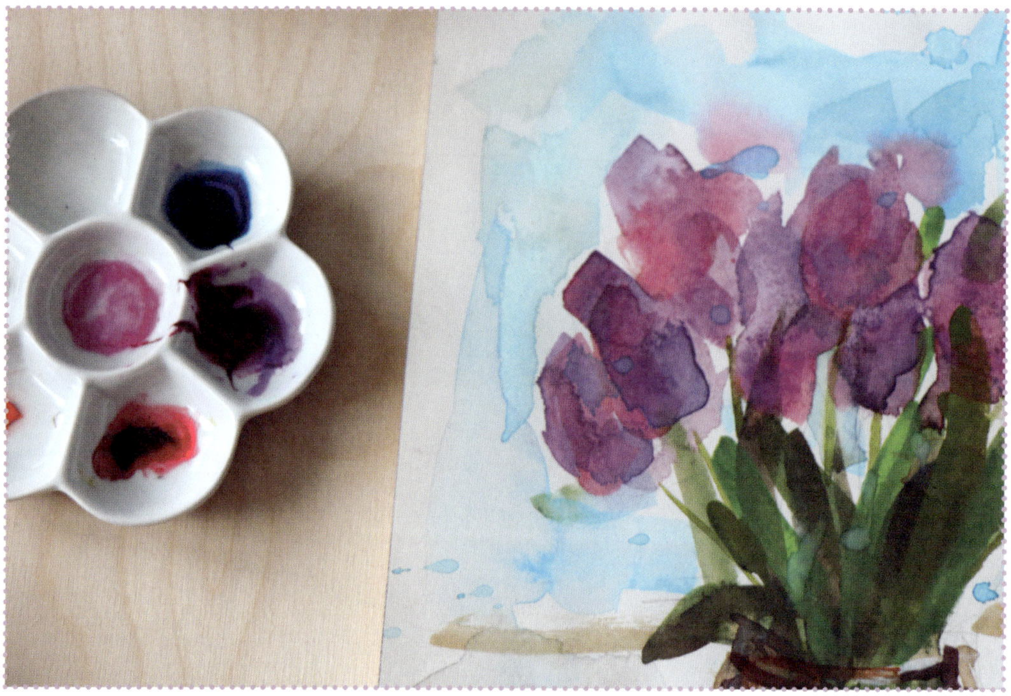

Hot-pressed paper is very smooth and usually lighter in weight than cold-pressed paper. The paper has been pressed with heat, resulting in a smooth surface. Hot-pressed paper is suitable for smaller works, fine-detailed work, and especially portraits. I say "smaller" works because it is thinner and more likely to buckle, but it can be stretched for larger sizes.

Quick Tip

Paper weight is usually measured in pounds. The heavier the weight, the thicker the paper. A heavier paper is a good choice when using multiple washes of paint.

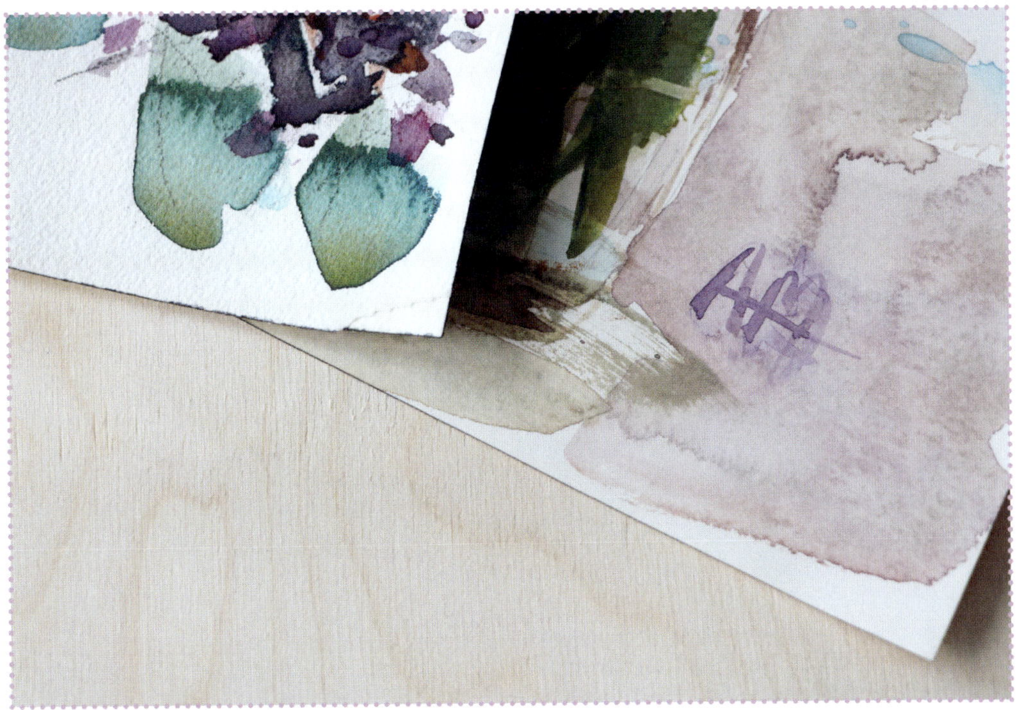

Cold-pressed paper has a rougher texture and is heavier than hot-pressed paper. There is a definite tooth to the paper that absorbs more paint and water. Cold-pressed paper is suitable for many types of artwork, from landscapes to figures. I think it is the most adaptable of all the watercolor papers.

Rough paper is the roughest paper, with a definite and pronounced tooth. It is great for large washes of paint and for landscapes where a rough texture adds depth to the foliage and atmosphere.

Stretching watercolor paper involves completely immersing it in water (usually in a tub of water), and then laying it flat on the plywood board and fastening with a paper tape. The paper shrinks as it dries and is "stretched."

Once completely dry, remove the paper with a straight-edge blade like a box cutter, a retractable knife, or an X-Acto knife. This process is a little time-consuming, but you are welcome to challenge yourself by using this technique.

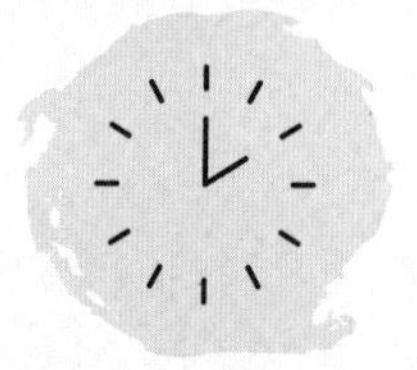

Quick Tip

Round brushes have a slightly different formula for measurement, as the measurement is based on the circumference. For this book, don't worry too much about brush size. Just use your eyes to judge which sizes you want to work with. Almost any small or medium brushes will be suitable.

BRUSHES

Watercolor brushes are made especially for use with watercolor paints. They come in both natural and synthetic bristle. The handle is usually either wood or metal. Brushes can be super soft or stiff and coarse. Brush handles can be long or short.

The brush is made up of a handle; the metal ferrule, which is crimped where the bristles are fastened; then the heel (closest to the metal ferrule), belly, and toe (tip) of the brush.

Brushes come in many different shapes and sizes. Sizes are numbered from 20/0 to 30+. There are a few rare specialty brushes finer or larger than these, but above are the most common sizes. In general, medium and smaller brushes are good for these projects because they are easy to use and adaptable to all the projects. I suggest a smaller brush for detail work and medium brush or two for larger and broader strokes.

Small and extra-small brushes are great for detail work. Medium brushes are adaptable for most items painted in this book. Large brushes are used for preparing large areas with washes of color. Long handles are great for working on large projects or on an upright easel. Short handles are good for smaller projects, detail work, and working on a flat surface.

BRUSH SIZE	IMPERIAL	METRIC
9	9/32"	7.2 mm
10	10/32"	8.0 mm
12	12/32"	9.5 mm
14	1/2"	12.7 mm

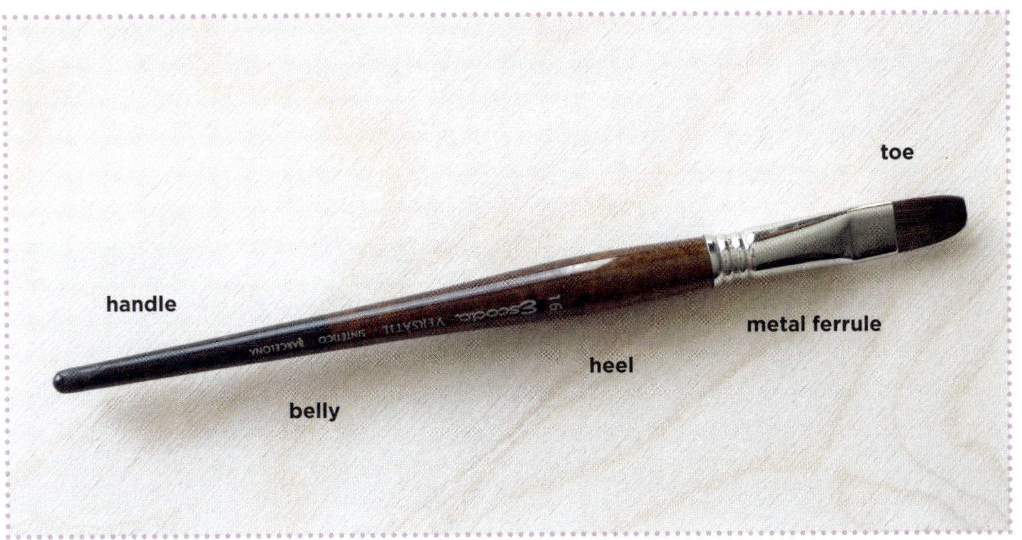

BRUSH SHAPES

Watercolor paint brushes come in flat, bright, round, liner, mottler, fan, filbert, and other shapes. For this book, you really only need a couple of flat or bright brushes and a small round brush.

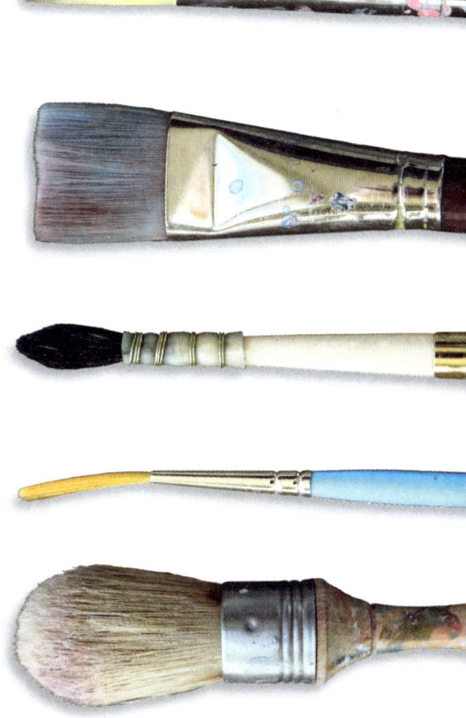

Flat brushes are flat and wide with an even tip. They are great for large washes of paint. The thin edge is good for painting straight edges and for some detail work.

Bright brushes are similar to flat brushes but are shorter in length. They are good for more detailed and controlled work and for loading large amounts of paint onto an area of your painting.

Round brushes are round in shape at the ferrule, usually with a pointed tip. They are great for washes of paint and detail work.

Liner brushes are round in shape with longer bristles. The liner brush is great for long lines and hand lettering.

Mop brushes are round in shape with a thick bunch of bristles. This brush is appropriate for large washes of color.

Paints

Pan sets are affordable and easy for starting out with watercolor painting. You may remember the classic tempura pan painting set from elementary school. It usually comes with its own brush and a lid with water wells for mixing paints.

Artist-grade pan sets are similar in that they usually include a preselected set of paint colors. Sometimes they include a brush or watercolor pen brush. Some professional watercolor pan sets are sold with optional individual pans so you can customize the colors within the set.

Watercolor paints come in both tubes and pans. Both are used in this book; however, pan sets can be used for all of the projects, if preferred.

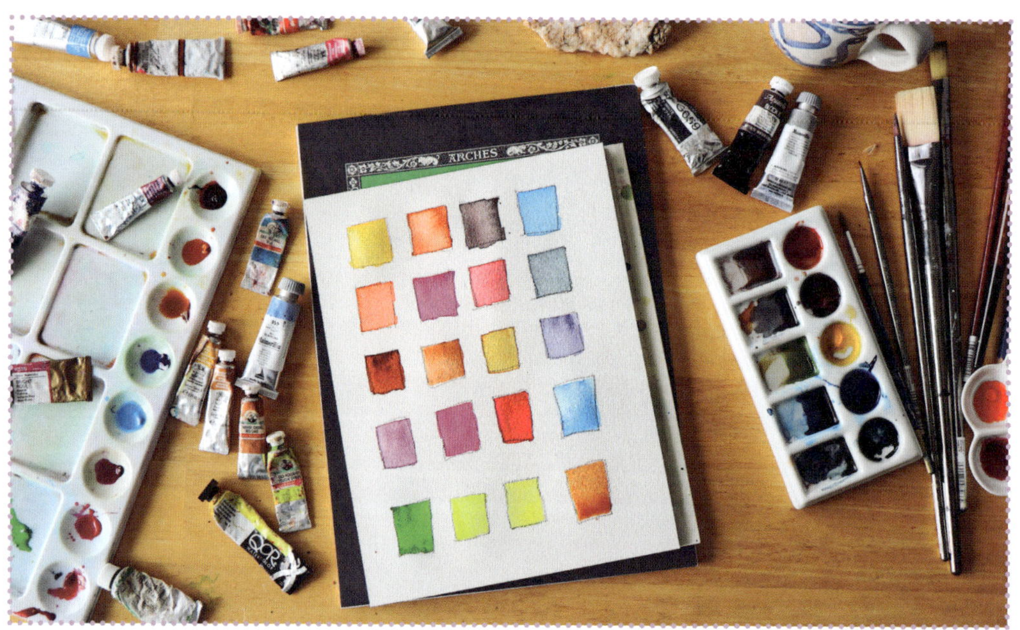

Mix tube paints with water on a palette to create and mix your own colors. If using tubes, as much or as little paint can be used, as desired. Additionally, there are many more color options than found in a ready-made pan set.

PALETTES

Watercolor palettes come in many different shapes and sizes. There are plastic, acrylic, enameled metal, and ceramic watercolor palettes. I prefer using plastic or ceramic palettes. The palette you choose should have enough wells for both setting up your colors and for mixing colors.

Plastic palettes are lighter weight and low cost. I find ceramic palettes look nicer and are easier to clean. The paint seems to slide off easily without staining. Ceramic palettes are sturdier but heavier. If traveling, I use plastic palettes because they are lightweight, flexible, and less likely to break.

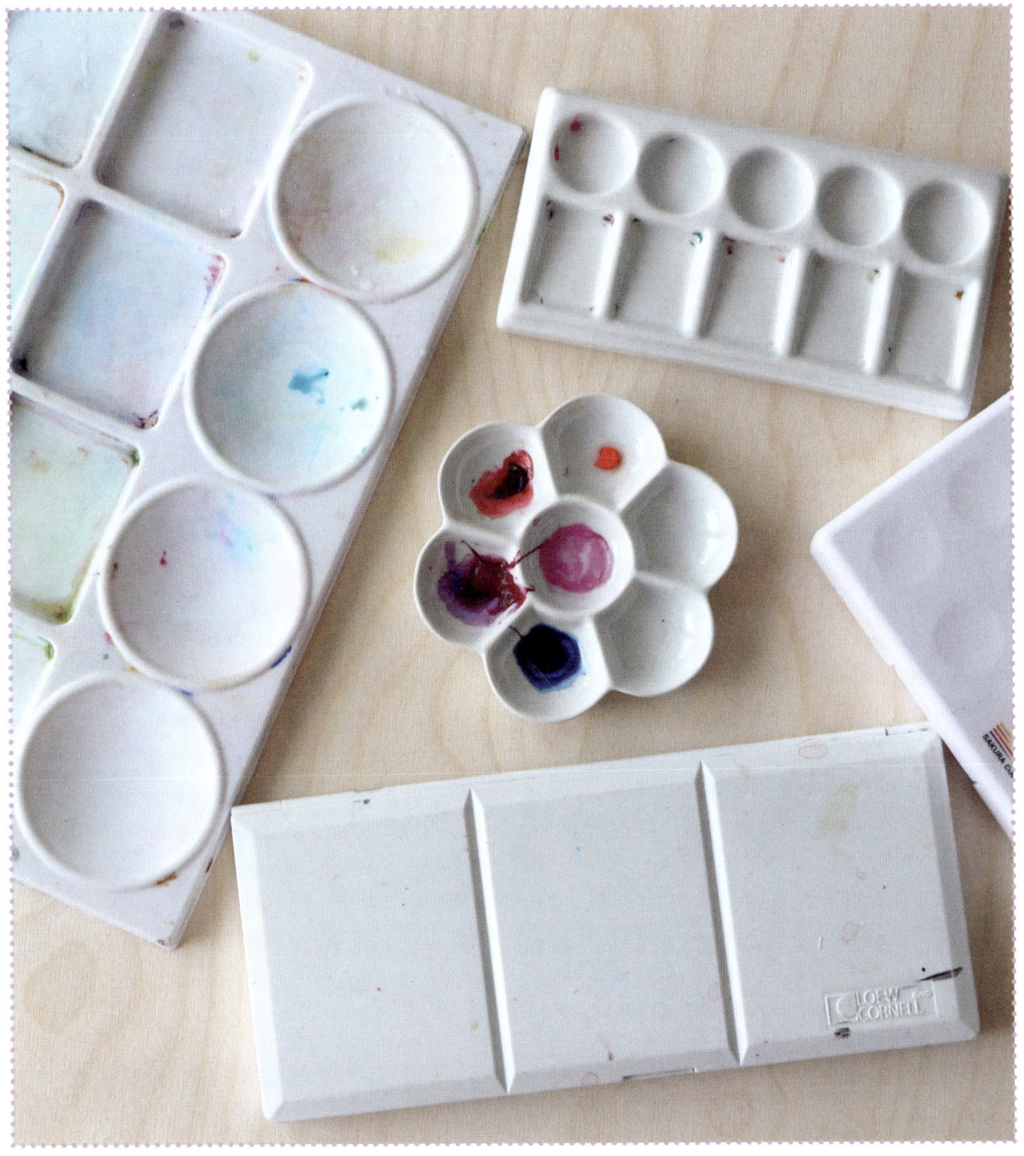

WATERCOLOR PEN BRUSHES

Watercolor pen brushes are a portable type of brush for painting on-the-go. Some paint sets come with a watercolor pen brush and are convenient for traveling. There are also some complete sets of watercolor pens in different pre-mixed colors that can be used as conveniently as markers.

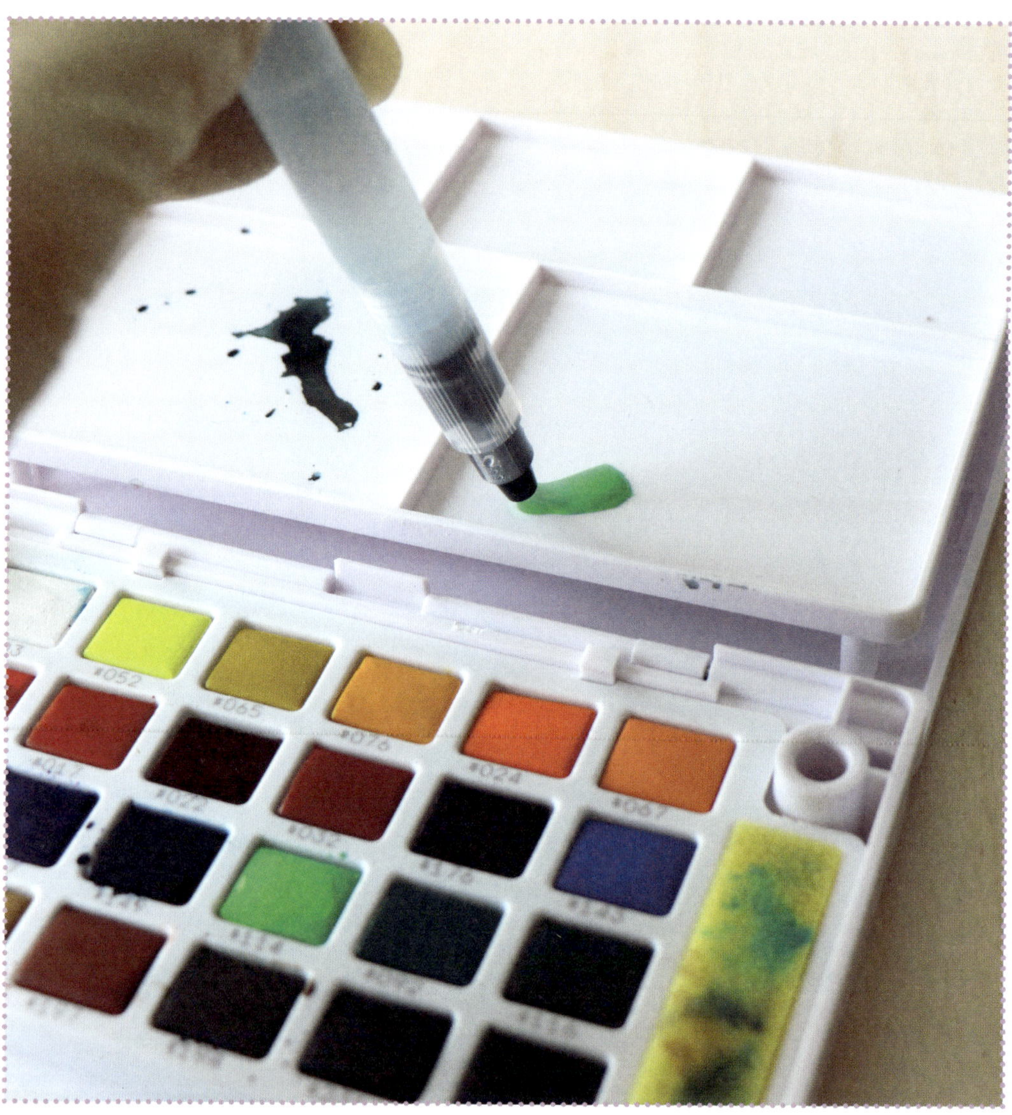

Unscrew watercolor pen brushes and fill them with water. Then simply dip into pans of watercolor paint and mix as desired. Squeeze the handle to release more water as you paint. Use sponges for cleaning the brush tip between colors.

All brushes should be cleaned after use with plain water. Because watercolor paint is water-based, warm water is all that is needed for cleanup. There are some brush soaps and conditioners available but are not necessary.

PENCILS, PENS & MARKERS

While you can use a liner brush to "sketch" directly onto the paper with paint, I often prefer to use pencils and pens to do my initial sketching. Light pencil marks can give the work just a hint of foundation and extra lines can be erased. Pens add a more dramatic look, with definite lines that can complement the watercolor painting. If using pencils, make sure to have a sharpener and erasers on hand. Test the erasers on your paper to make sure they do not tear or smudge the surface.

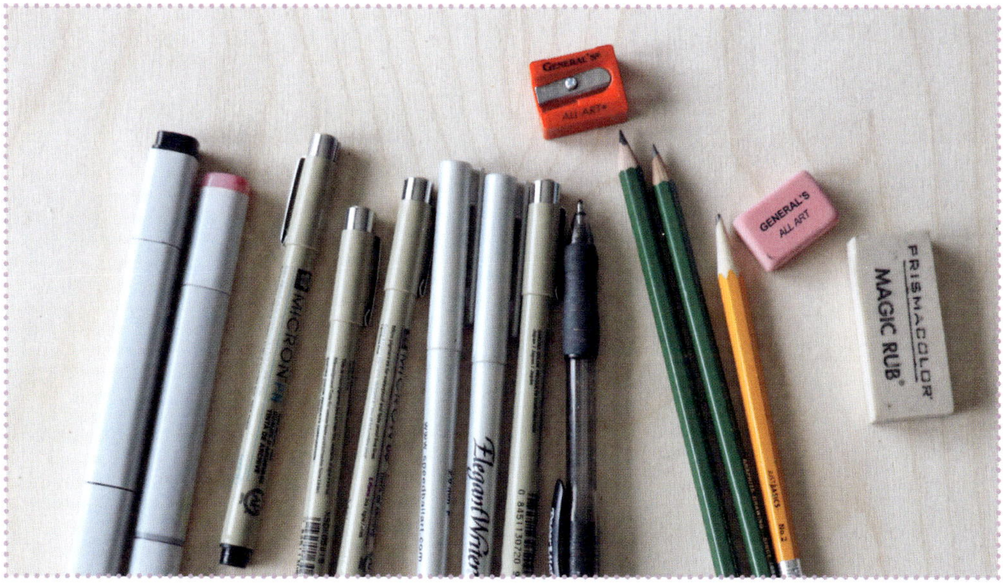

Markers can bleed through watercolor paper or run when mixed with water. Make sure to test them first on a small sheet of paper to see if you like the finished results.

ADDITIONAL SUPPLIES

- Rags, paper towels, or tissue for cleaning brushes and spills
- Jars for holding water
- Palette knife or rubber spatula for mixing paints
- Tape for securing papers
- Scissors, ruler or straightedge, X-Acto blade (for removing stretched and dried watercolor paper)
- Block or object to place under the board to lift one side slightly
- Portable table easel (optional) that can be adjusted from vertical and horizontal angles
- Erasers and pencil sharpeners
- Rubber gloves (optional for keeping your hands clean)
- Storage container for supplies

Find a quiet location where you can work without distraction. Make sure there is enough lighting so you can see your work and colors clearly without straining your eyes. Have a source of water close by for refilling your water jar and cleaning up.

Brush Techniques

For these exercises, the following brushes are useful: a round brush, flat brush, and liner brush. Other watercolor brushes you may find useful are a deer foot brush, mop brush, cat tongue brush, and filbert brush. (But these additional brushes are optional and simply fun to have on hand.)

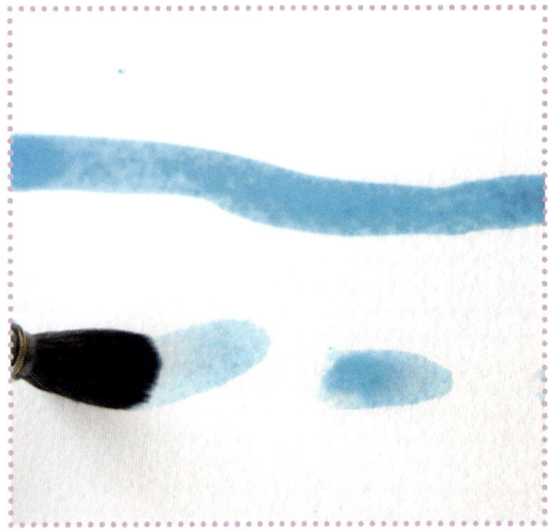

Straight and broken lines with a round brush.

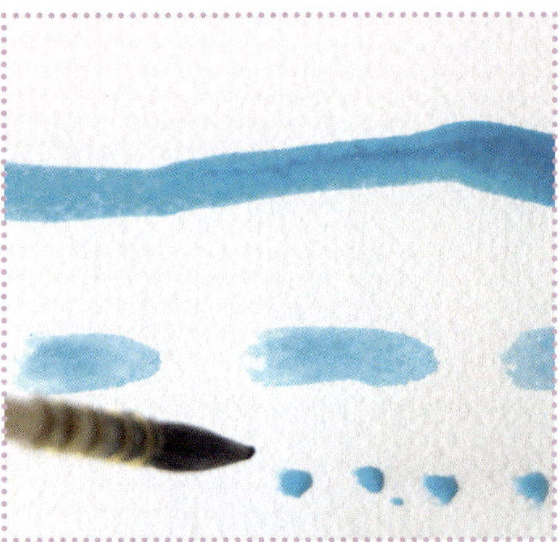

Dots with the tip of a round brush.

Curvy lines with a round brush.

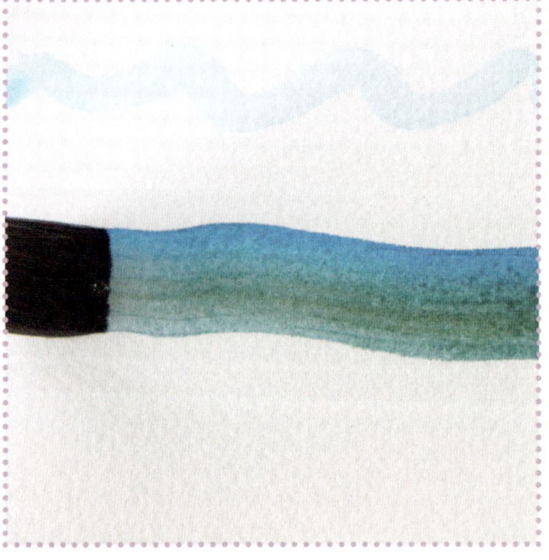

Broad strokes with a flat brush.

Round brushes are standard and very useful for watercolor painting. For me, they are the workhorses. If desired, you can paint an entire painting with just a round brush.

Flat brushes are the second most important brushes for watercolor painting. They are great for broad strokes of color or straight continuous lines. They can be used for large washes of color, as well as getting into those tight spaces.

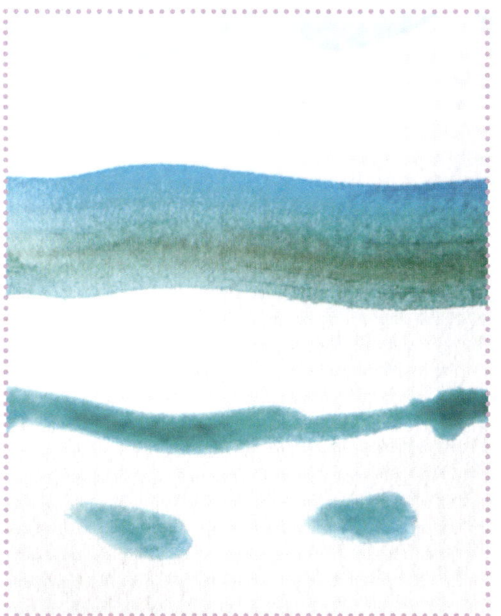

Thin and broken lines with side of a flat brush.

Curvy lines with a flat brush.

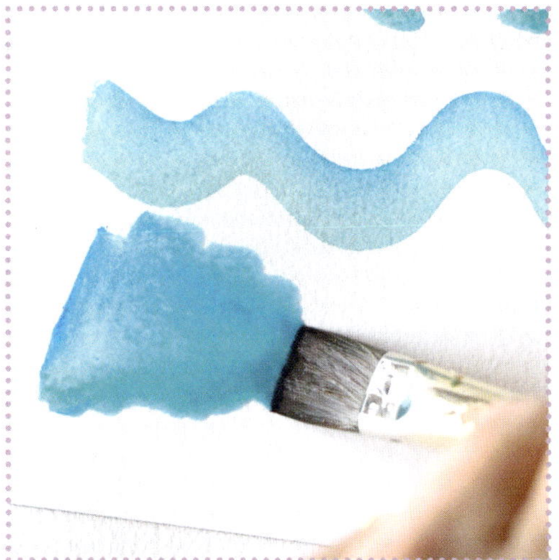

Wash of color with a flat brush.

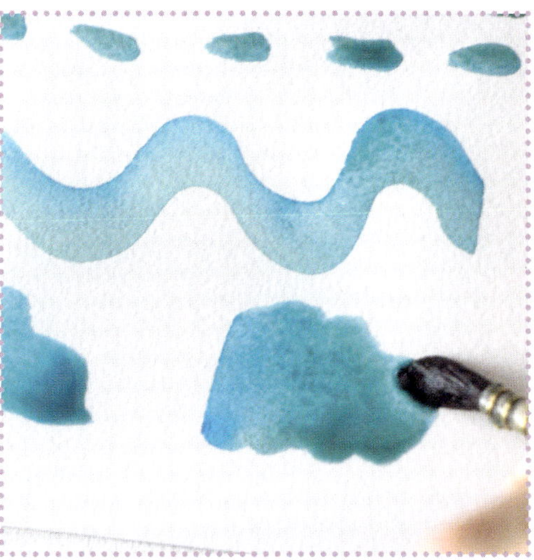

Wash of color with a round brush.

Filbert brushes are flat brushes that are rounded at the ends instead of square. While not as good for tight corners, they are great for curvy, rounded lines and washes of color.

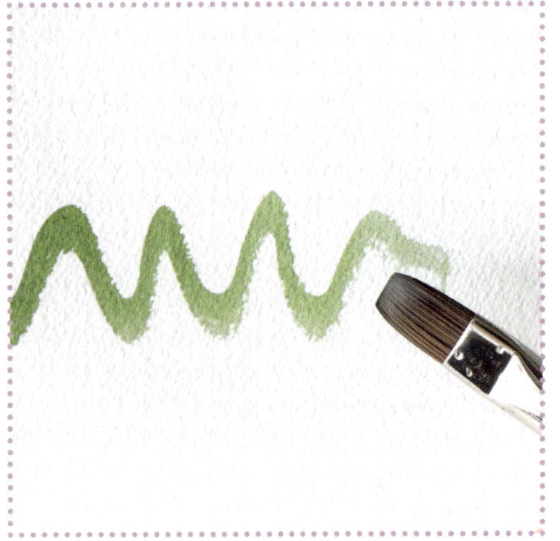

Curvy lines with a filbert brush.

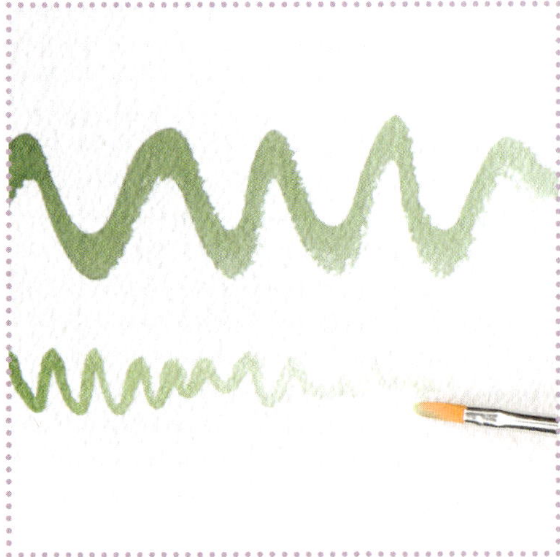

Curvy lines with a small filbert brush.

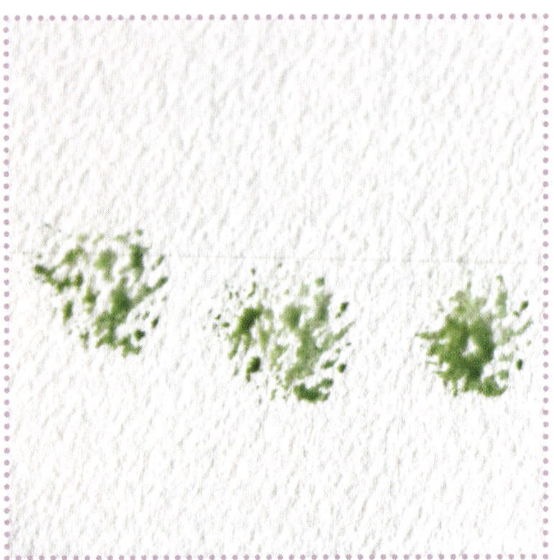

Stippling with a deer foot brush.

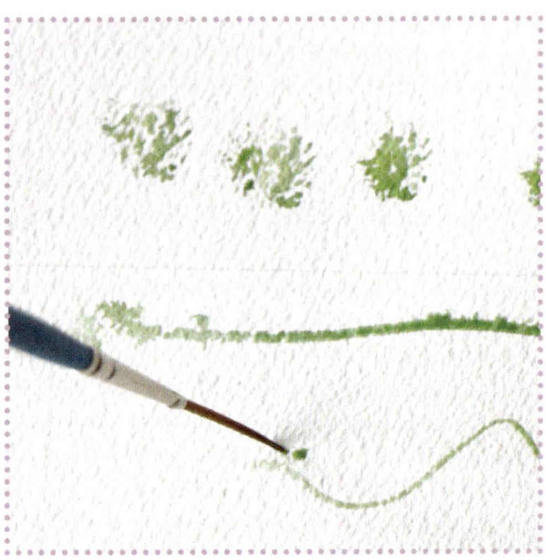

Straight and curvy lines with a liner brush.

Deer foot brushes are good for stippling with a drybrush technique. With drybrush painting, only small amount of paint is picked up on the brush. Add very little water to the paint. This will create a stippling pattern when pressing the brush lightly against the paper. The longer the brush is held in place, the more paint is laid down on the paper.

Liner brushes are long, thin round brushes good for making lines, letters, and linear details, such as the veins on a leaf.

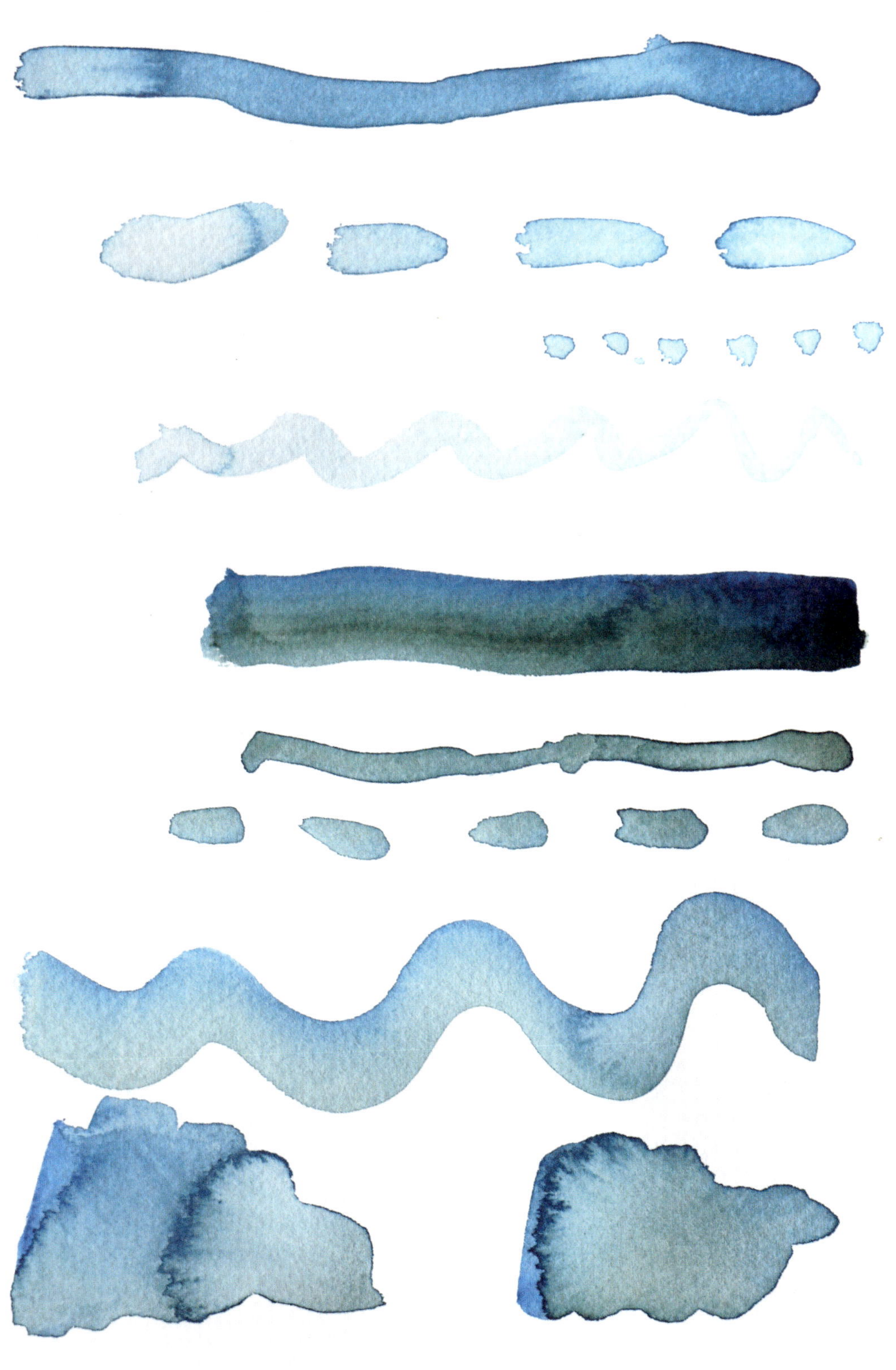

Mixing Colors

Mixing watercolors is quite fun and easy. It takes just a bit of practice to get used to your paints and the amount of water needed to get the desired results. One thing to remember is that watercolors are transparent, and they will show the paper underneath. Take advantage of this when painting. Also, instead of painting light colors on top of dark colors, remember to add darker colors over lighter areas. To create light areas, less is more—the lightest whites should be the paper itself. To lighten watercolors, instead of adding white (which is an option), try watering down the paint to a weaker mixture.

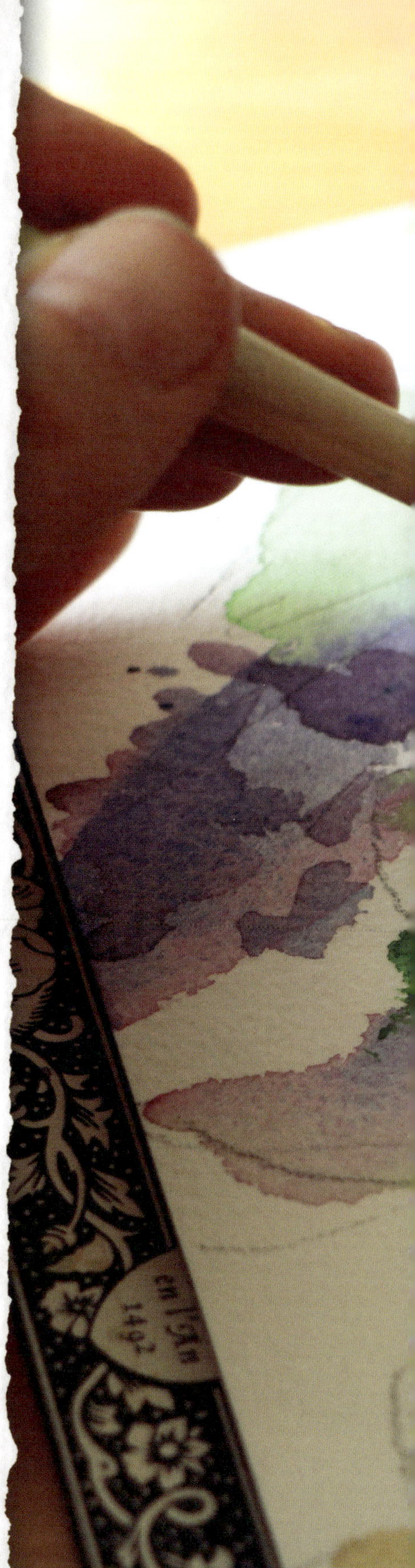

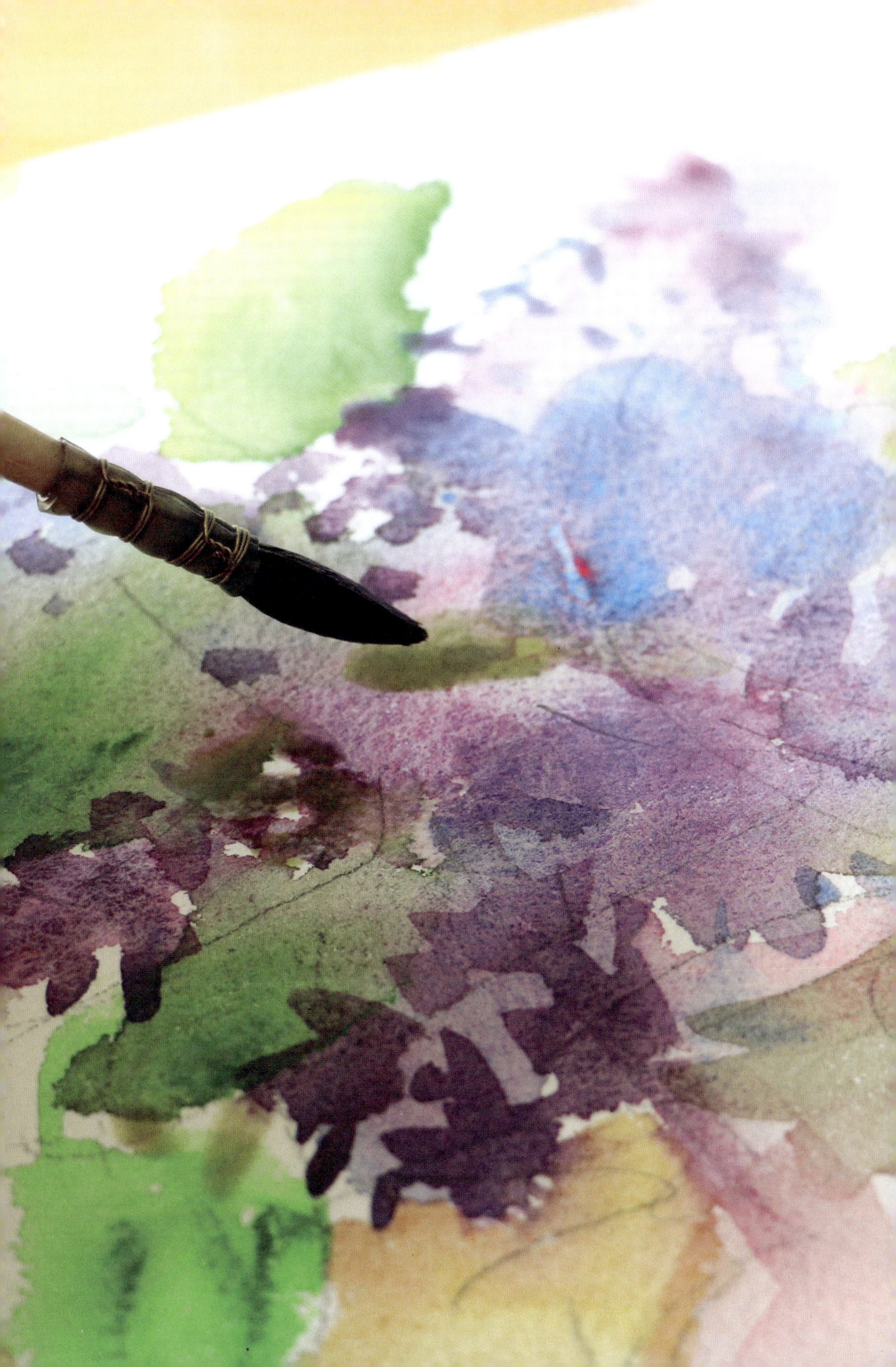

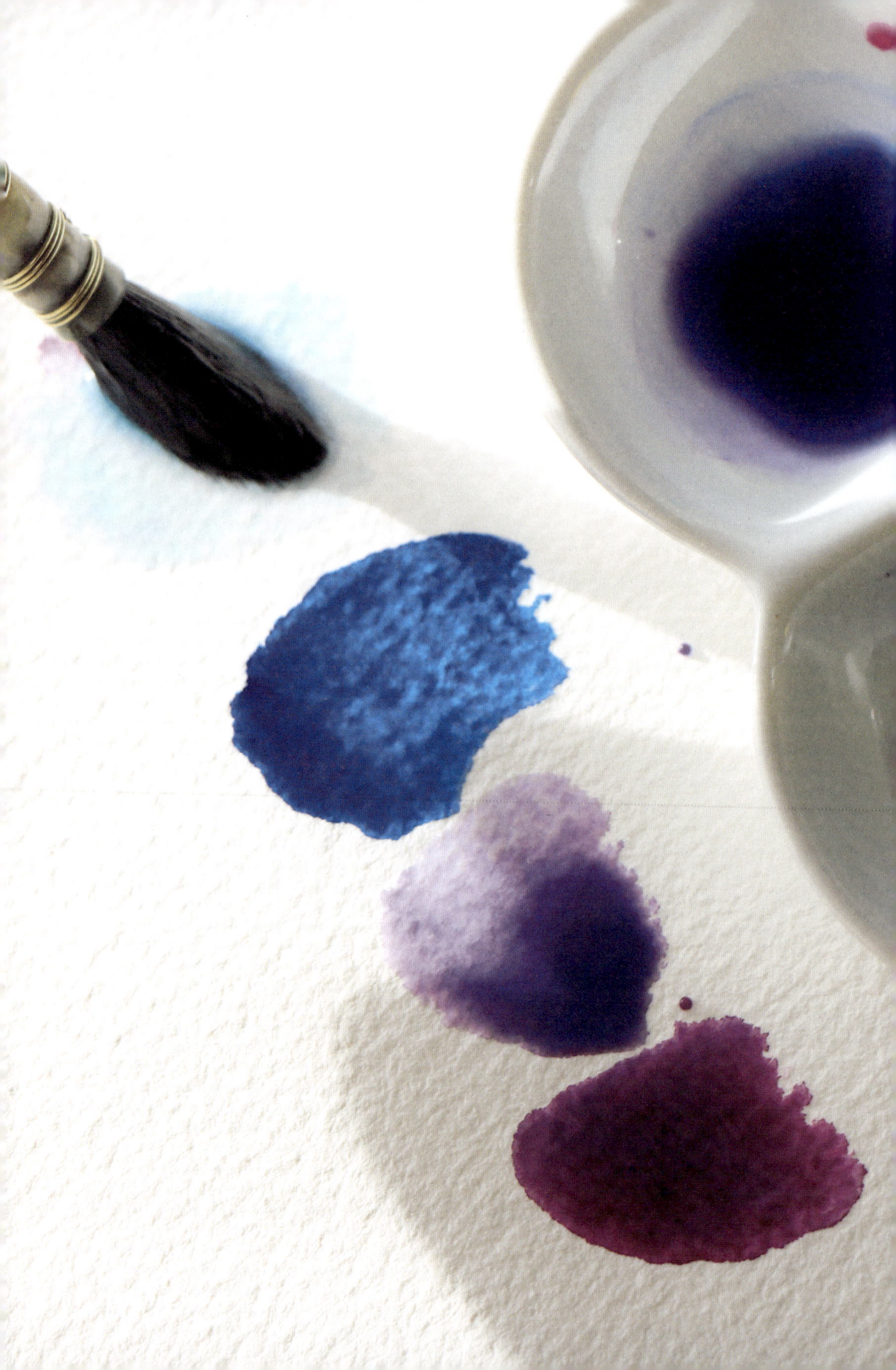

WET-INTO-WET

You can mix watercolors on the palette or on the paper by painting one color right next to (or on top of) another color. This technique is best practiced on scrap paper or in a sketchbook before trying on your artwork. Go ahead and experiment with mixing your colors.

Here I paint one color next to another while both are still wet. The colors meet and blend to create a secondary color. As I mentioned, you can mix these same secondary colors on the palette, but it is also fun to see how they naturally blend together directly on the page.

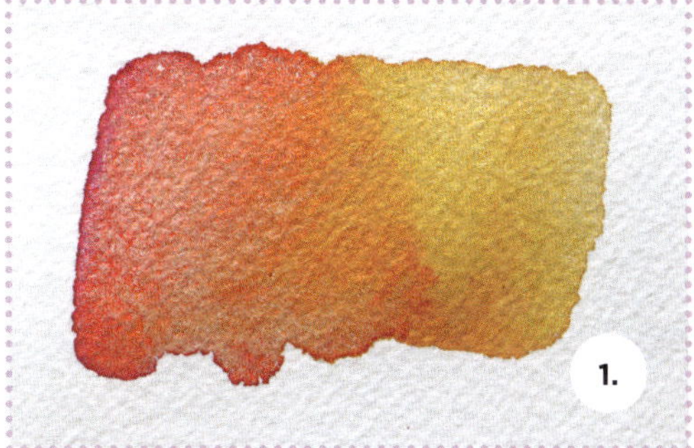

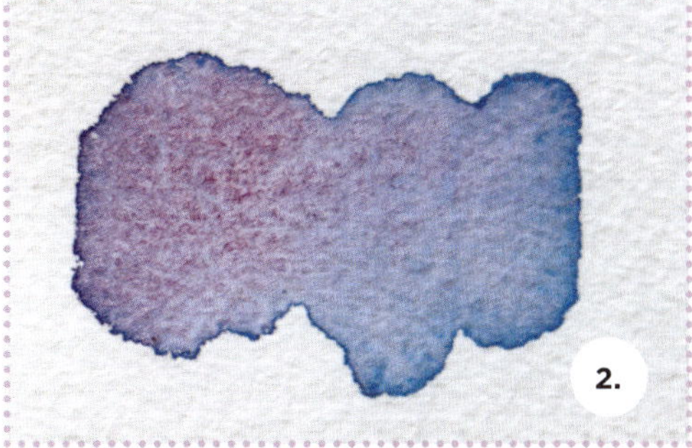

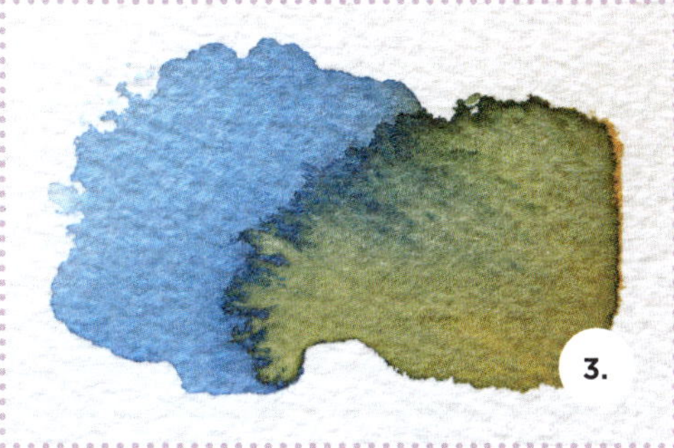

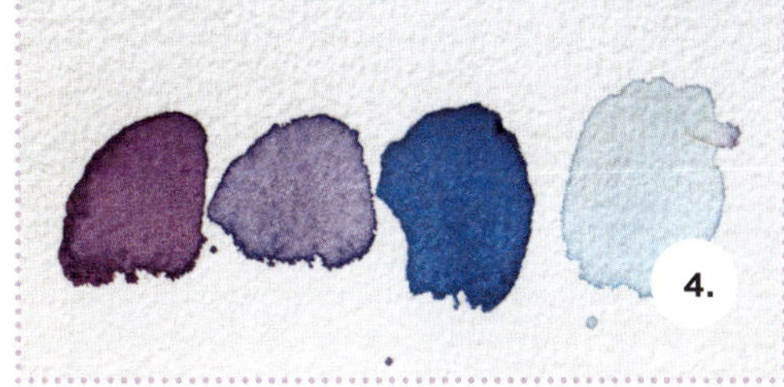

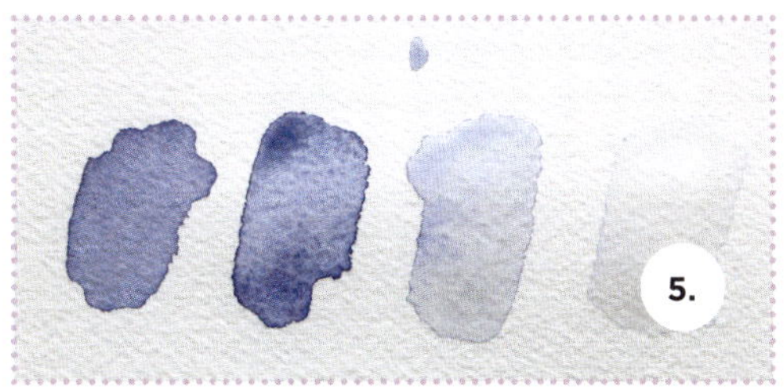

1. **Red and yellow blend to create orange.**
2. **Red and blue blend to create violet.**
3. **Blue and yellow blend to create green.**
4. **Pure violet, and then with one dip into water; phthalo blue, and then with one dip into water.**
5. **Four transitions from dark to light using violet and water. The more water, the lighter the applied color. I simply dipped the brush into a container of water between each brushstroke.**

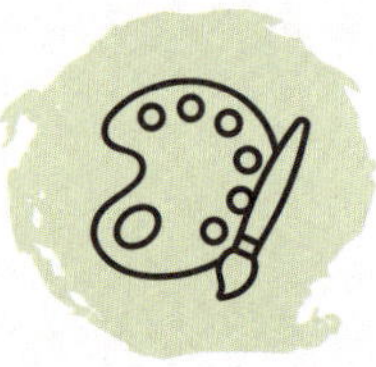

Creative Exercise: Leaves

Use the creative exercises on the next few pages to practice what you have learned so far. Start by painting some basic leaf shapes. You can imitate leaf varieties in your area or look in books or online for ideas. Sketch the basic shapes with a pencil. This way, if you make a mistake, you can erase it before adding the paint.

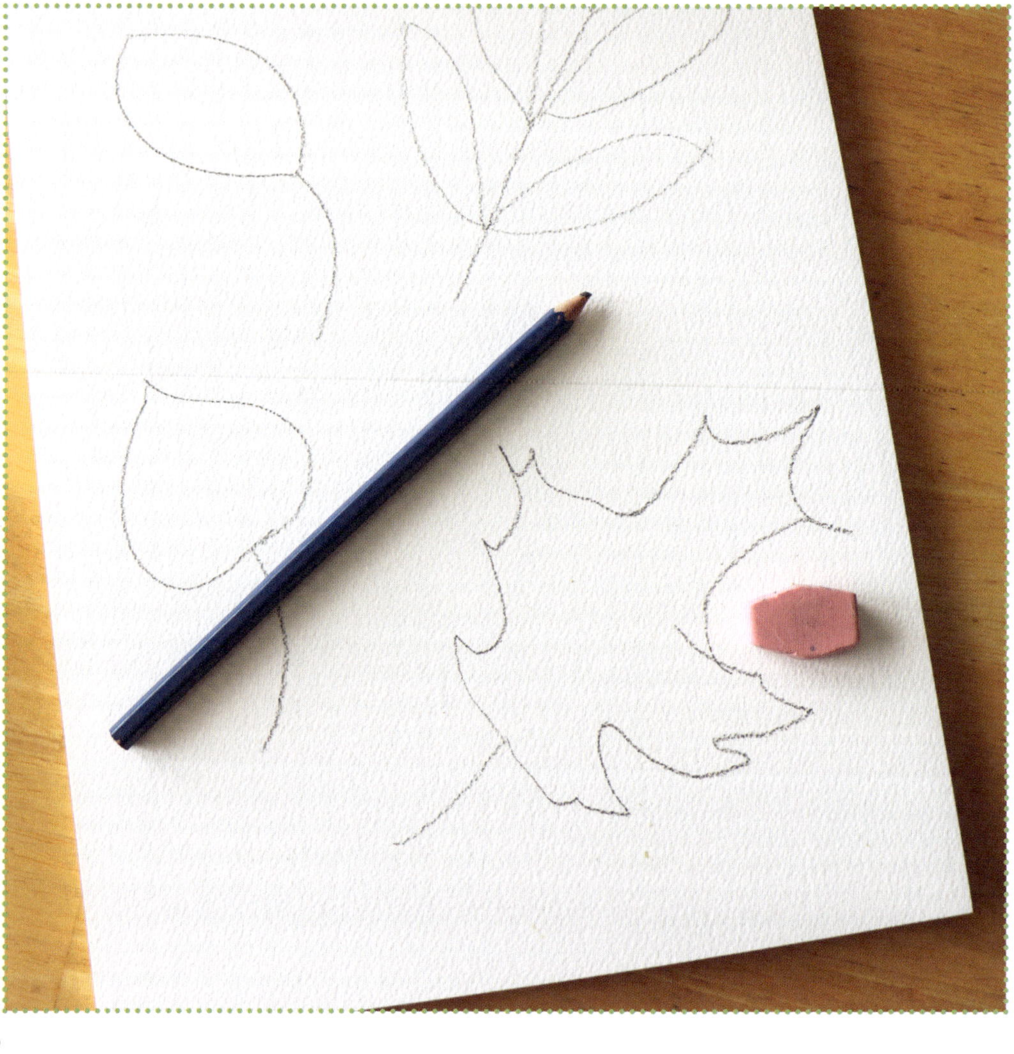

Use your flat brush dipped in water to "pull" the paint from the outline into the middle of the leaves. This creates a transparent layer of color. If the leaf is large or the outline has dried, go ahead and add more paint to the center of the leaf and blend to fill in the shape.

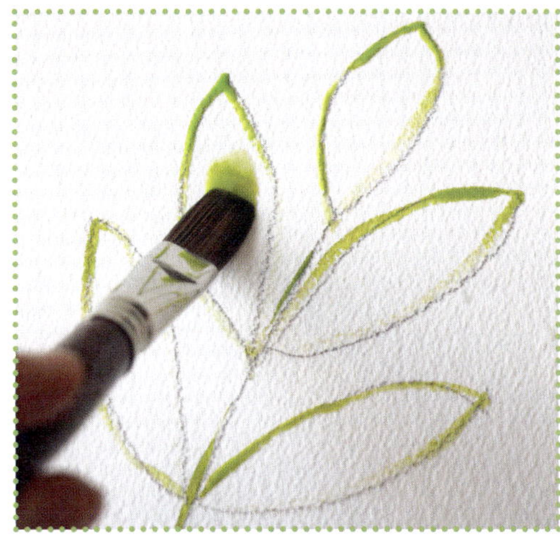

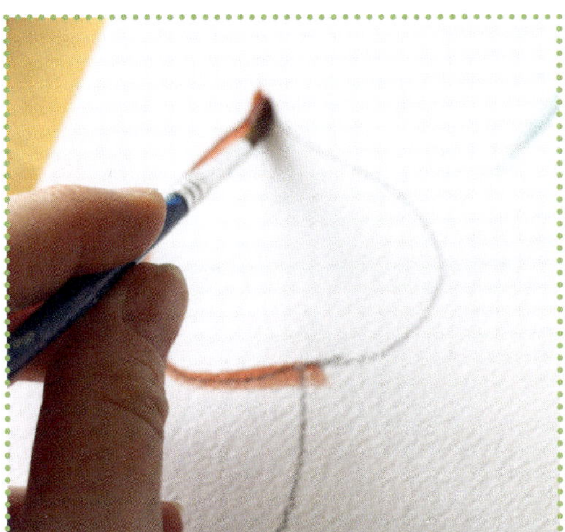

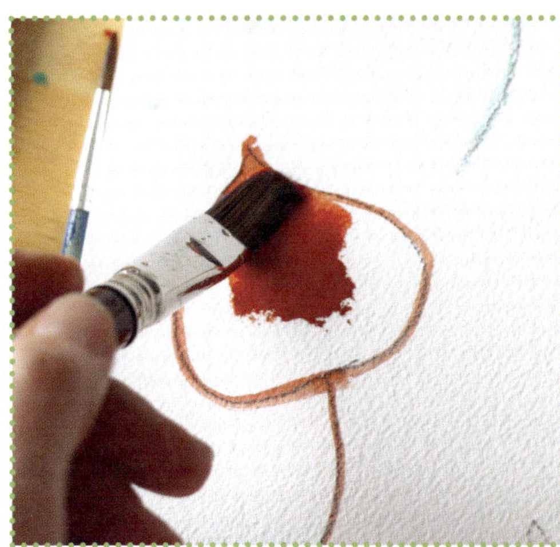

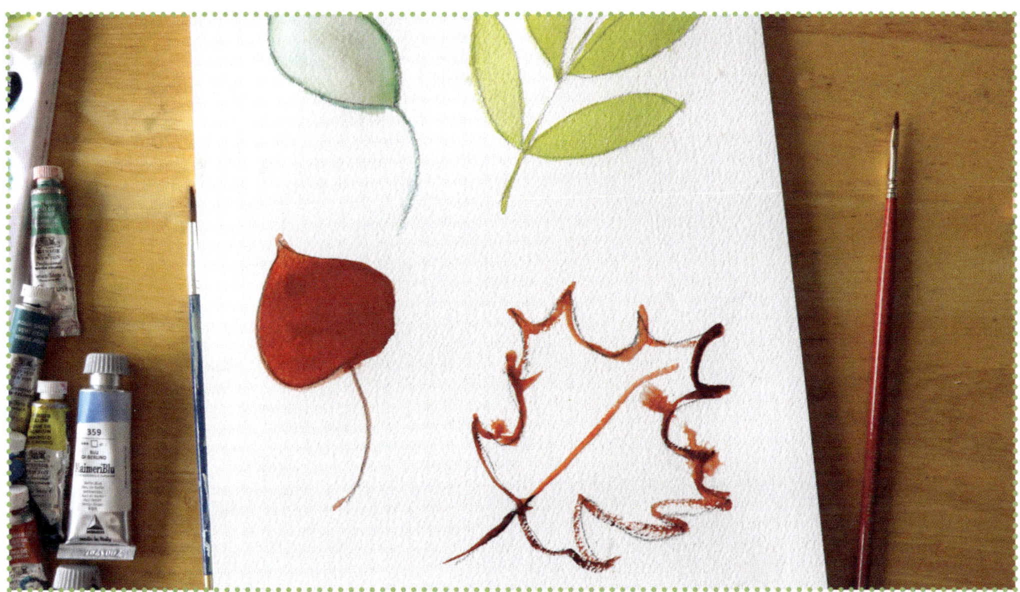

Use a liner brush to make pine needles. Start with darker colors and end with lighter greens for the needles.

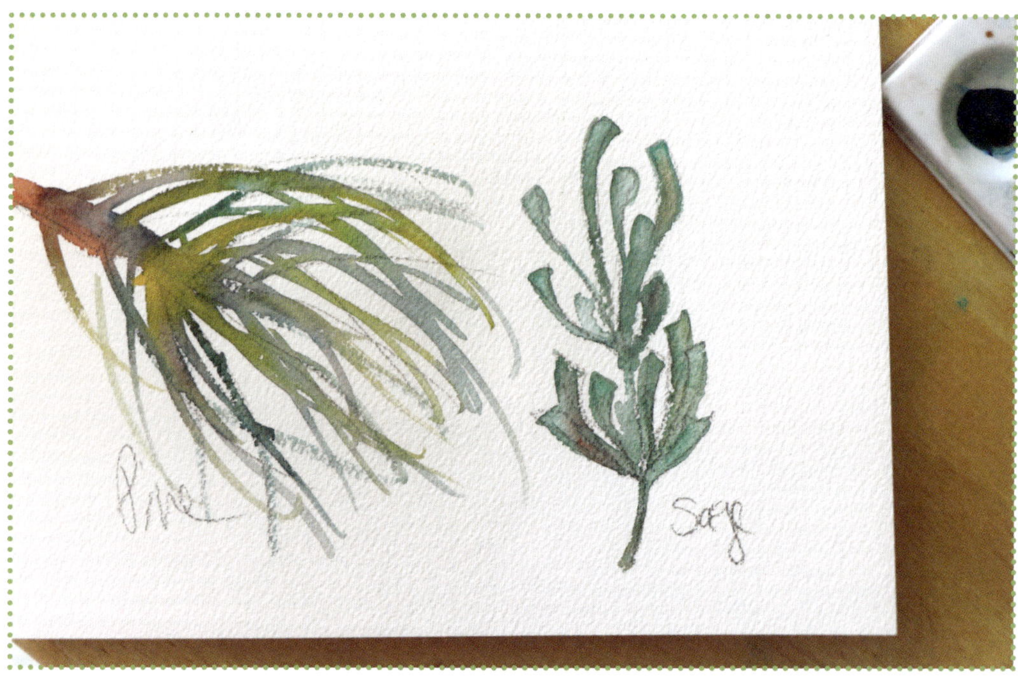

Try more complicated leaves or leaves from another part of the world. Try overlapping leaves or adding folded leaves. Try adding stripes and variations wet-into-wet or dry-on-dry for more defined lines.

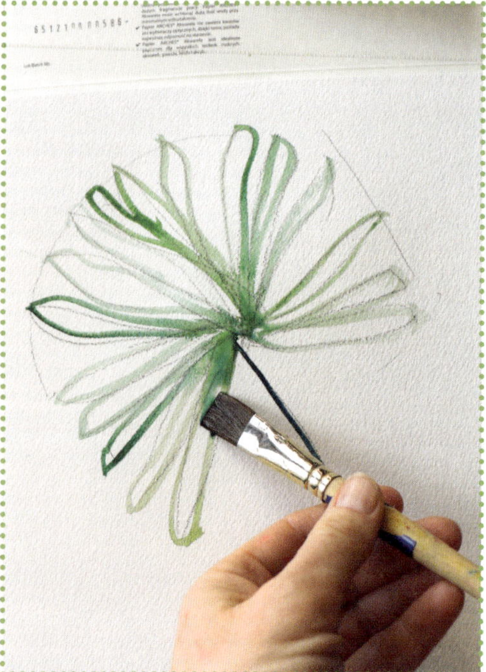

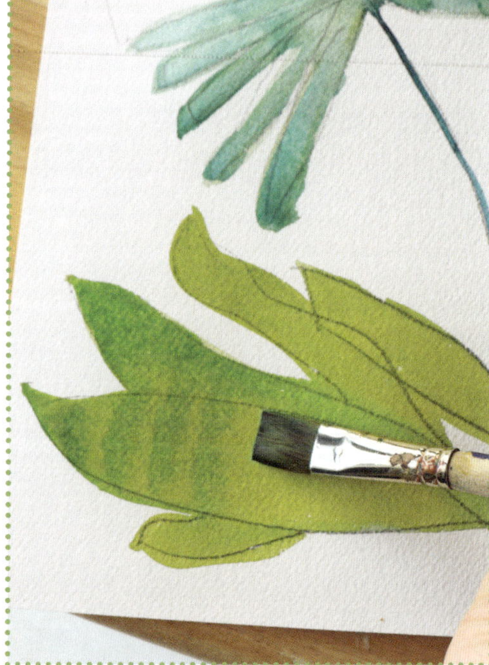

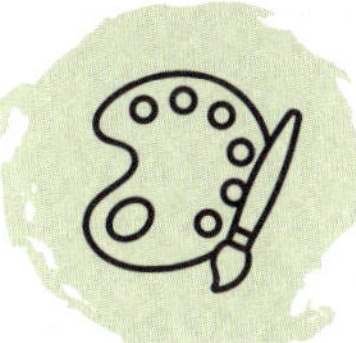

Creative Exercise: Jellyfish

Start by sketching two jellyfish. Mix up some red and blue to make a violet mixture. Then paint one jellyfish body blue and the other violet.

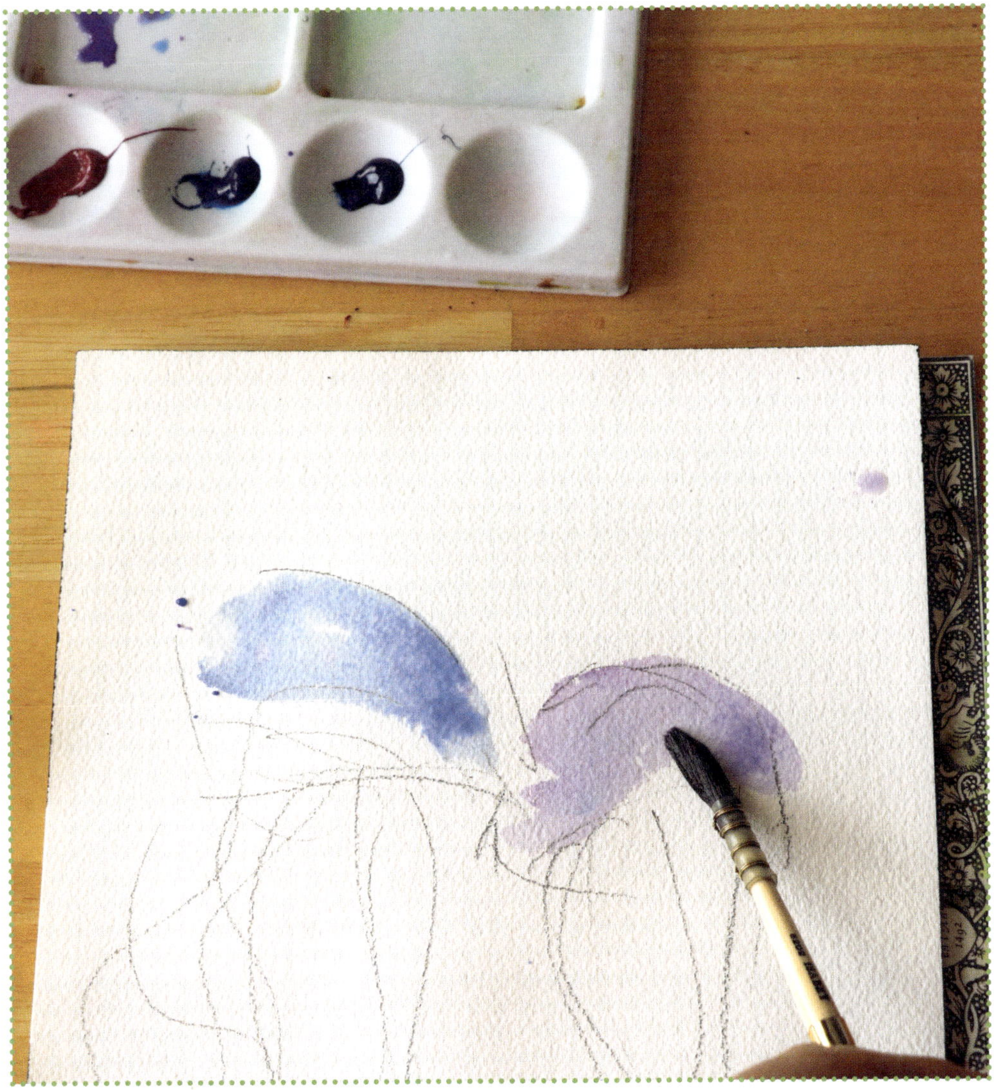

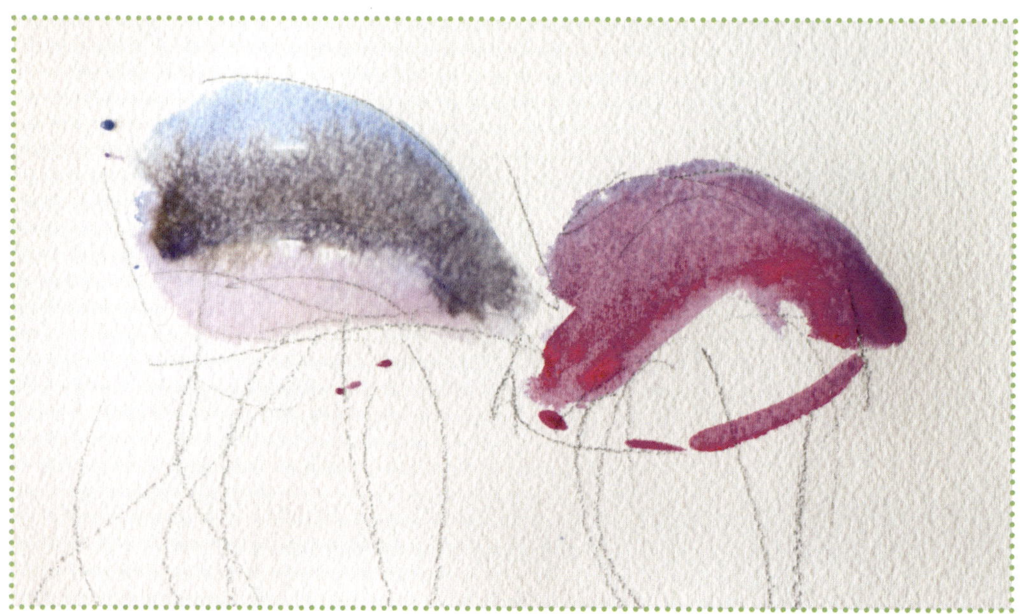

Add some saturated color to the middle and bottom edges. This will help delineate the top of the jellyfish from the underbelly where the tentacles hang down.

Combine a watered-down mix of the violet with a touch of added yellow. Use this to paint the underbelly of the blue jellyfish. Outline the underbelly of the violet jellyfish. Add some black to the blue paint, and spread along the base of the blue jellyfish.

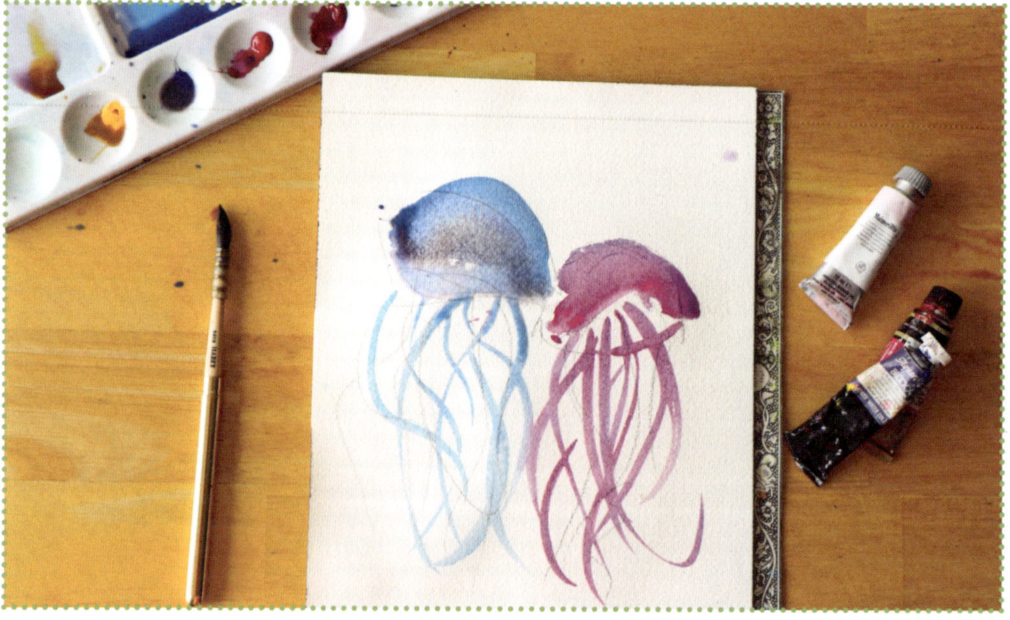

Paint matching tentacles with tip of the round brush dipped in paint. Again, add black to the blue paint and use to paint darker tentacles on the blue jellyfish. Add more blue to violet, and paint some darker tentacles on the violet jellyfish.

Fill in the underbelly of the violet jellyfish with a mixture of gray paint mixed from all three primary colors or by adding brown to the violet or blue paint. After the tentacles have dried, paint the underbelly of the violet jellyfish.

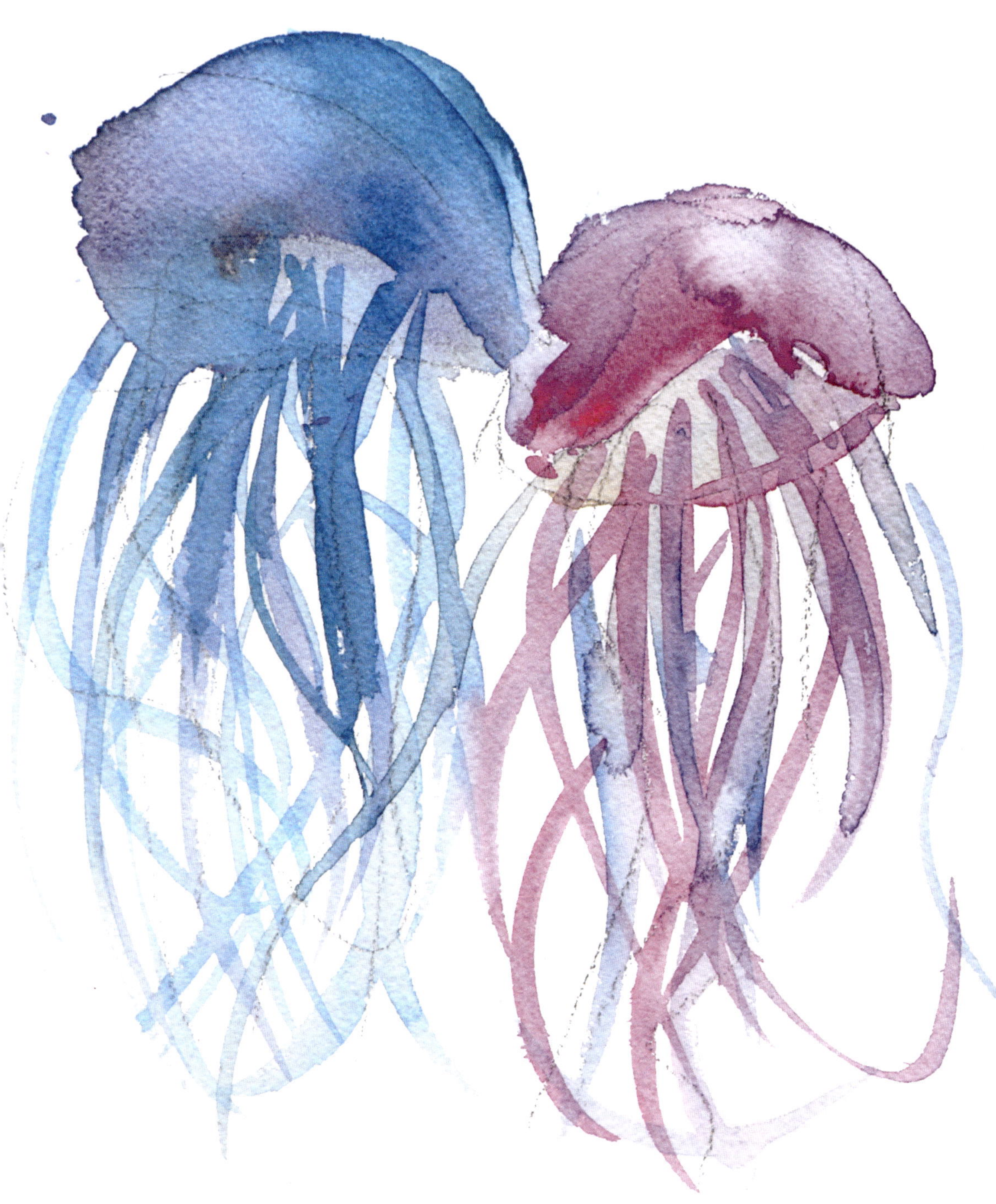

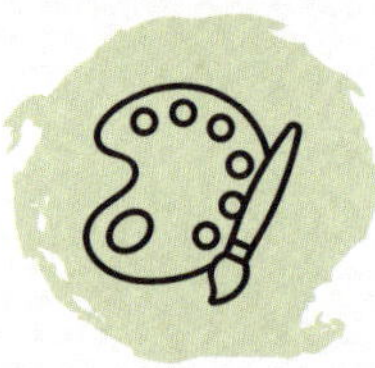

Creative Exercise: Abstract Drip Art

When using watercolor, you can tilt the painting and use the angle to create unique and colorful dripping effects. Abstract drip art possibilities are endless. But here are a few ideas to get started.

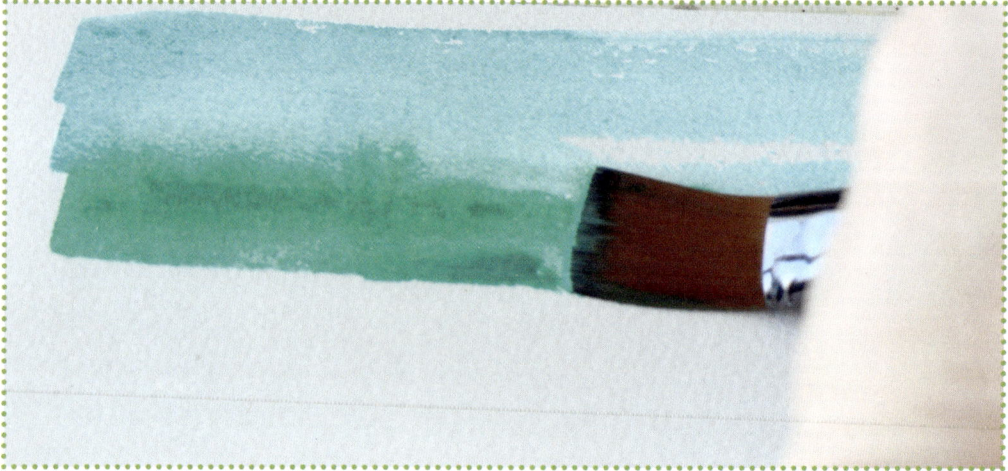

STEP 1:

First, pick four or five colors for your project. I use two different blues, a pink, and a burnt sienna.

Use a flat brush to make two horizontal brushstrokes from left to right using the color of your choice. Now add a second similar color underneath. Notice how the stroke becomes drier toward the right side of the painting.

Place an object beneath the surface of your watercolor paper block or painting board to create an angle. The object should be flat enough that the board does not wobble.

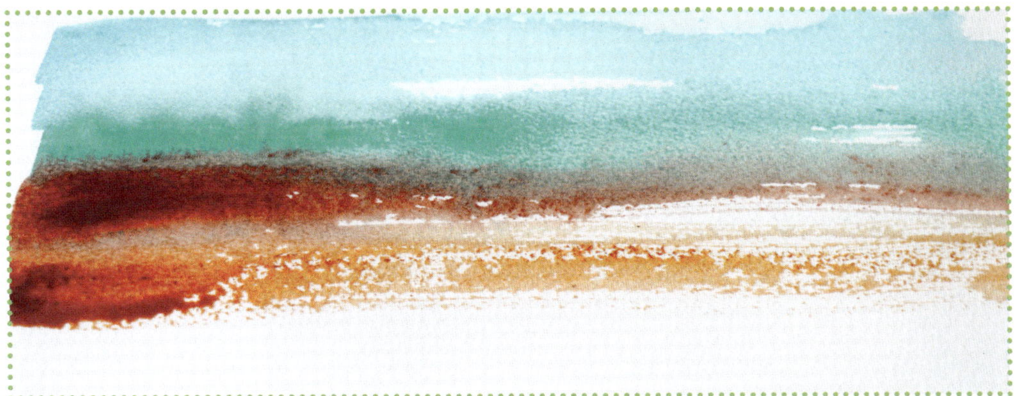

STEP 2:

Now switch to burnt sienna. This color will break up the painting with a more dramatic shift in color and value.

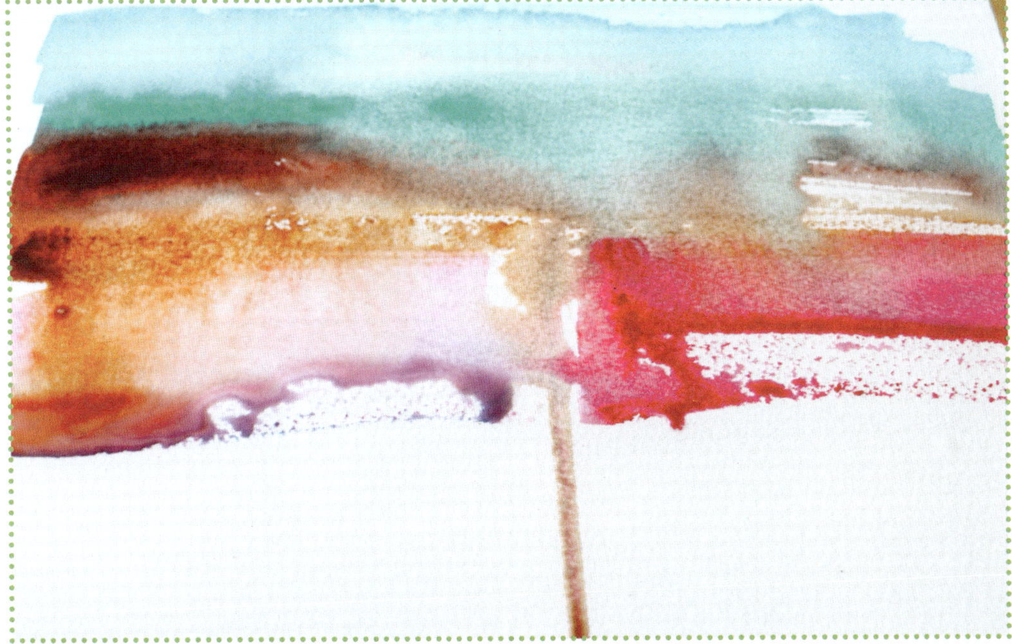

STEP 3:

Add water to your flat brush and apply to your painting. Watch as the colors blend into each other. Don't use your brush to blend the paints; rather, gently press the brush to the surface and slowly stroke where you want to soften the lines and mix the colors.

Where the drip divides the paper, I added some pink horizontal brushstrokes to the right. Make sure not to touch the drips or the paint will blend and mix. Then mix blue with some pink to create a light violet color and apply a couple more brushstrokes to the left of the drip. Add more water to further blend the colors.

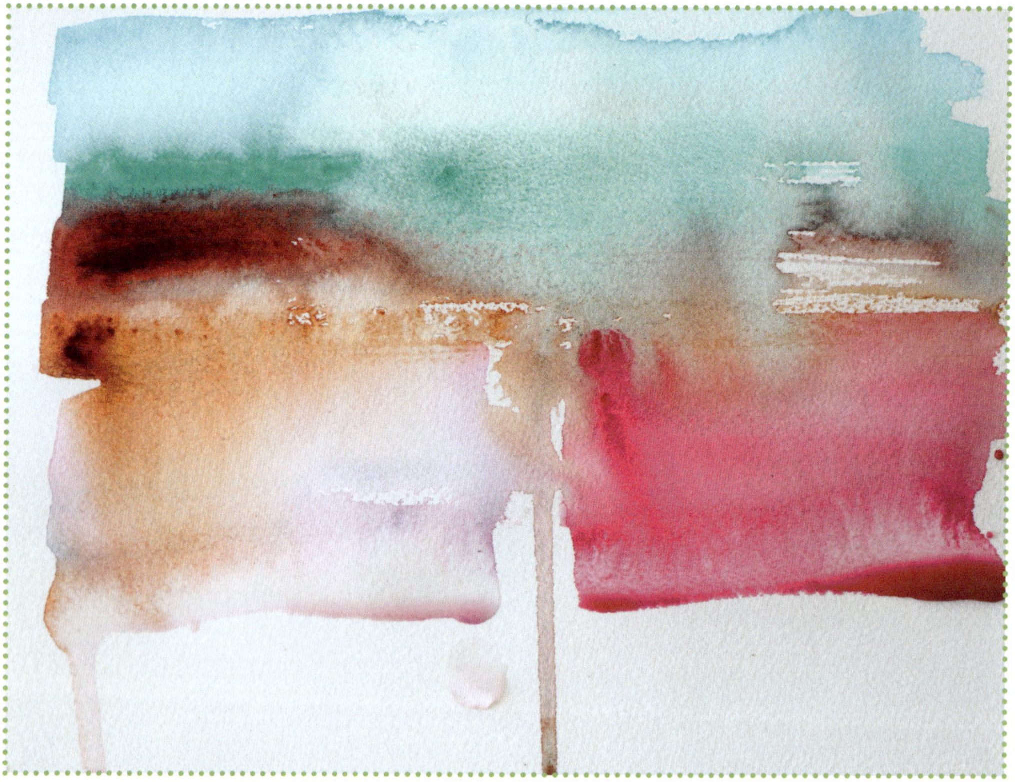

STEP 4:

Finally, decide when to stop painting. I decide to leave some white paper showing. As the painting dries, the colors start to absorb into the paper, creating blooming and pooling of pigments.

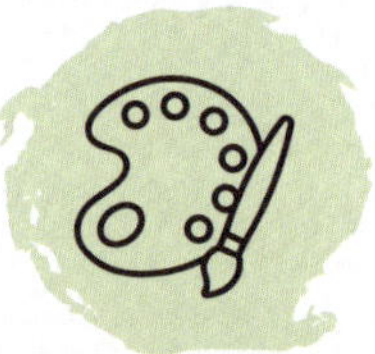

Creative Exercise: Choosing Colors

Now choose colors for your own abstract project. It's a good idea to choose colors that are near each other on the color wheel. The addition of an earthy tone will offset the brighter colors.

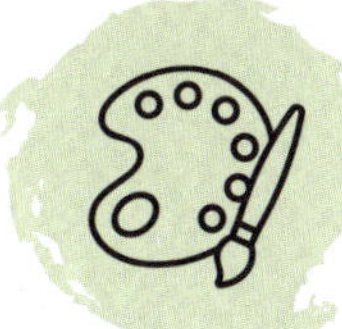

Creative Exercise: Drippy Dots

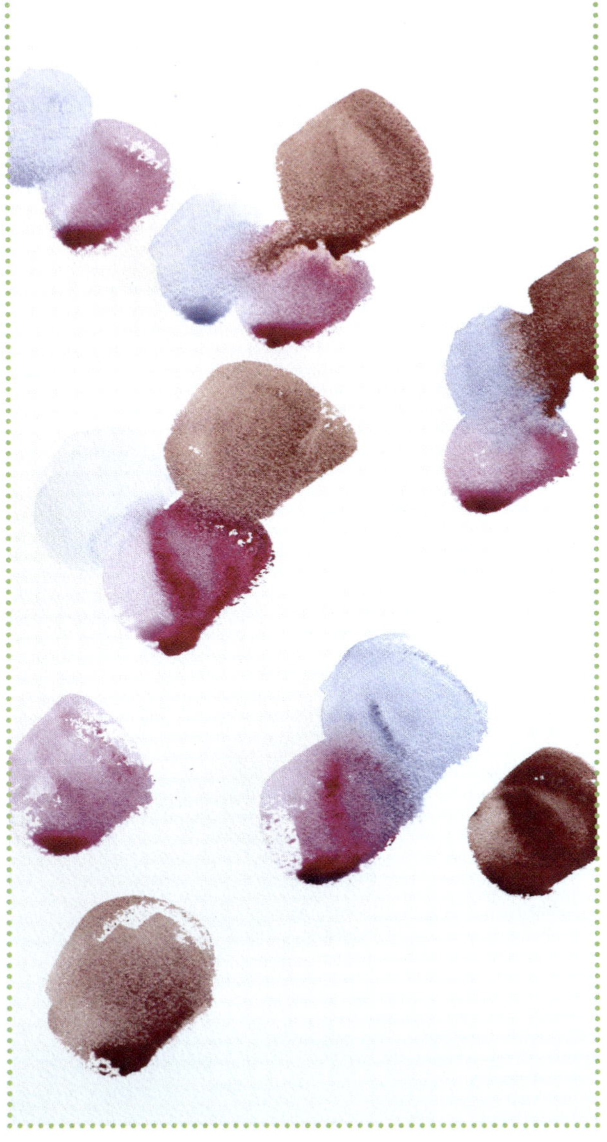

STEP 1:

For this project, use a round brush and a medium flat brush. Start by applying one of the colors in random circles around the paper. I chose ultramarine violet. Using a similar color, such as magenta, paint more circles that attach to the first circles.

Use a third color (I used violet-brown) to continue with the drippy dots. Notice when the colors connect wet-into-wet, they blend together at the connection point.

Lift the back edge of your paper with something about 3 to 5 inches high, such as a tissue box.

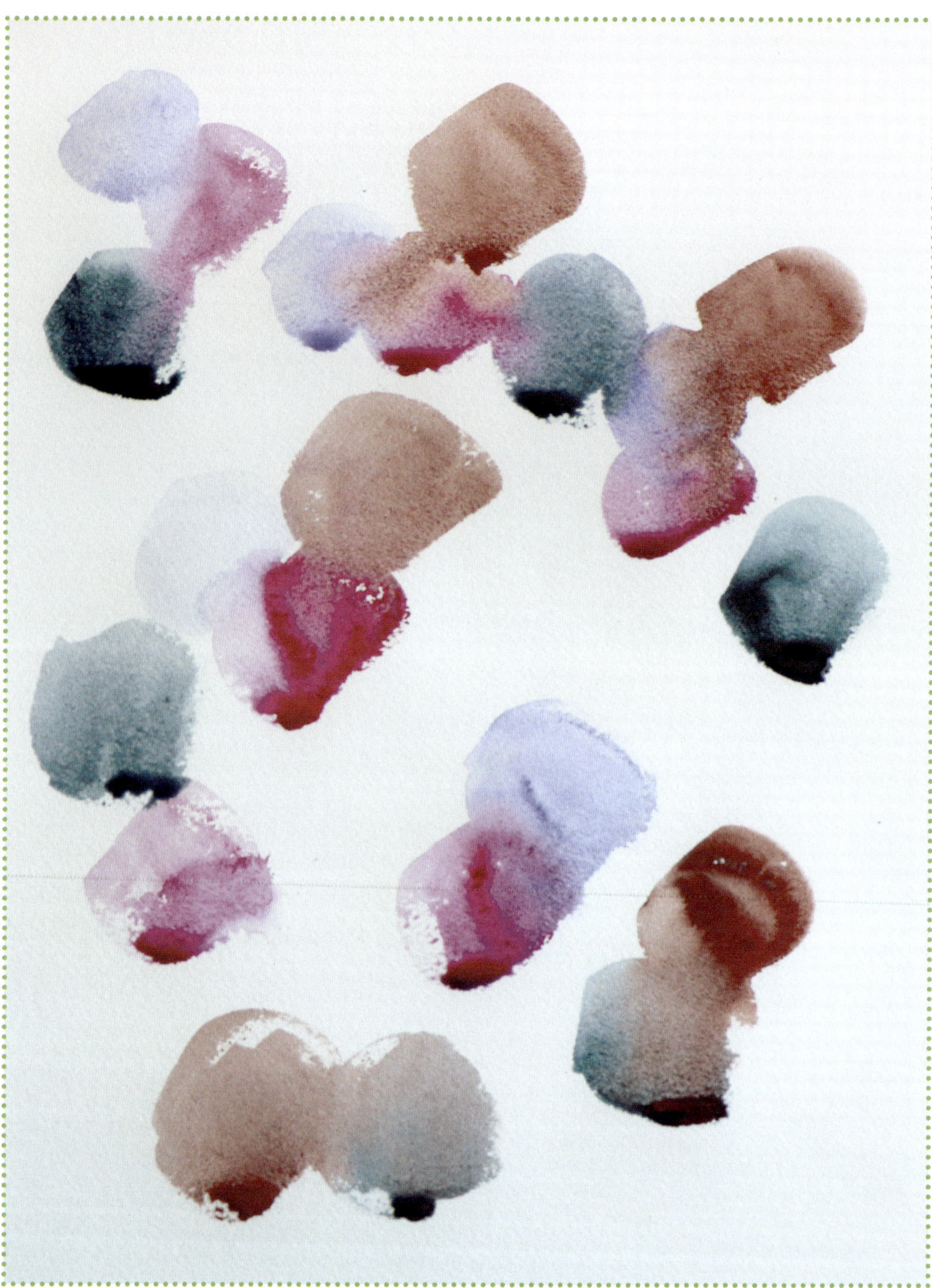

STEP 2:

I use a dark Payne's gray for the next set of connecting dots. Fill in areas to create a balanced effect on your paper. While the dots are random, choose what looks most pleasing.

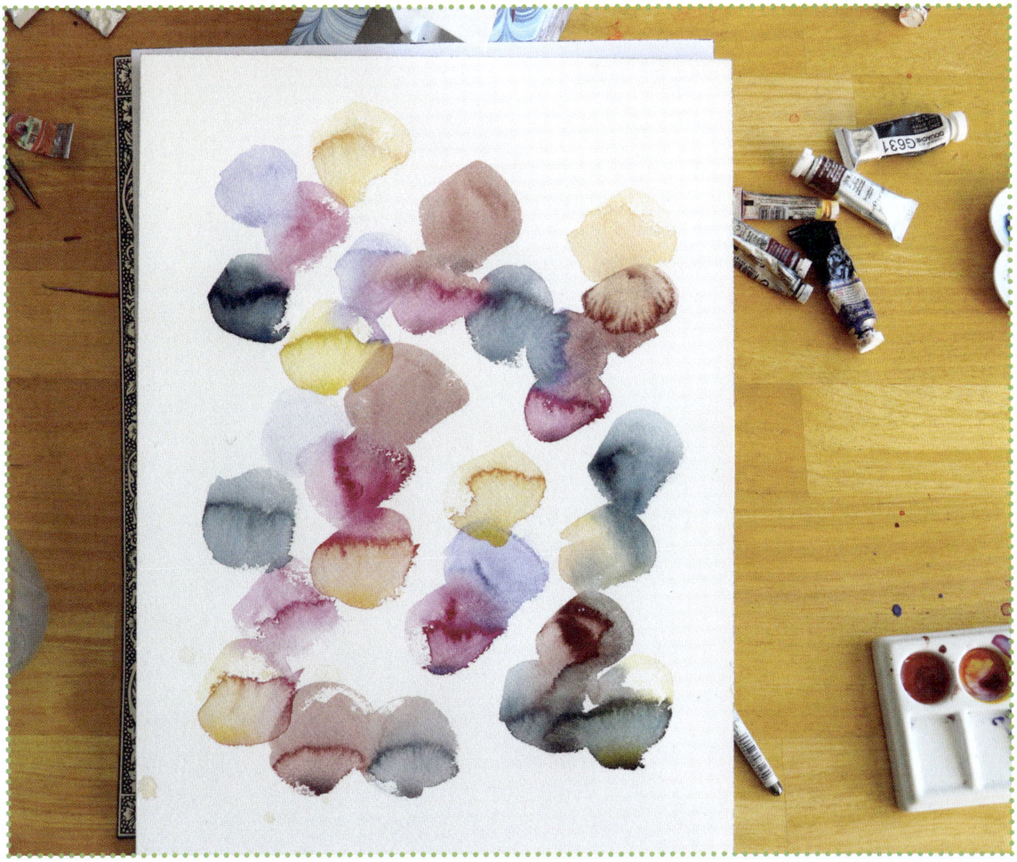

STEP 3:

On your palette, blend a touch of magenta and Payne's gray into yellow paint to tone it down. You don't want the bright yellow to overpower the other colors on the paper. Allow the painting to dry.

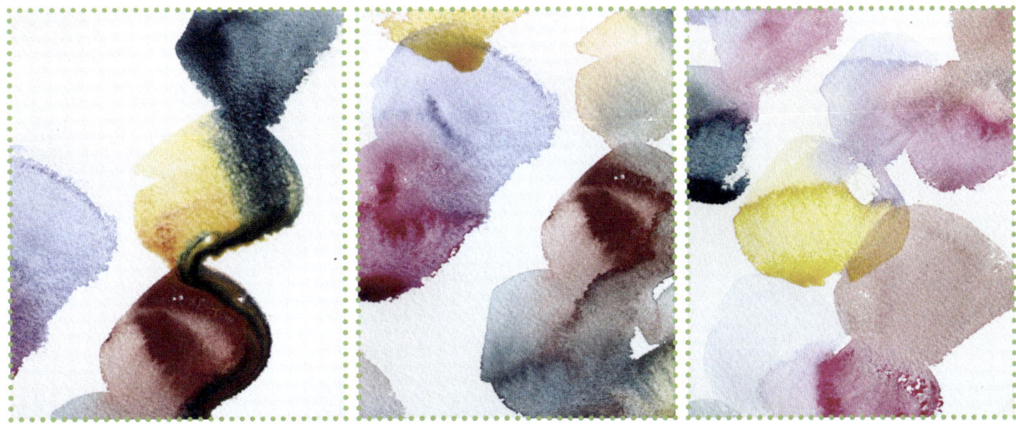

See how dramatic the flow of colors can be, especially when the colors contrast in value or hue.

Flowers

While you can learn to paint intricate details, we will instead focus on fast and lively techniques that merely suggest flowers. You can spend more time adding details, but here we will focus on quick paintings that celebrate the fluid qualities of watercolor paints.

Supplies

- Watercolor paper (block or secured on board)
- Small round and flat brushes
- Medium round and flat brushes
- Watercolor paints
- Colors: Holbein® antique green, cadmium yellow, permanent rose, Maimeri dragon's blood red, ultramarine violet, transparent earth orange, cerulean blue, phthalo or Berlin blue
- Palette for mixing paints
- Spray bottle (optional)
- Jar of water
- Tissue or paper towels for cleanup

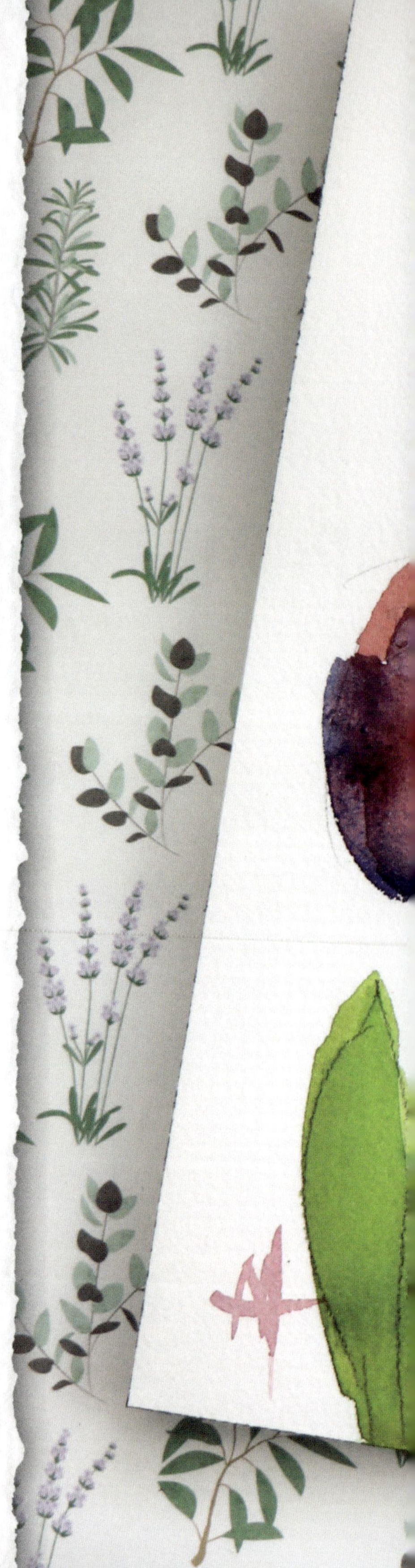

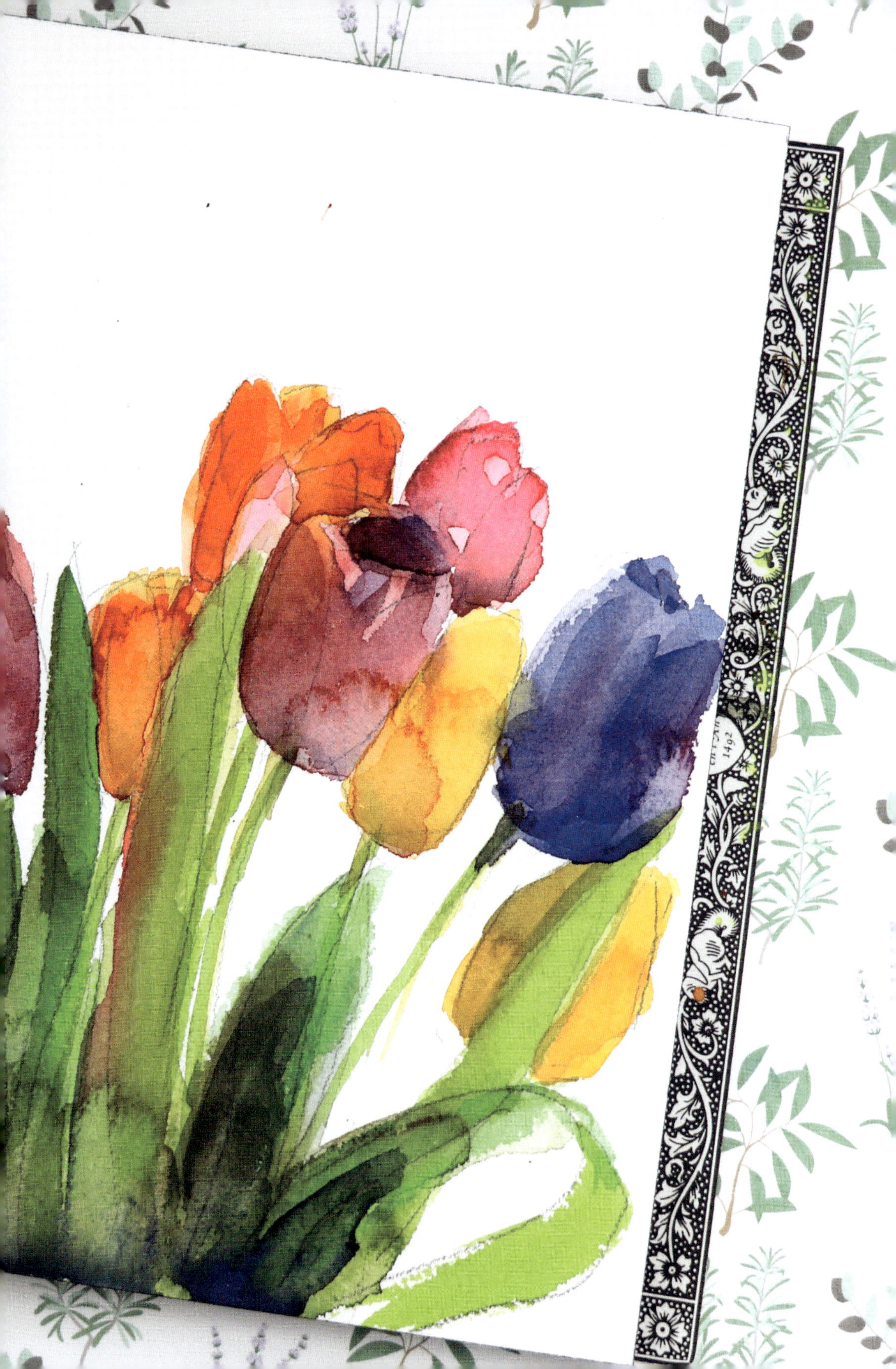

POPPIES

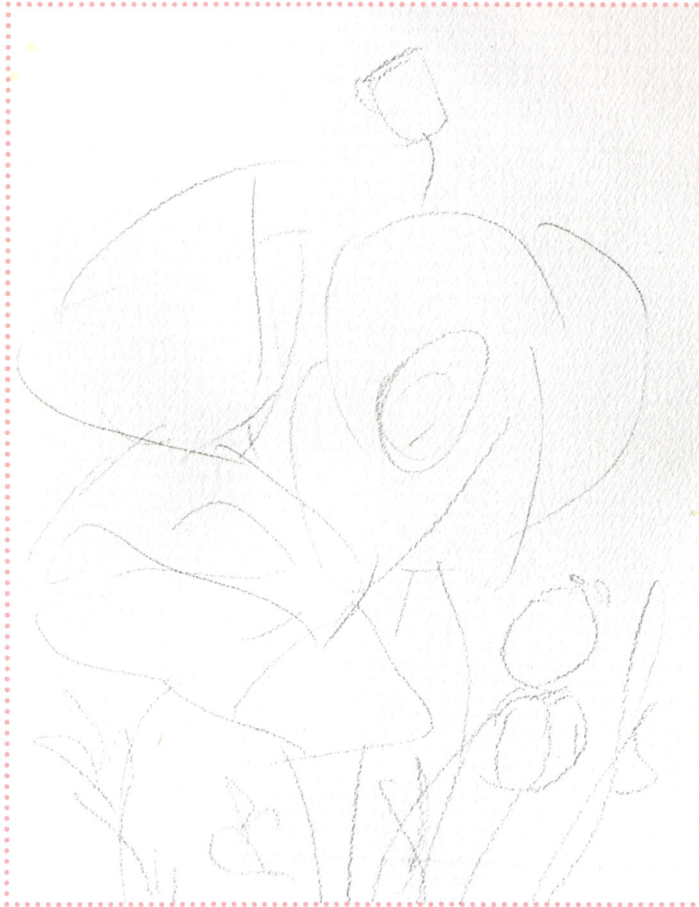

STEP 1:

Choose any color you like. Poppies usually have a dark or yellow center. Create a quick pencil sketch of the flower. Start with the basic outline of the flower, followed by the seedpods and stems. Make each flower a little different to add variety and interest to your composition.

Next add the stems and leaves. Poppy leaves are variegated with fringed edges. Don't add too much detail—simply create a rough sketch to get started.

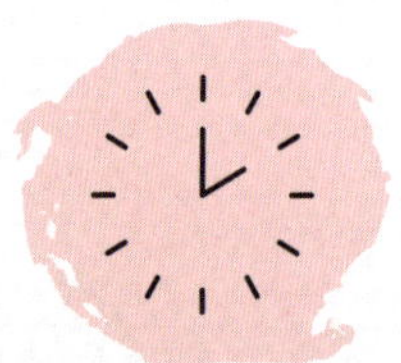

Quick Tip

Start with a basic palette of sample colors straight from the tube mixed with a little water. You can create a collection of swatches (see page 14) to test out your chosen colors. Try to use a variety of vibrant colors and earth tones.

Knowing the general shape of the flower you wish you paint will help you lay down the basic outline for the painting. Then let the watercolor create the layers and effects through the blooming and blending of colors.

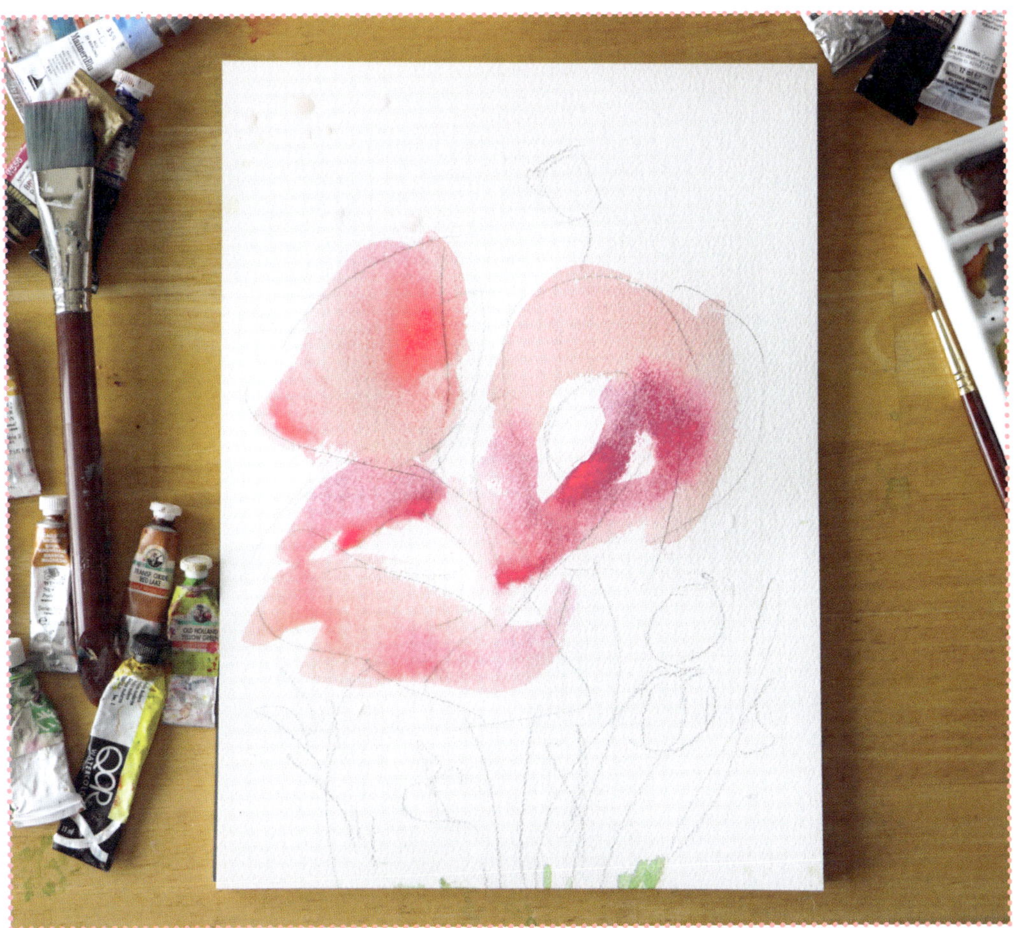

STEP 2:

Add a layer of paint to the flower petals. Here I used pink mixed with some yellow and a bit of green to tone and warm the cool pink color. Then I added some pink onto the wet paint. You want the colors to mix together a bit on the page.

With watercolor, always add the petals before the leaves and stems. If I were to need more room for the flowers, I would have a hard time using watercolor paint to cover the stems and leaves.

STEP 3:

Add green paint to create stems, leaves, and seedpods. Keep them loose using quick strokes. Hold the paintbrush near the end of the handle. Gripping the brush close to the paper is more appropriate for controlled detail work.

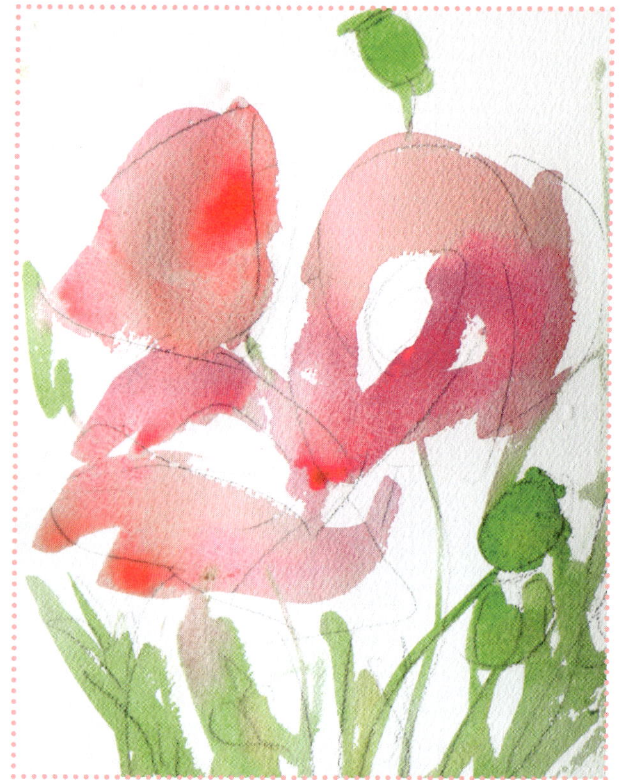

STEP 4:

Add a dark or light center to your still-wet poppy centers. You can also add a touch of this center color to each upright closed or cup-shaped poppy where the stem meets the base of the petals. This gives a hint of the center color shining through the petals. Because we are working wet-into-wet, the dark or yellow center will bleed into the petal colors.

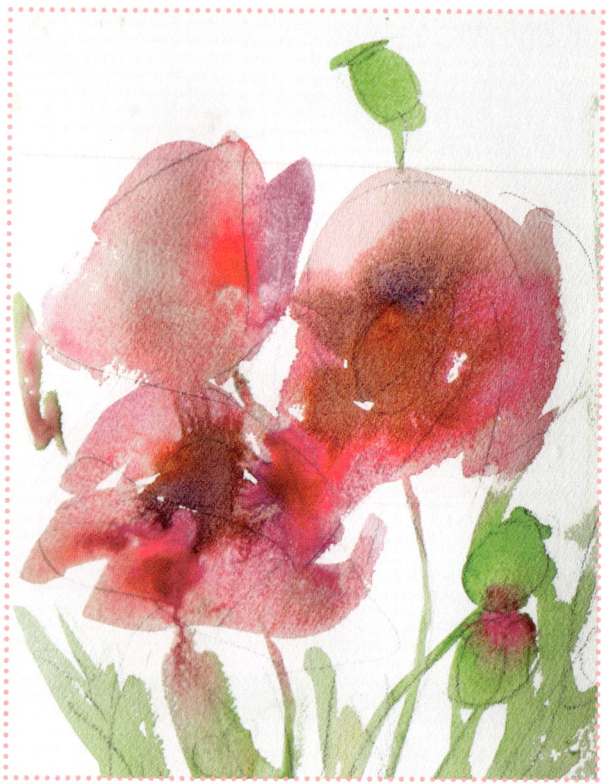

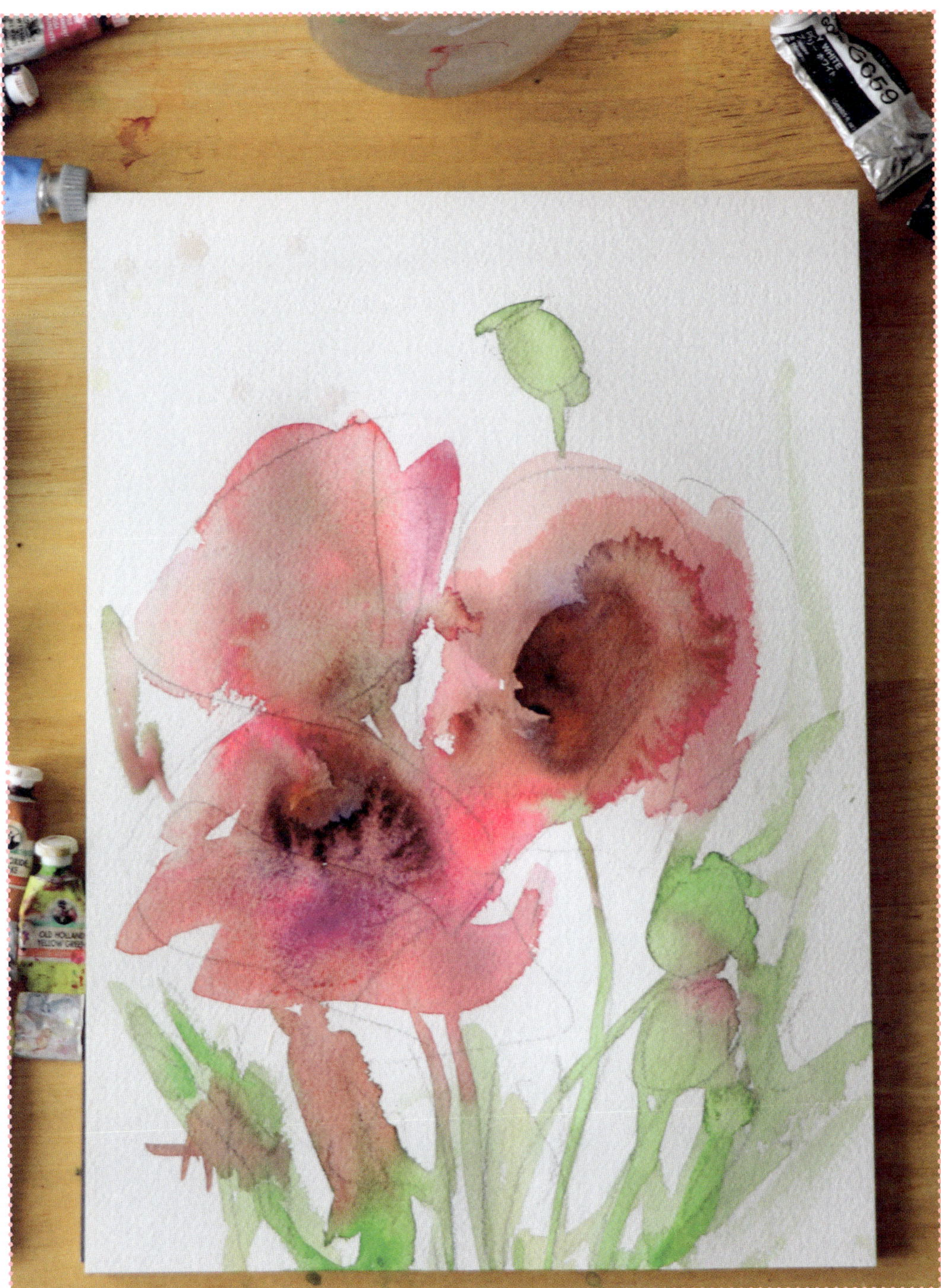

STEP 5:

Create a light wash of the dark or yellow center, which bleeds a bit into the petals. When the petals are mostly dry, add a second wash of darker or more yellow, which dramatically colors the center without bleeding into the petal paint.

AZALEAS

Azaleas are a quite dramatic because of the color and value contrasts between the flowers and leaves. They also provide the perfect opportunity for loose and quick painting, as you can suggest the flowers and leaves without painting each individual petal.

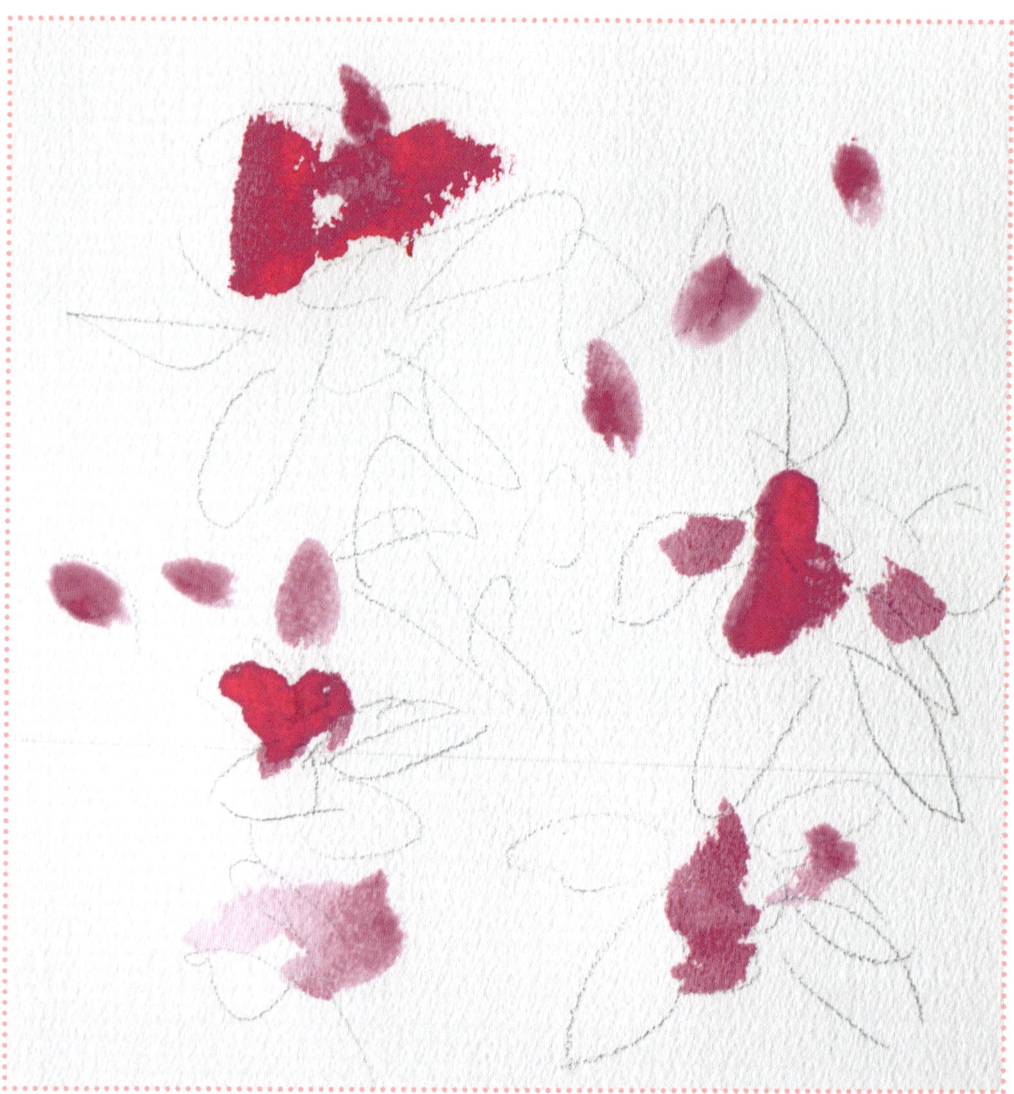

STEP 1:

Start with a basic pencil sketch, laying out where you want your flowers. The basic shape of azalea leaves are single, smooth undulate almond-shaped leaves. The leaves are quite dark and shiny.

STEP 2:

Next lay down bright washes of color for the flowers. Add water as needed to lighten the saturation of color. You can mix either yellow, green, or blue into some of the pink to tone down the color.

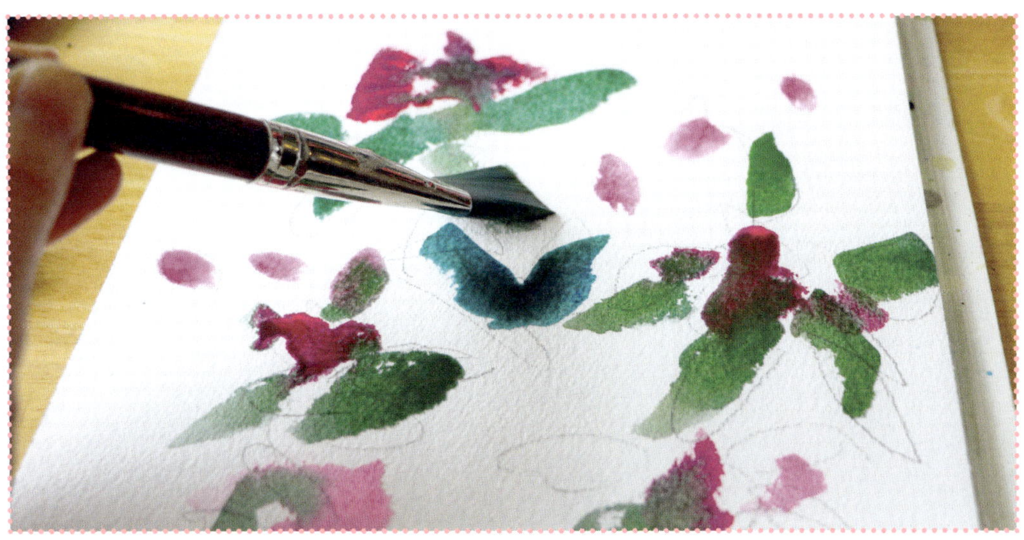

STEP 3:

For darker leaves, mix a dark blue, such as ultramarine blue or phthalo blue with a yellow, such as cadmium yellow. To make the darkest leaves, use more of the blue paint. To make the lighter-colored leaves, use more yellow in the green mixture. If the color seems too bright, tone it down with some of the pink or red paint on your palette.

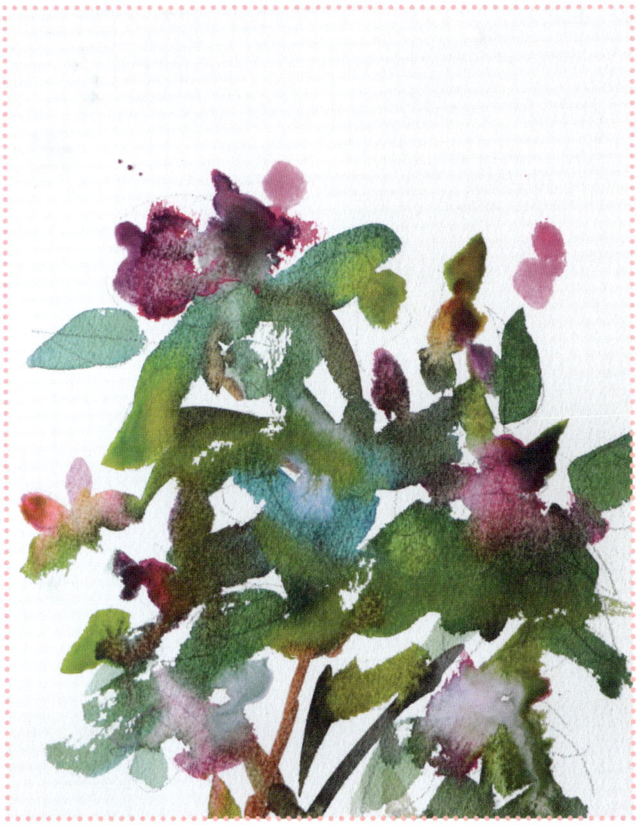

STEP 4:

Working wet-into-wet will create some interesting effects, such as blooming (washed out areas with delineated color deposits) and blending of colors. Add more flowers as needed to balance out the composition.

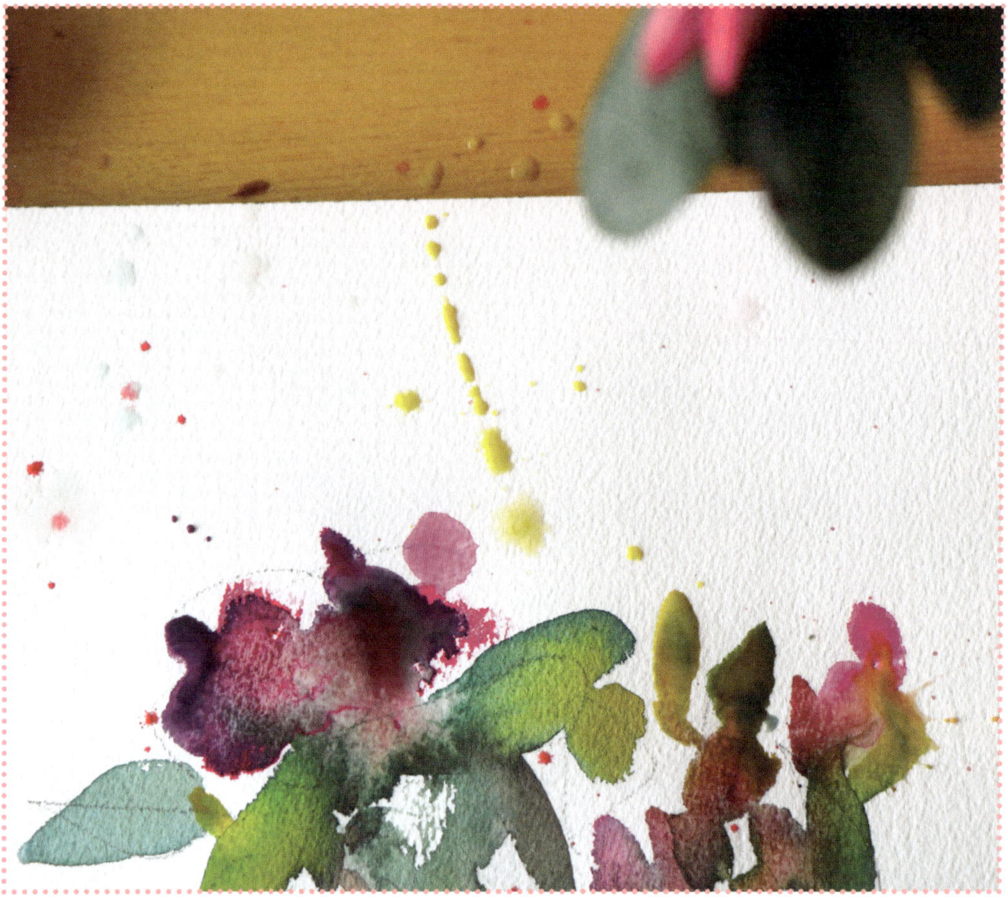

As mentioned earlier, use splatters of color and large brushstrokes near the base of the plants to add weight and color balance to the final painting.

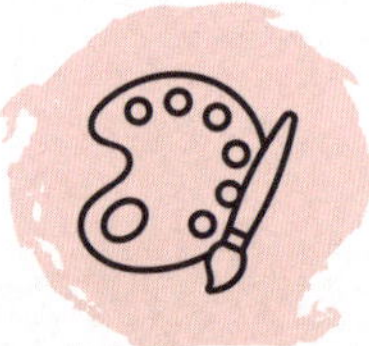

Creative Exercise: Flower Shapes

Try drawing your own flower shapes. Flowers come in basic shapes such as star, trumpet, pom-pom, cup or bowl, spike, and lace. Focus on fast and quick sketches of the general shapes.

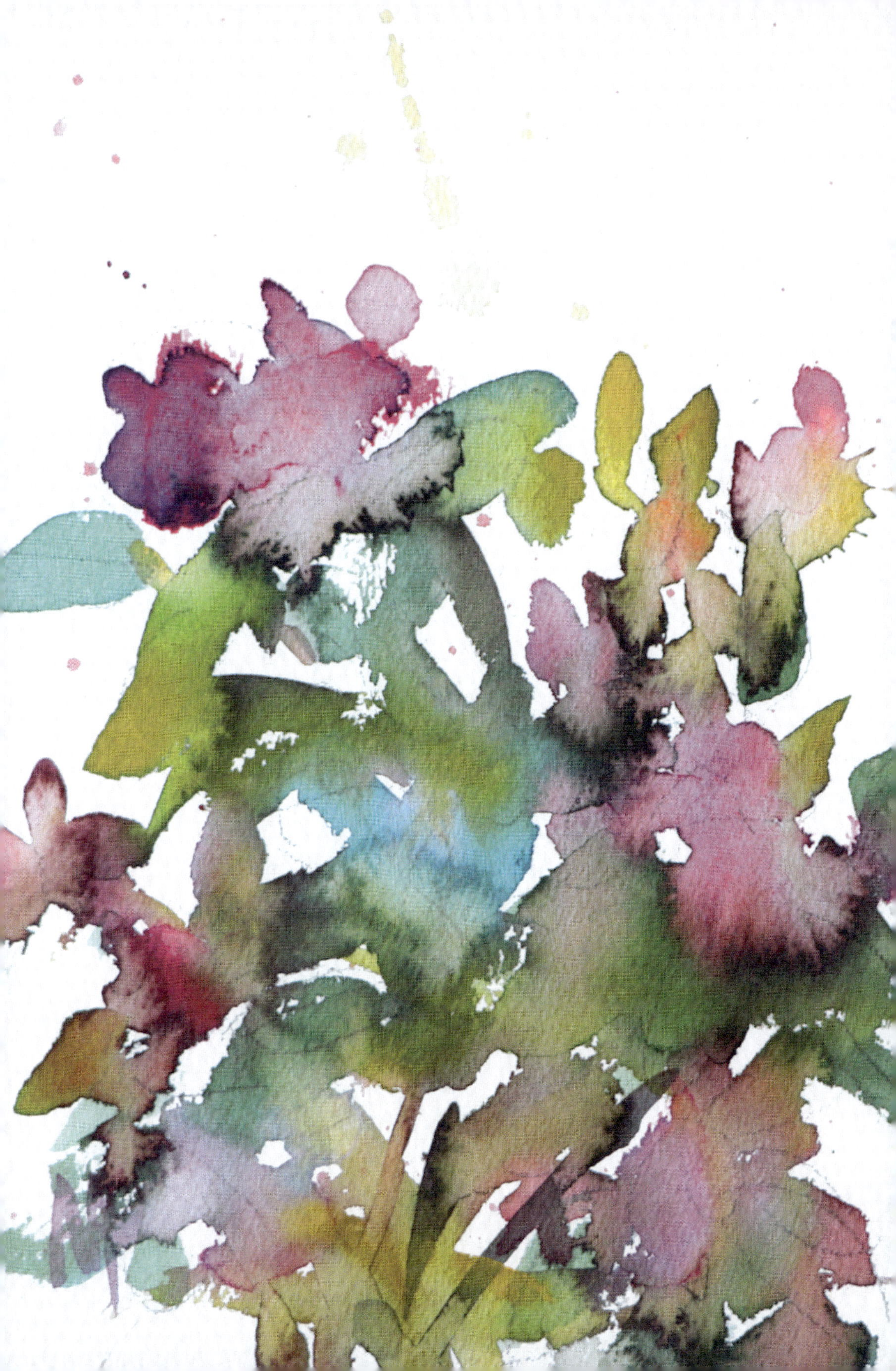

DELPHINIUMS

Now let's try a tall spike-shaped flower. We are going to keep this painting very loose and simply suggest the shape of the flowers with watercolor.

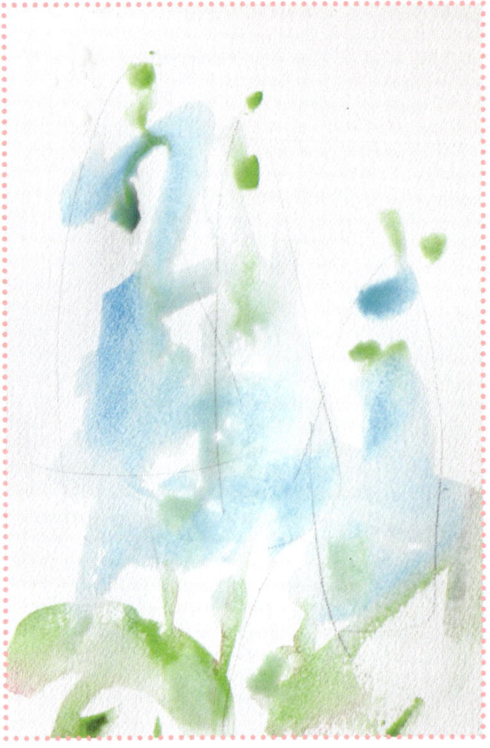

STEP 1:

Start with a basic pencil sketch of the shapes on your watercolor paper. Notice I do not actually sketch any of the individual flowers. Use your flat brush to paint a first wash of cerulean blue, blue green, and blue pink or violet to create the flowers.

STEP 2:

While the paint is still wet, use your round brush to add dots of ultramarine violet or a similar color to create more pronounced flowers. These dots of paint will softly blend into the background.

With watercolor, there is a fine line between letting the paint and water work together and letting them get out of control. Just enjoy the process and see what happens.

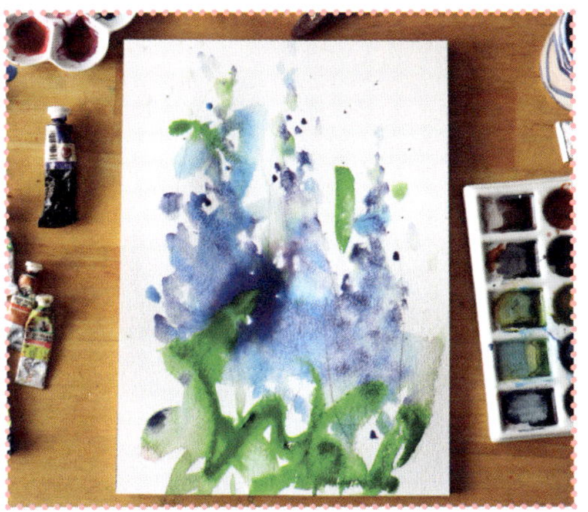

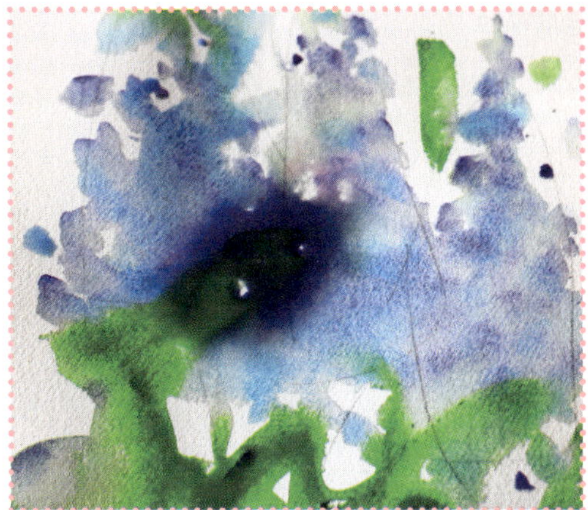

STEP 3:

Use your round and flat brush to create stems and leaves with green paint. With your round brush, add some green to the tops of the flowers with smaller flower buds. Notice the pooling effect created with this amount of water and paint. Sometimes these pooling effects can add a softness to the painting. Let the paint dry completely.

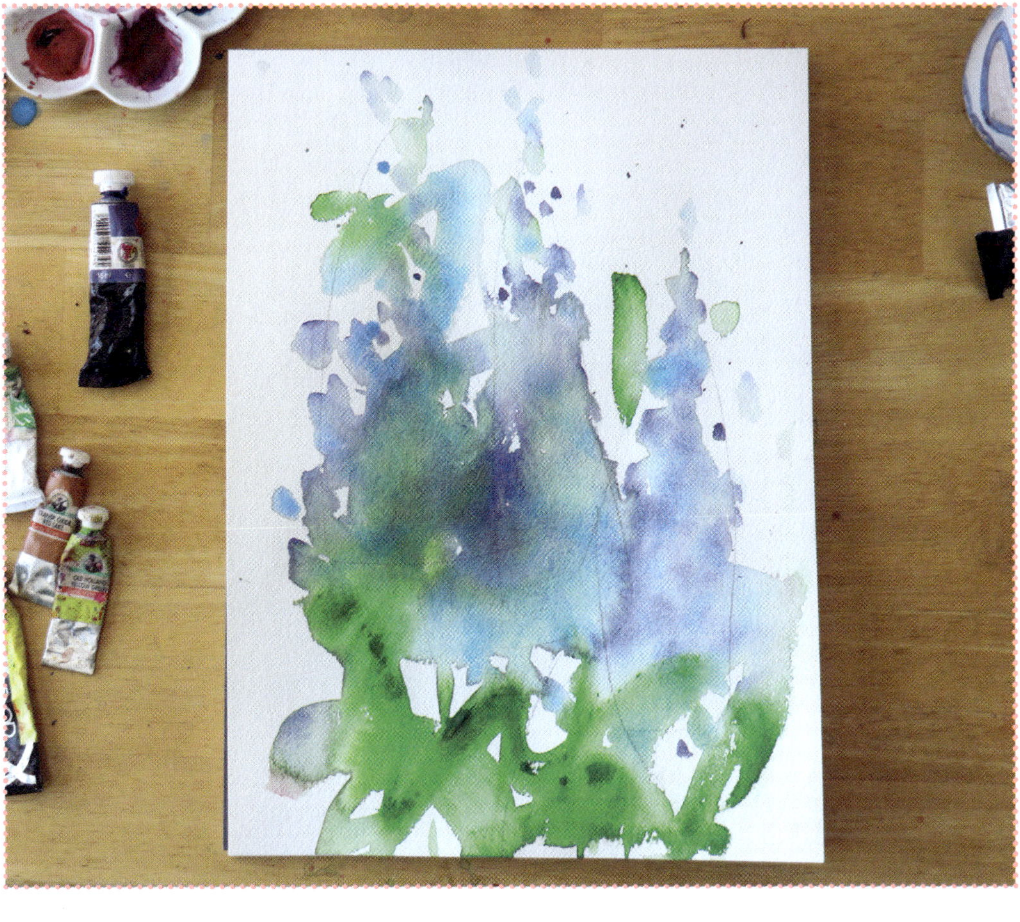

BOUQUET OF AZALEAS

Now we will create a still life from what you have learned so far. With watercolors, there may be some extra drying time needed between the background layer and the flowers.

STEP 1:

Start by adding a light background to give your painting some depth. Use a flat brush and some pale yellow ochre (or color of your choice) mixed with a generous amount of water. Starting at the top of your paper, paint from left to right (or right to left if you are left-handed).

Create a more saturated line about two-thirds down the paper, suggesting a horizon line that will become the table. Leave the center area blank for the flowerpot. Once completely dry, sketch the flowerpot, flowers, and leaves with a pencil.

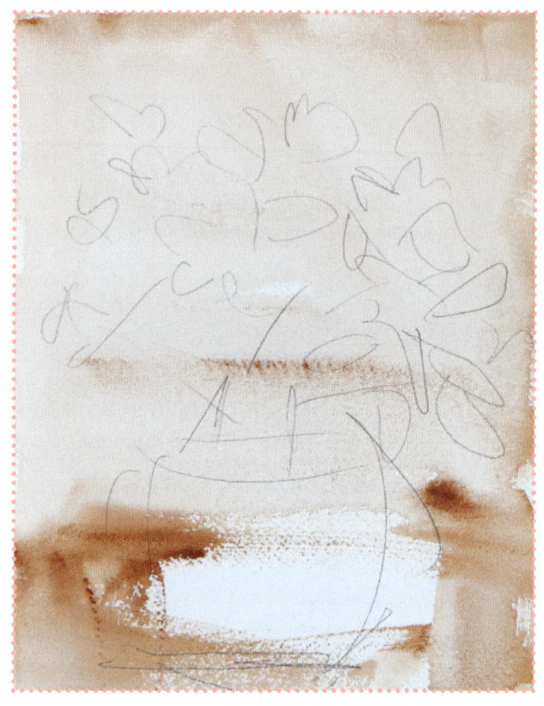

STEP 2:

Use a flat brush and turquoise blue to paint a round flowerpot. Using a mixture of turquoise blue and dragon's blood (or any transparent earth-red paint), add a darker shaded area to the left side of the flowerpot. Make sure to use clean water and replace whenever your water is no longer clear.

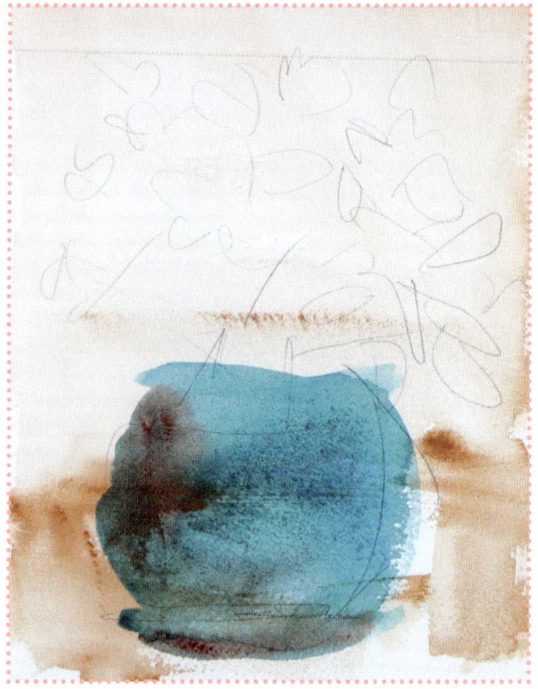

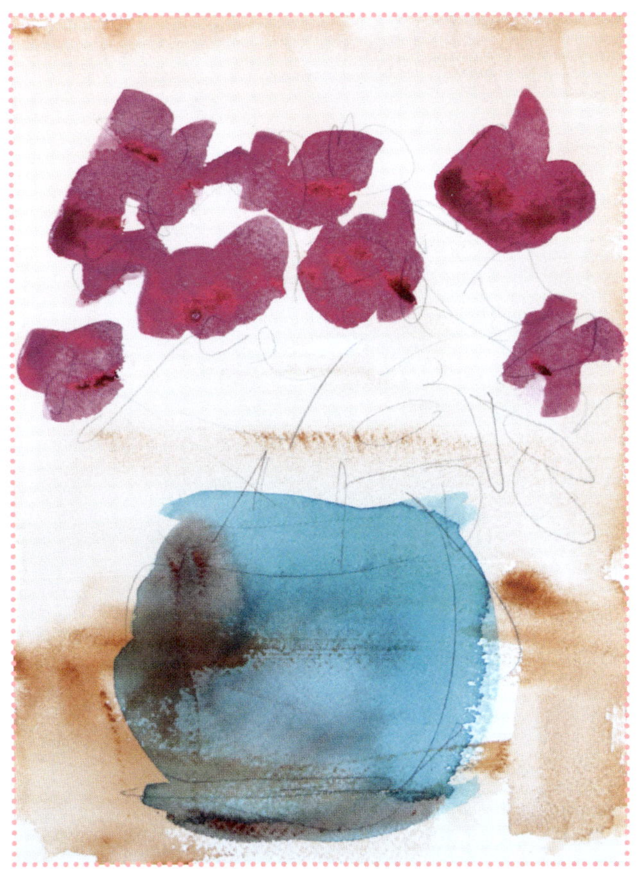

STEP 3:

Using a cool pink, such as permanent rose, and a flat brush, add watered-down pink flowers to the paper where you sketched the flowers in pencil. Let the flowers dry.

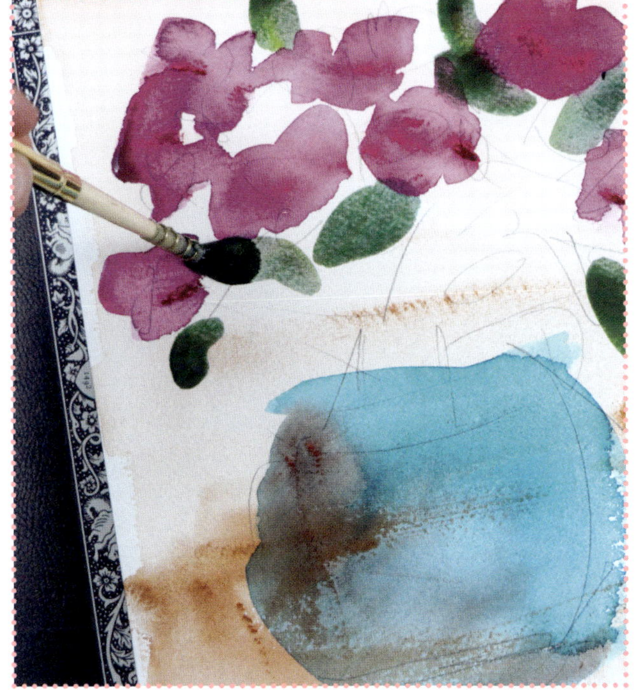

STEP 4:

Now add some leaves using a mixture of blue and yellow paint. Add some of the pink or transparent earth orange to create darker shades of green.

Using a round brush, paint leaves in all directions around the flowers and close to the opening of the flowerpot. Leave some space between the leaves and flowerpot for the stems (step 5).

STEP 5:

Use the round brush and either a dark green or violet mixture to add a dark shadow for the opening of the flowerpot. Mix some of the pink with either a little blue or green and add some darker flower petals with the round brush.

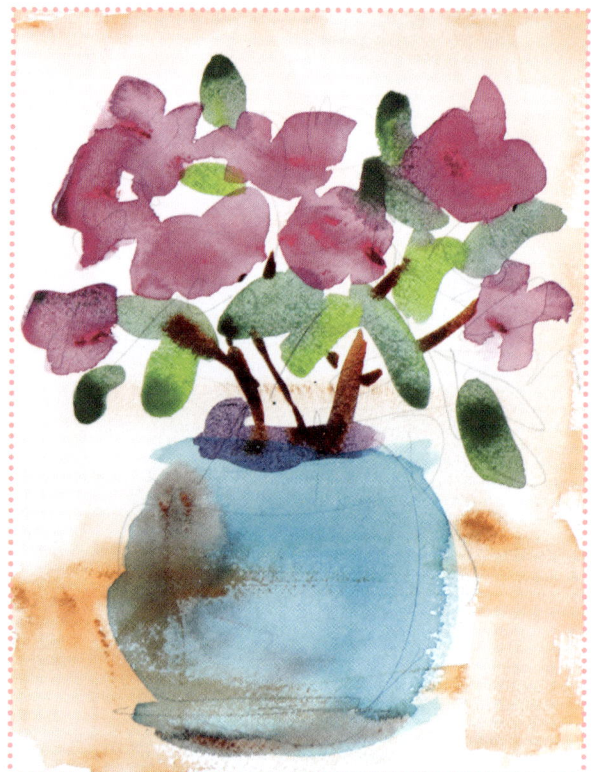

STEP 6:

Now add some yellow to the pink and some of the green paint mixtures to make some warmer shades of pink and green for the flowers and leaves. Add a few more leaves and flower petals in these warmer tones with the round brush.

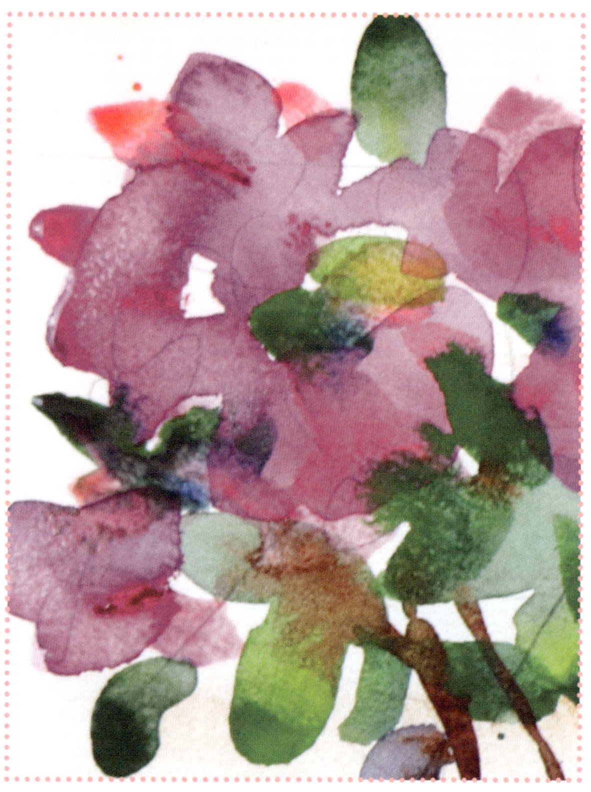

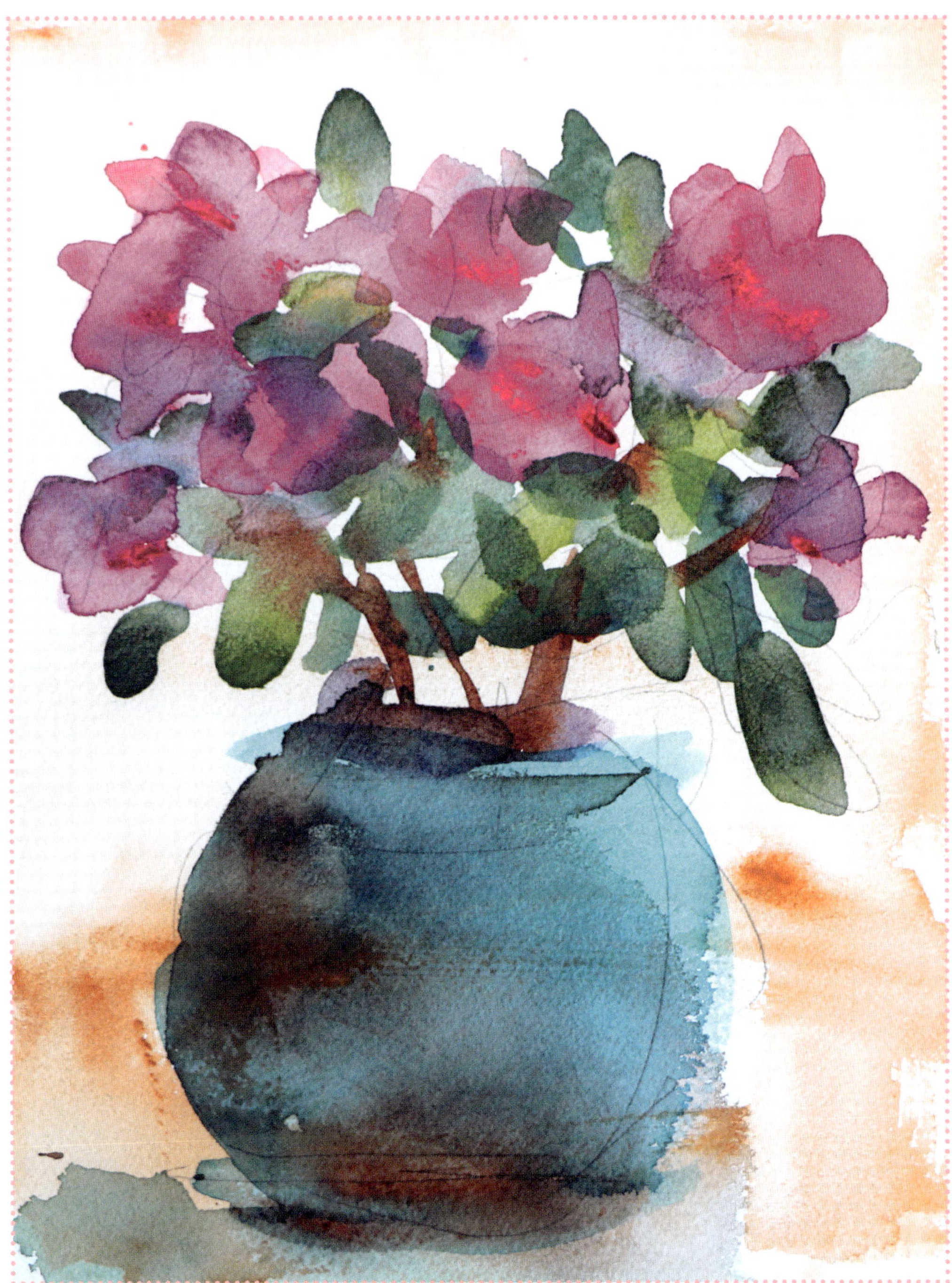

STEP 7:

Add another wash of the turquoise blue and transparent red mixture to the left side of the flowerpot. Add a shadow to the base of the flowerpot using a dark green. Let dry completely.

STEP 8:

Apply a dark shadow to the left side of the flowerpot and along the bottom. While the paint is still wet, immediately apply a spritz or mist of water using your spray bottle. This will soften the brushstrokes and blend them into the existing paint.

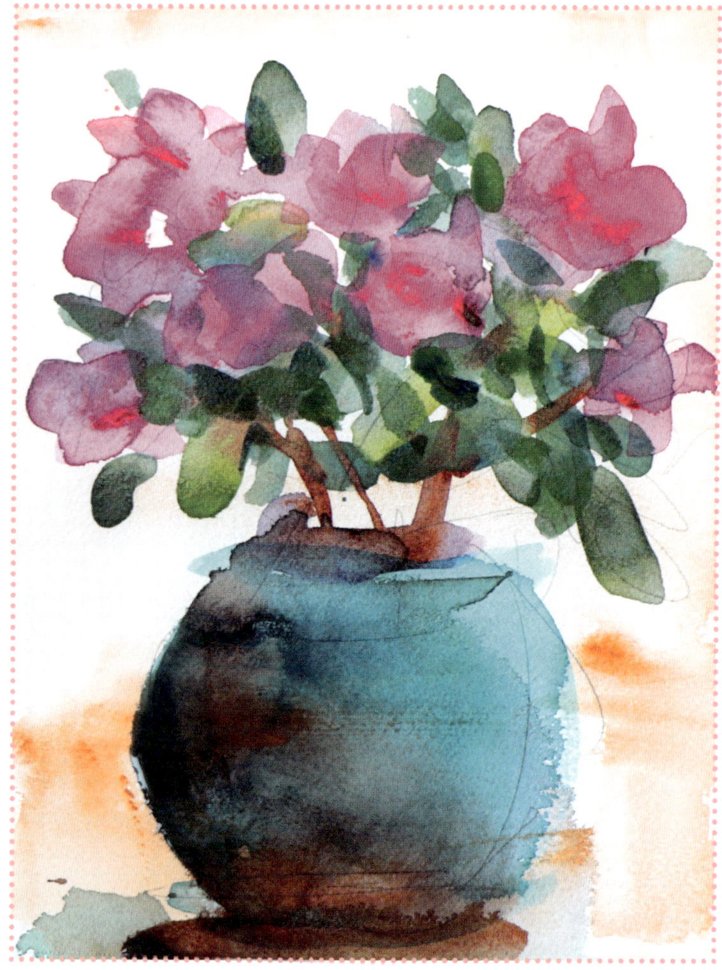

STEP 9:

Let dry completely before removing from your watercolor block.

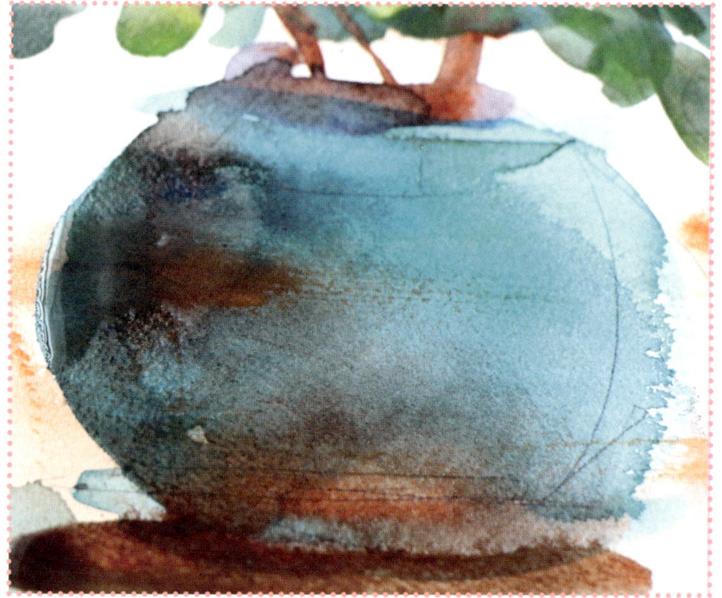

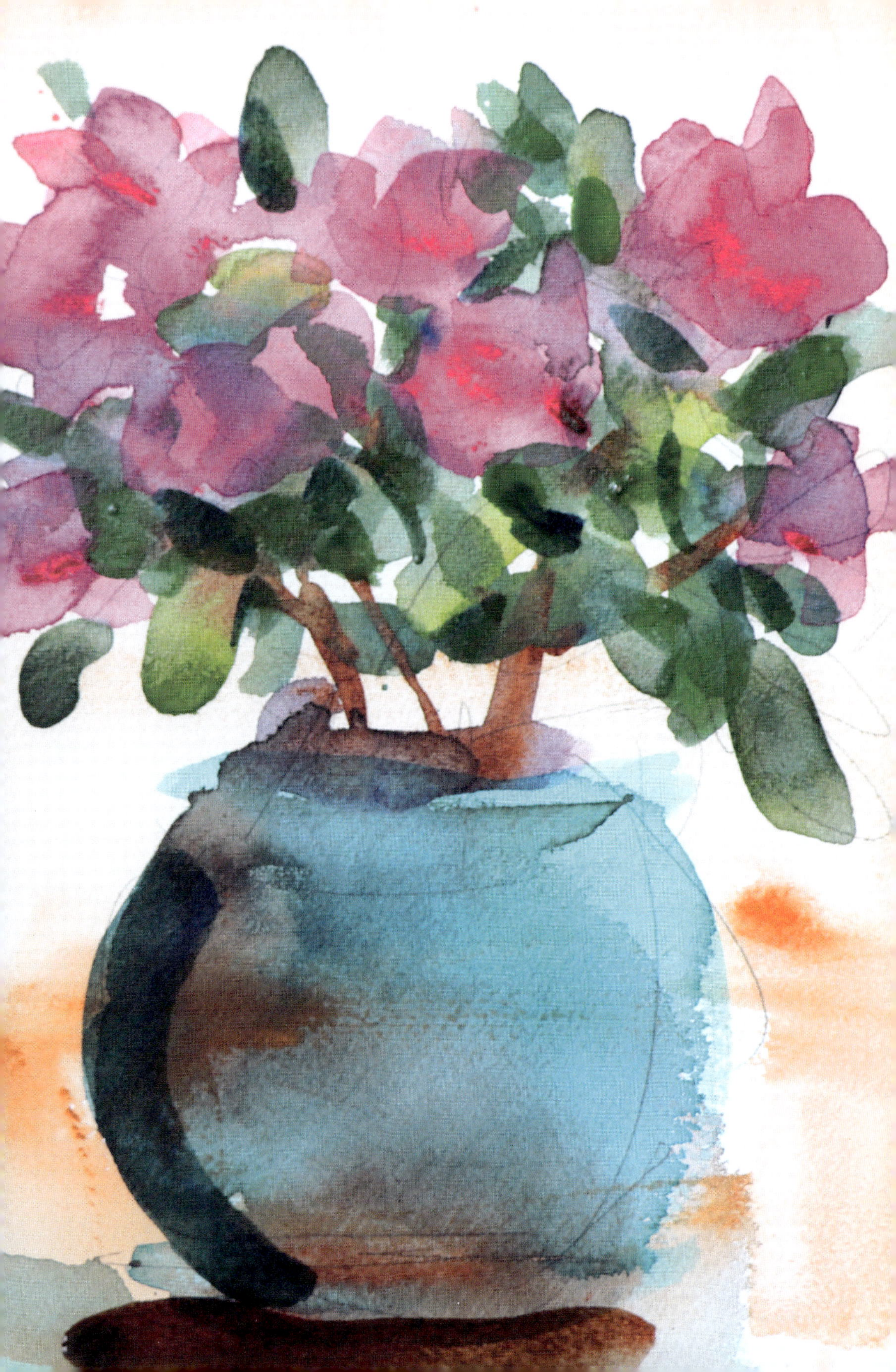

Birds

Once you learn the basics, you can apply them to many different varieties of birds. We will paint two types of birds, European robins and a mountain bluebird.

Supplies

- Watercolor paper (block or secured on board)
- Medium round and flat brushes
- Small round brush
- Watercolor paints
- Colors: cerulean blue, burnt sienna, permanent rose, cadmium yellow, transparent earth orange, black lake, titanium white
- Palette for mixing paints
- Spray bottle (optional)
- Jar of water
- Tissue or paper towels for cleanup

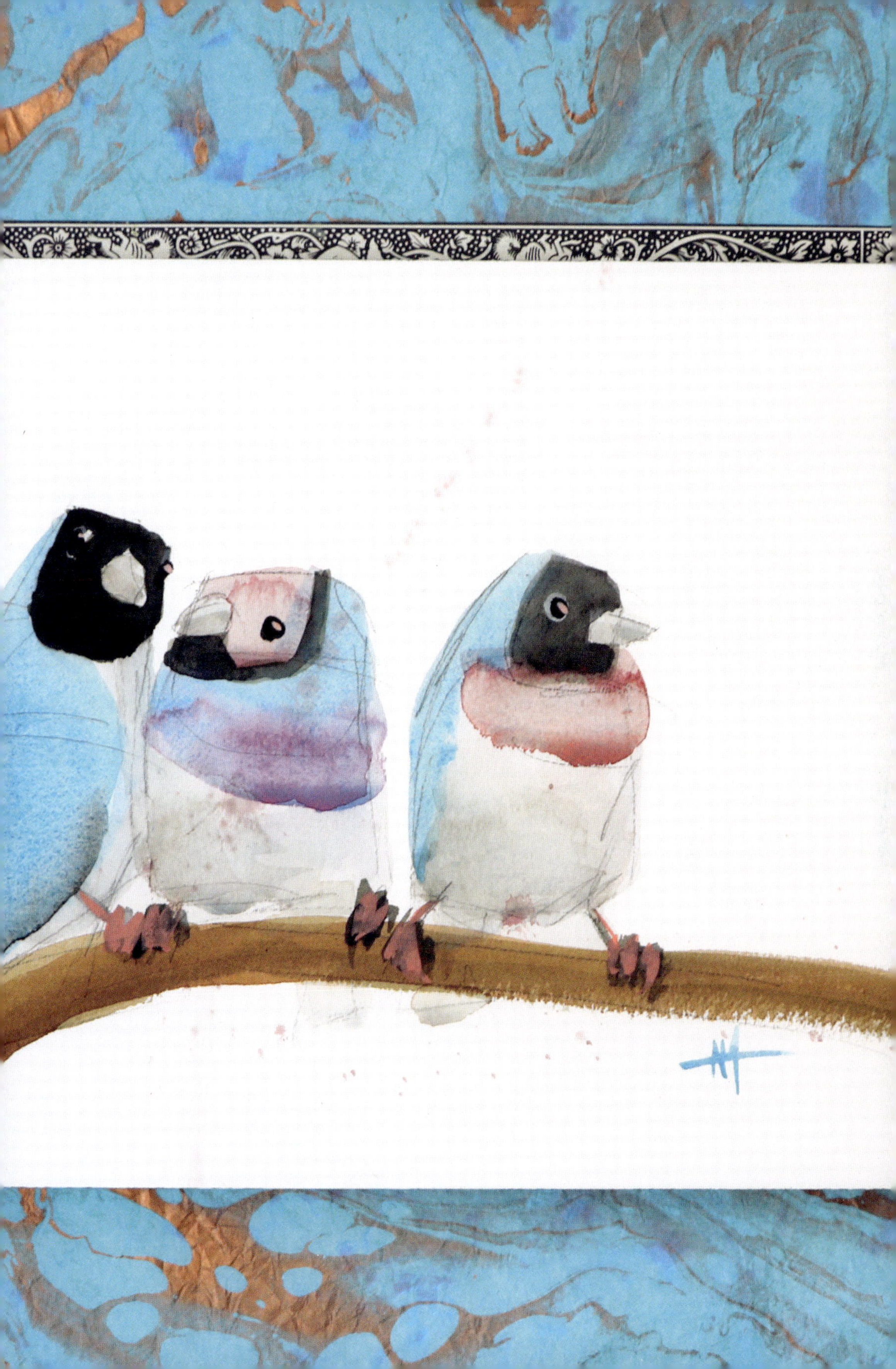

MOUNTAIN BLUEBIRD

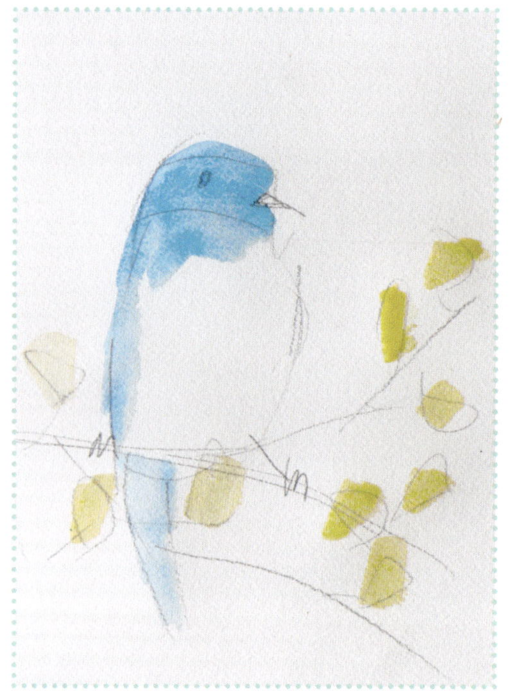

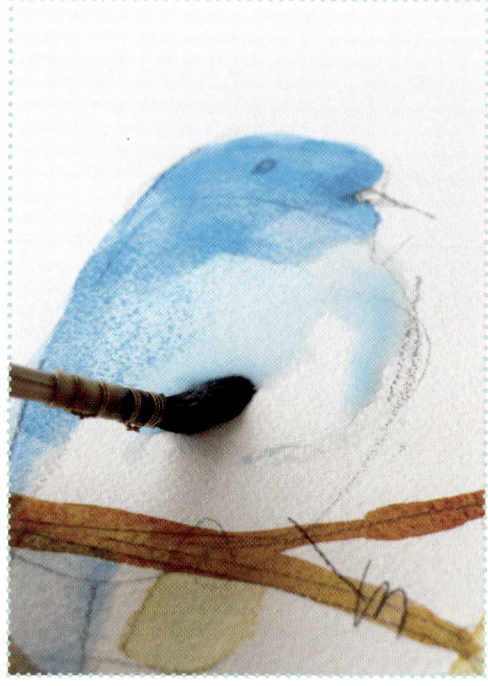

STEP 1:

Draw the bird, branch, and willow buds. Pick up some blue paint for the head, wings, and back of the bird. Mix yellow and white to make a pale yellow for the willow buds. Add a touch of blue, if desired, to make more of a yellow-green.

STEP 2:

Now that the blue on the bird has had a chance to dry for a few minutes, add a watered-down version of the blue paint to create a lighter blue belly on the bird.

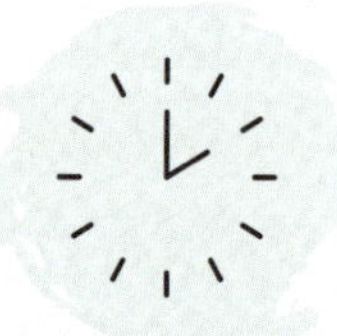

Quick Tip

Make sure to avoid touching the branch until the paint is completely dry. Stop before the branch, if necessary. If the branch is still wet, the brown paint will run into the body of the bird. You can always go back later and add more watered-down paint to the edge of the branch.

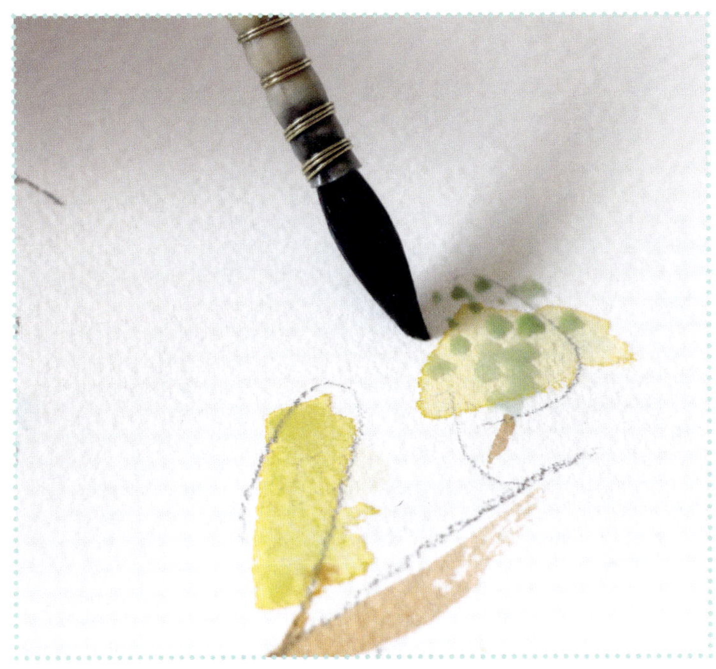

STEP 3:

Use the tip of a round brush to make yellow-green dots on the buds. Start with the yellow buds that are dry. Some may not be dry yet. It's okay if the dots run a bit into the wet paint.

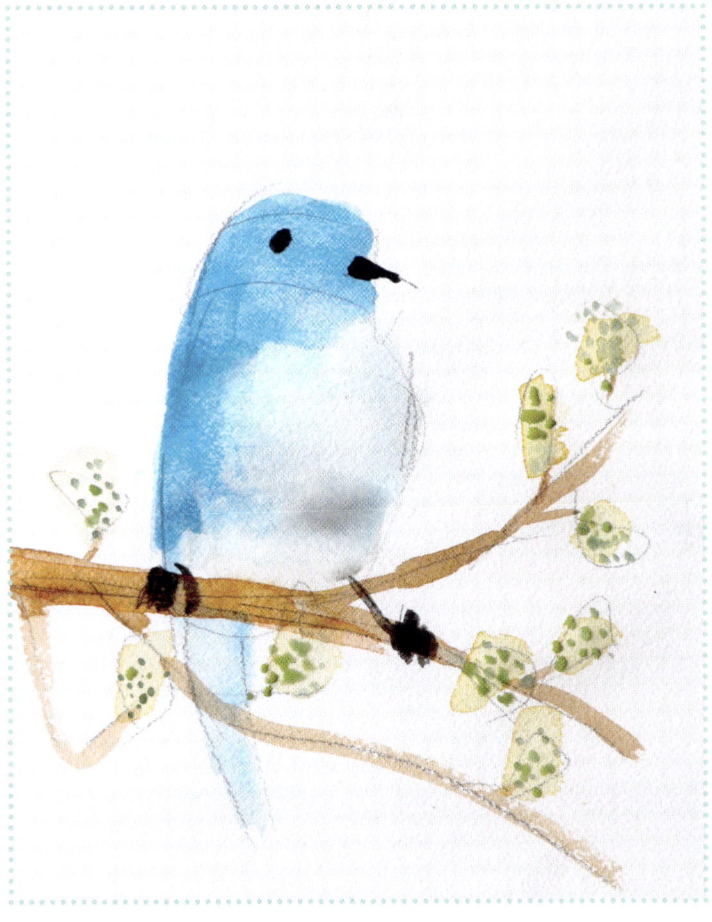

STEP 4:

Finish the belly with watered down blue or gray paint, so it completely touches the now-dry branch. Add the black eyes, beak, and feet.

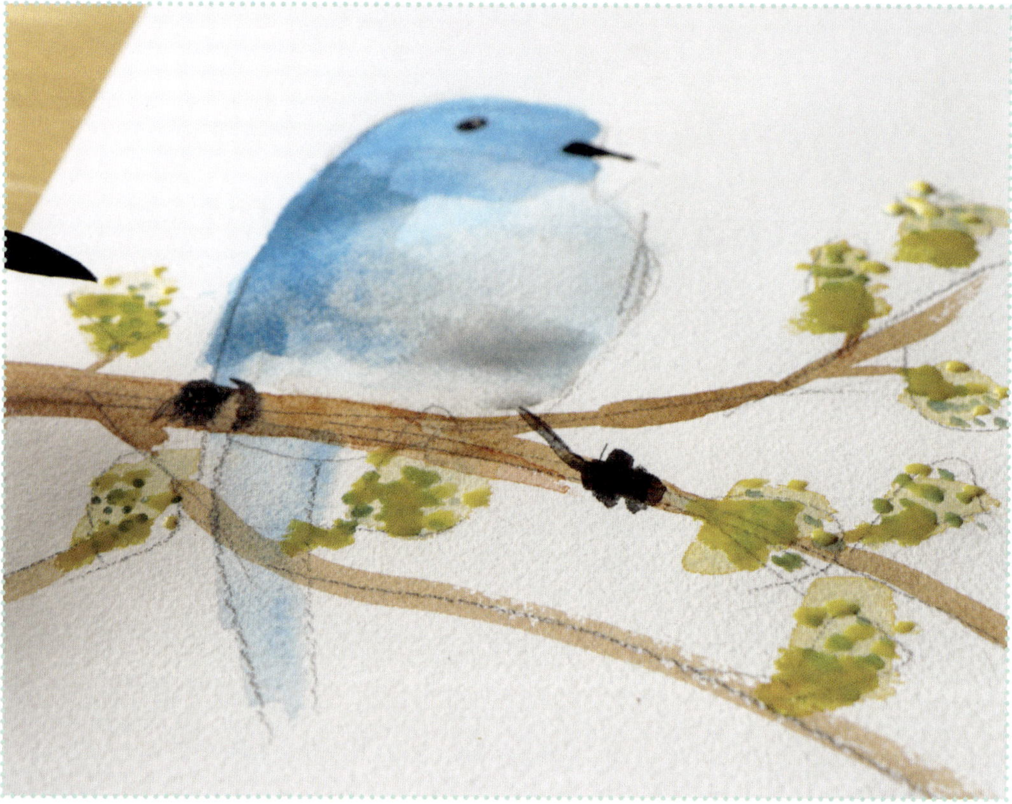

STEP 5:

Use the tip of a round brush to add more white-yellow dots to the willow buds. Some can extend beyond the yellow bud to create the willow catkins.

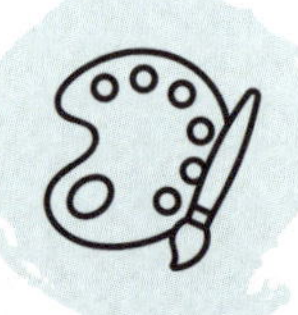

Creative Exercise: Swatches

When selecting a palette of colors, use your watercolor sketchbook or a separate piece of paper to create a list of swatches or color mixes. Experiment with color mixing and blending and take notes to find the right combinations.

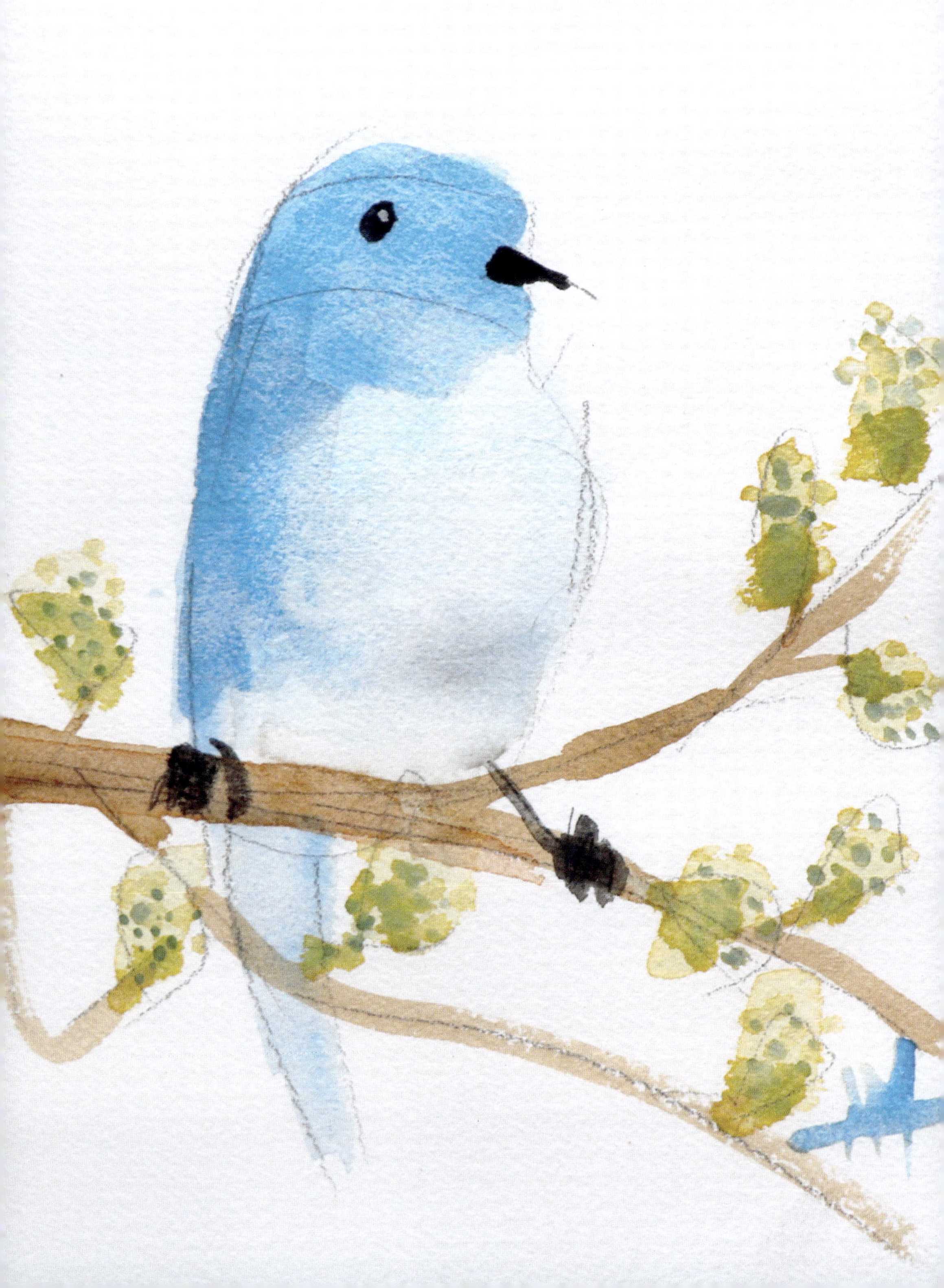

EUROPEAN ROBINS

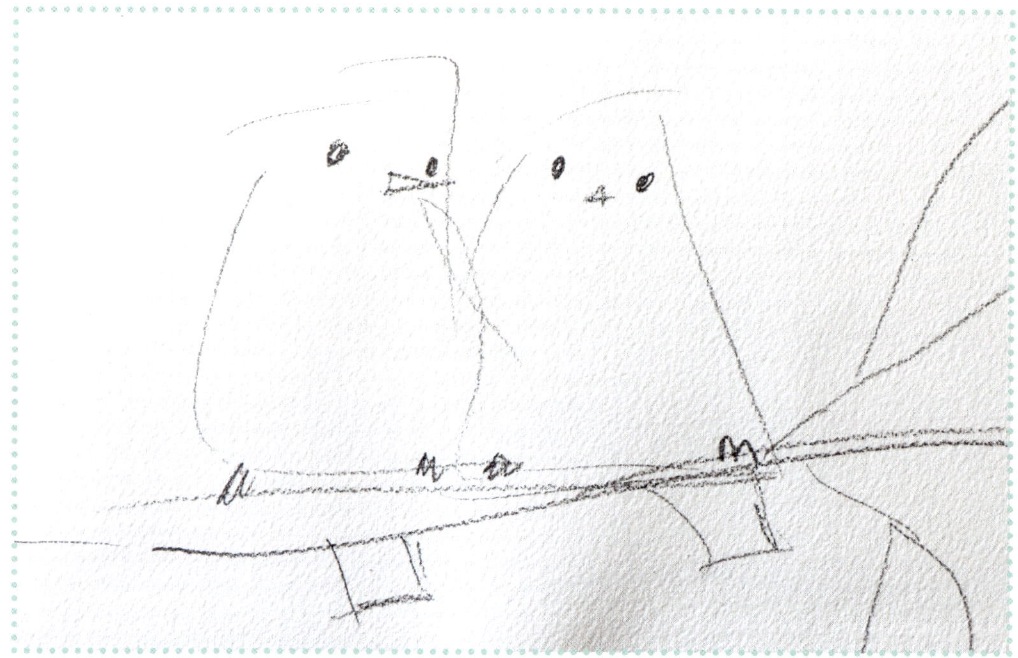

STEP 1:

Start by sketching the basic shape of your birds. Don't fuss with feathers and small details. Make sure to draw the eyes, beaks, and feet of the birds. Add some leaves to the branch, if you like. Try to balance the composition by placing the birds slightly off-center and adding leaves to the branch on the other side of the birds.

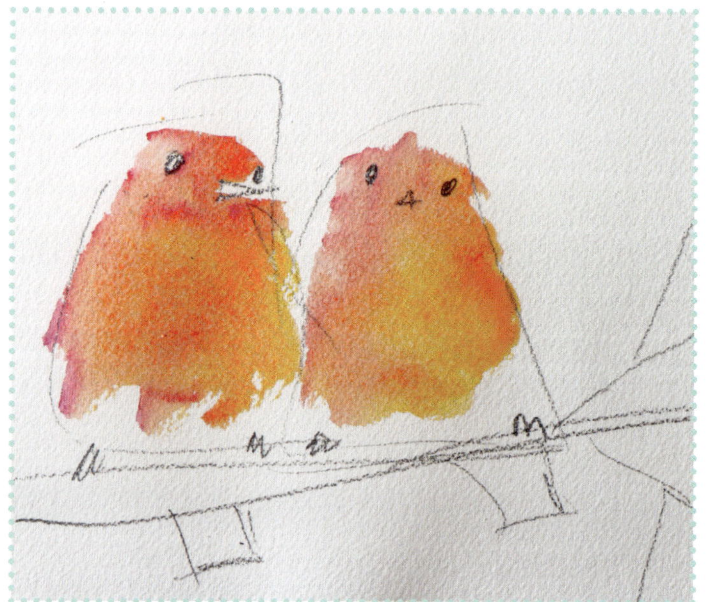

STEP 2:

Mix yellow and rose with a touch of burnt sienna. Lay down the red-orange paint mixture on the bodies of the birds. The red-orange color should extend to the face area of the head.

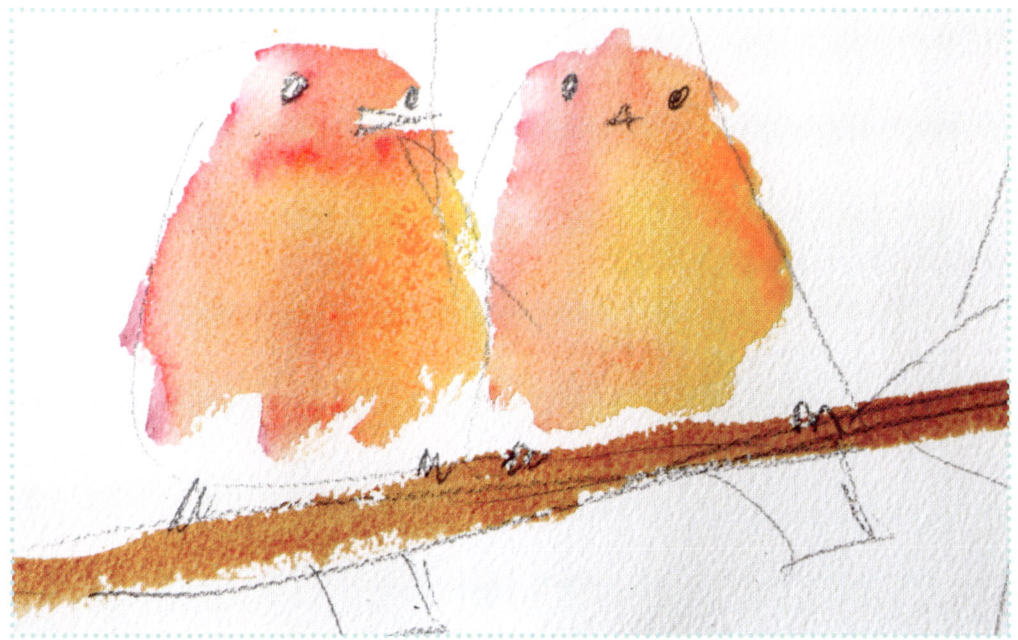

STEP 3:

Mix a brown for the tree branch. You can use just the transparent earth orange or burnt sienna, or you can mix a bit of burnt sienna into the transparent earth orange for a more reddish brown.

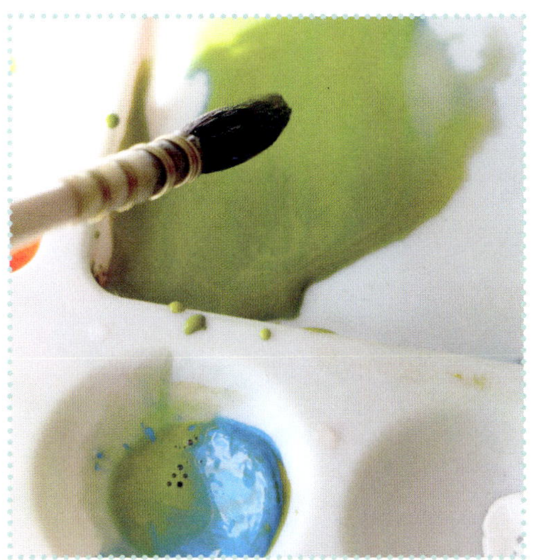

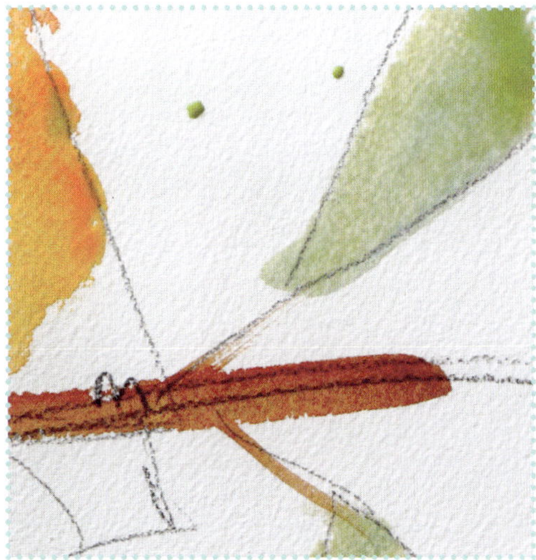

STEP 4:

Mix blue and yellow, and add a touch of rose or burnt sienna to tone down the green. Paint the leaves. It's okay if a few drops of paint splatter onto your paper. It creates an effect and tells the story that this is a watercolor painting.

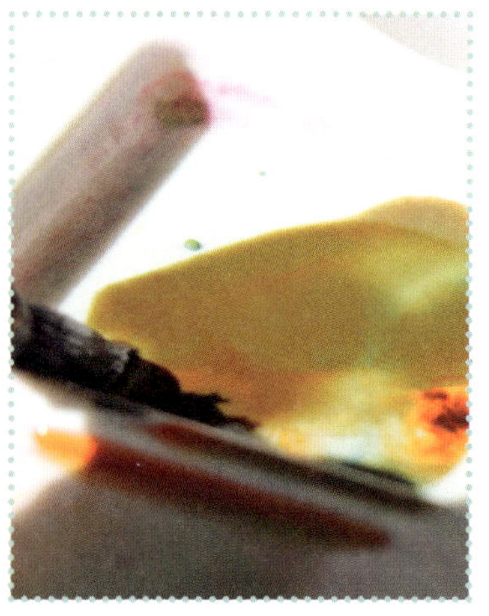

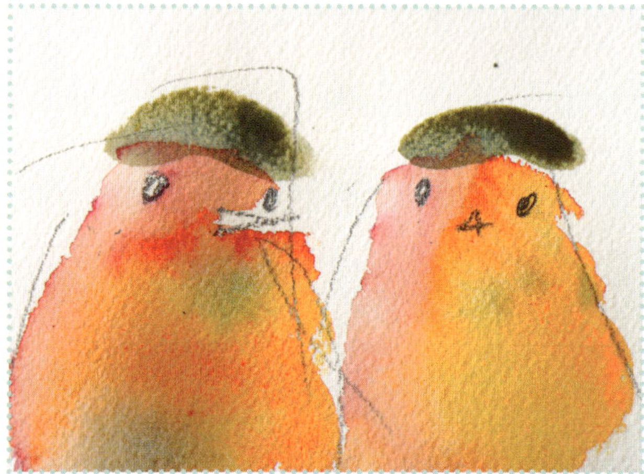

STEP 5:

Mix a warm gray for the body of the birds, using cerulean blue, burnt sienna, and touch of yellow. Add more blue if it looks too brown. Add some black to the gray mixture for the darker tail area.

Paint heads and wings on the birds. The wings are just suggested. If you want to try another bird later that has markings on its wings, let the base color dry completely before adding more color for the markings.

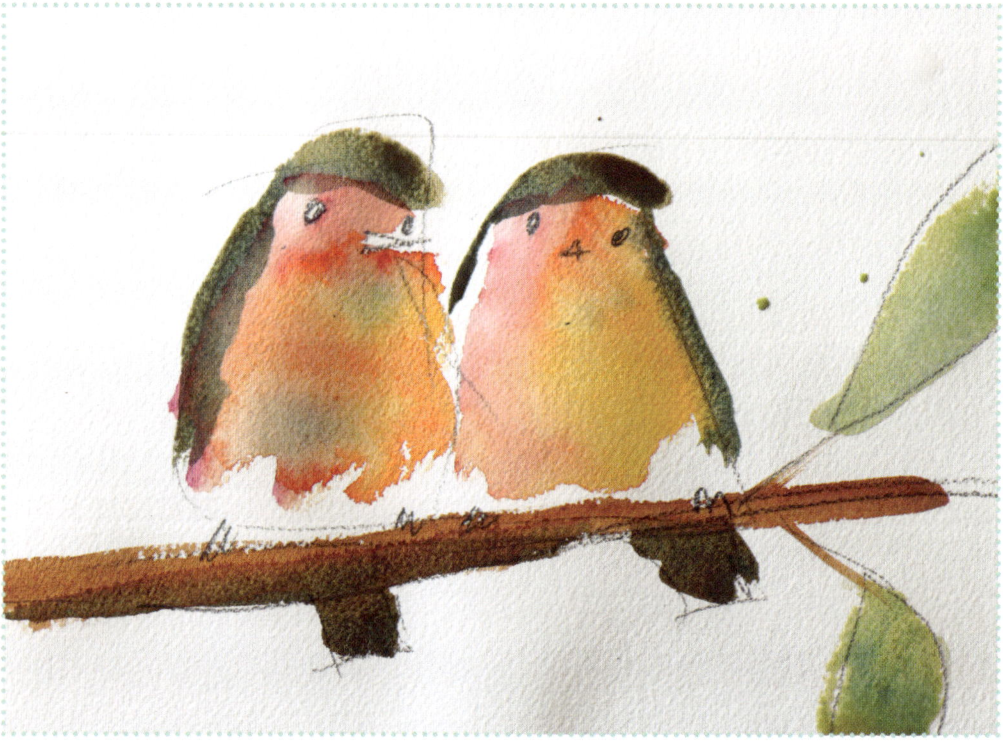

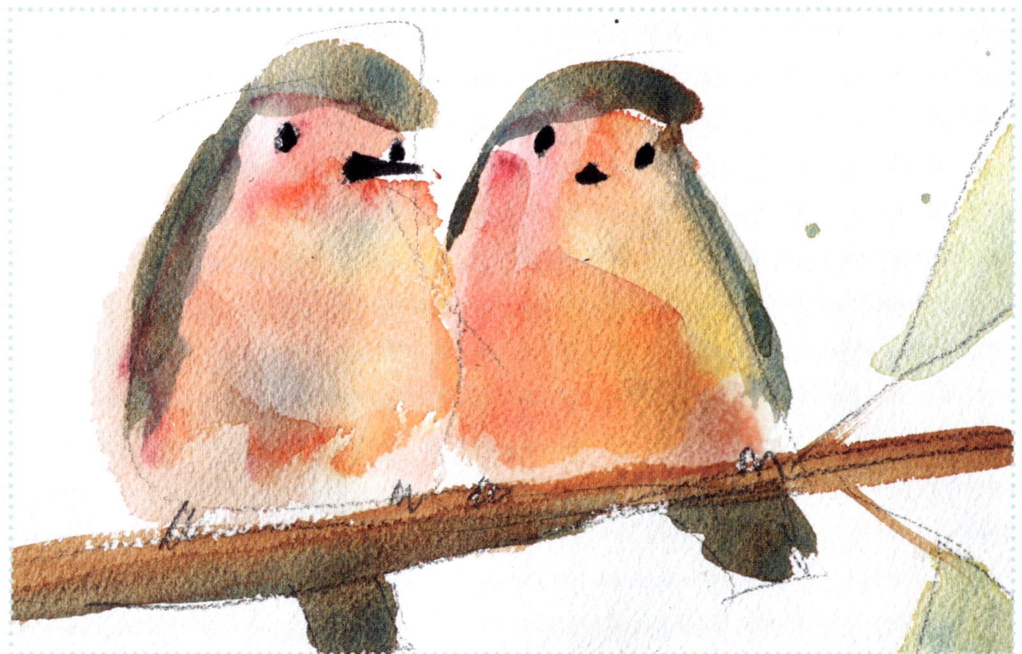

STEP 6:

Use titanium white mixed with gray (or just a watered-down gray) for the bottom of the bird bellies. If you have the time, add a shaded area with darker brown paint to the bottom of the branch and a more orange-red color to the middle of the bird bellies.

Use a small round brush to pick up some black lake paint for the eyes, beaks, and feet.

STEP 7:

Wait for the black paint to dry. Use your brush to add more shading and details to the leaves and birds, as desired.

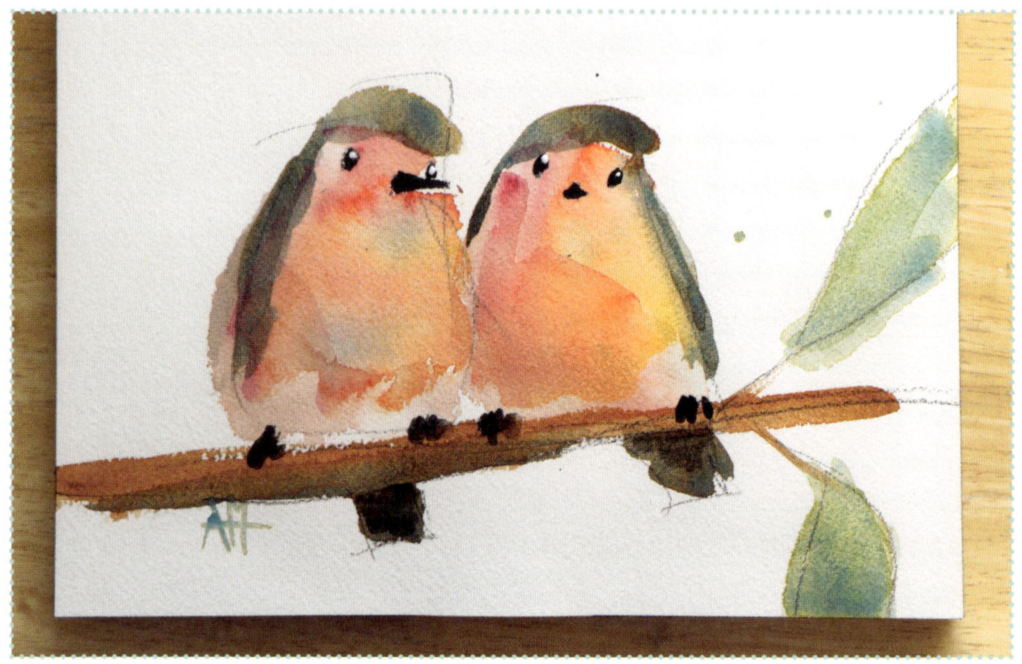

STEP 8:

To add highlights to the birds' eyes, use either a white watercolor in a very thick concentration or white gouache. But if you want to be a purist, use the transparent white or better yet, leave a tiny white spot in the black of the eye to be the highlight on the eye.

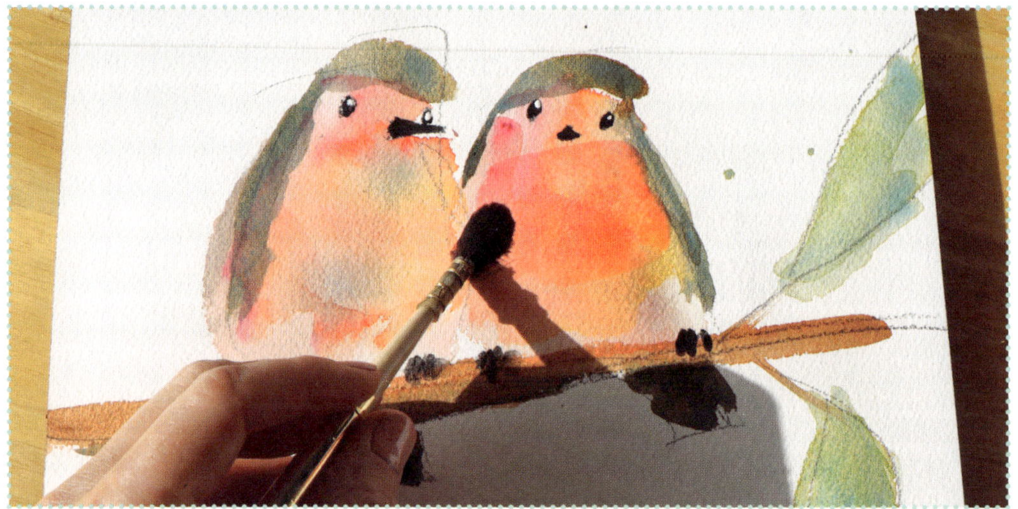

STEP 9:

For a finishing touch, mix more pink into the orange paint and add another wash of pink-orange to the center of the birds.

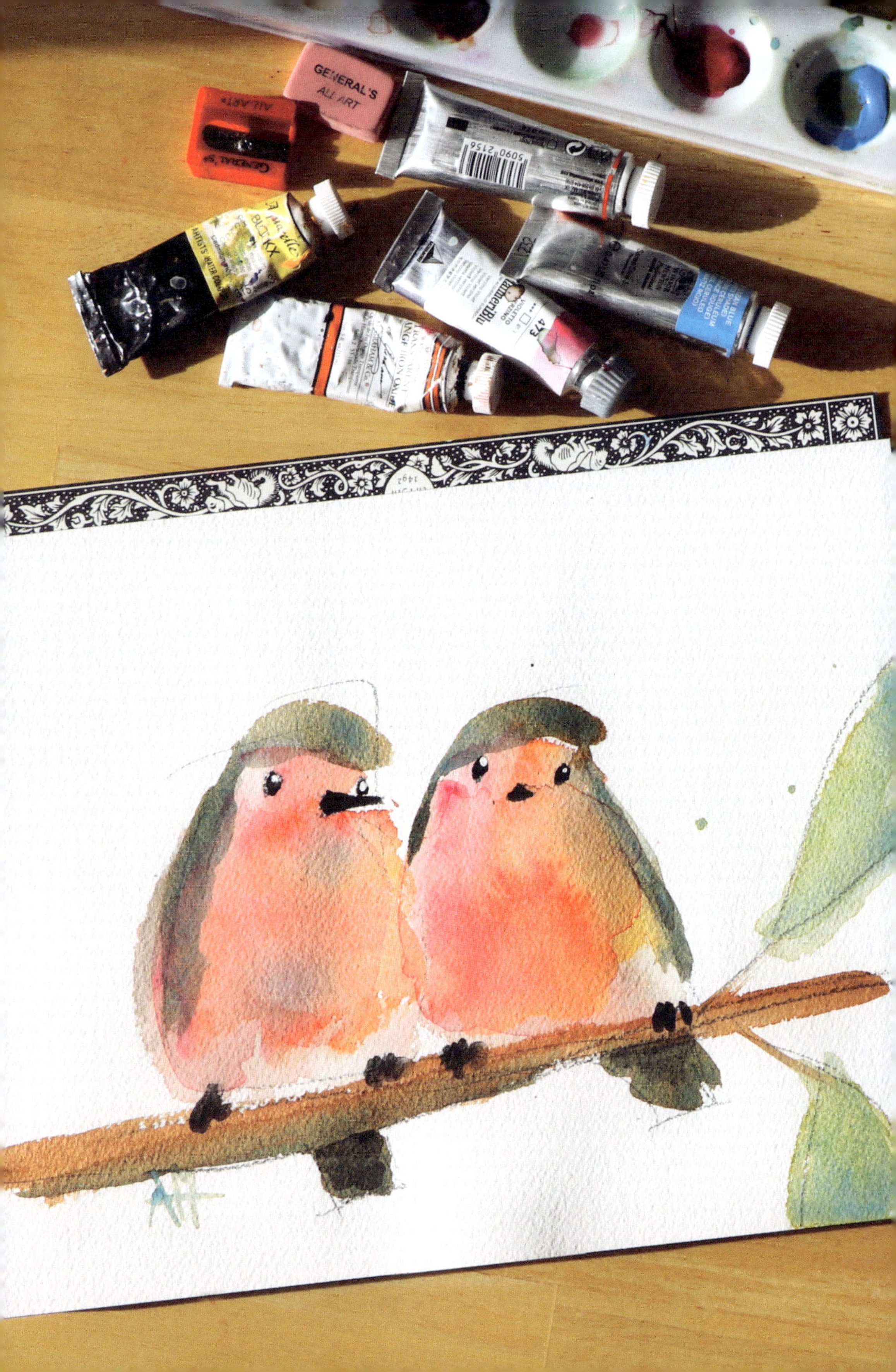
GENERAL'S
ALL ART

Still Life

Begin painting still lifes by practicing different types of fruit. Feel free to choose local fruits and challenge yourself with assorted shapes and colors.

Supplies

- Watercolor paper (block or secured on board)
- Medium round and flat brushes
- Watercolor paints
- Colors: cerulean and phthalo blue, black lake, burnt sienna, cadmium yellow, aureolin yellow, permanent rose, titanium white
- Palette for mixing paints
- Spray bottle (optional)
- Jar of water
- Tissue or paper towels for cleanup

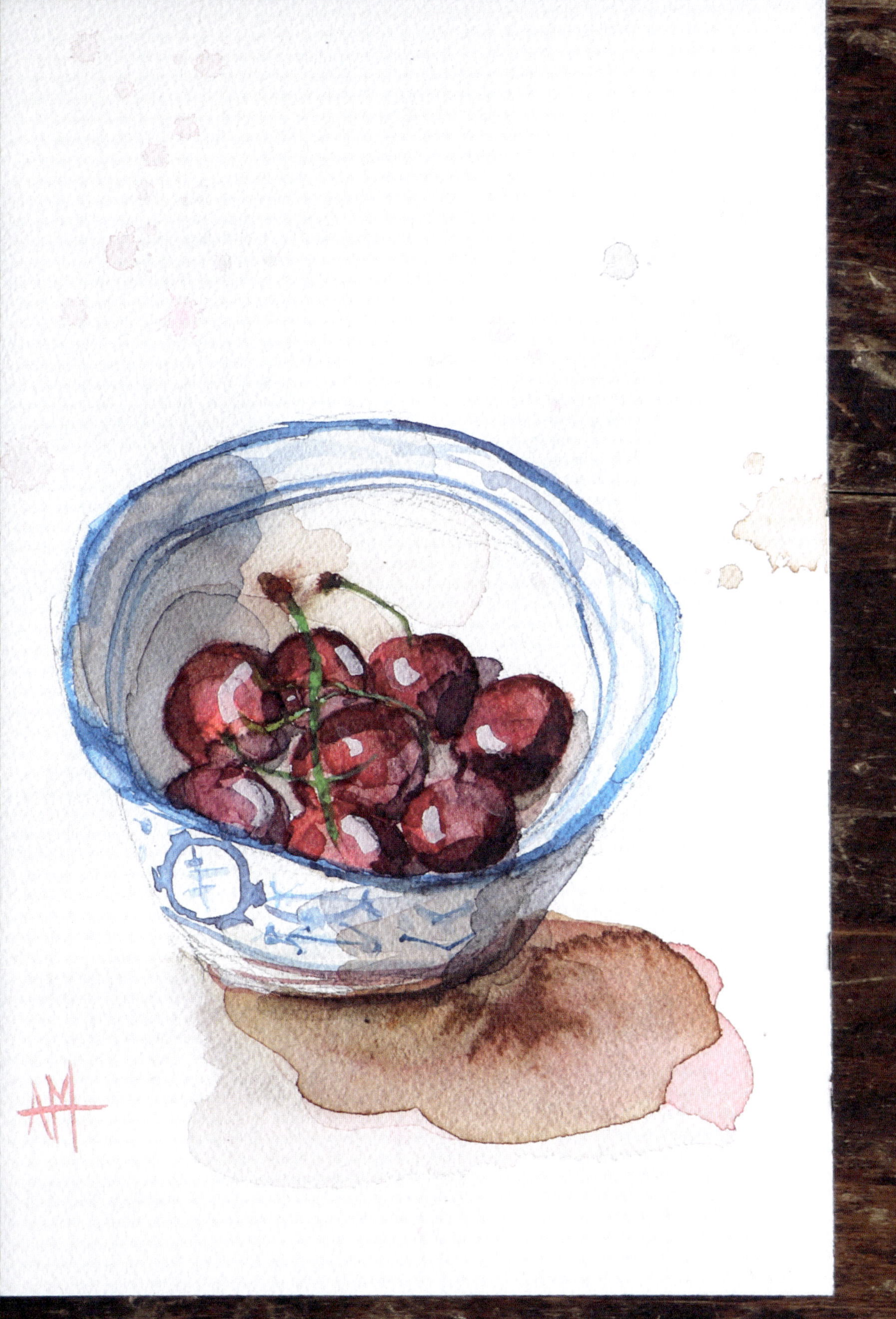

BLUEBERRIES

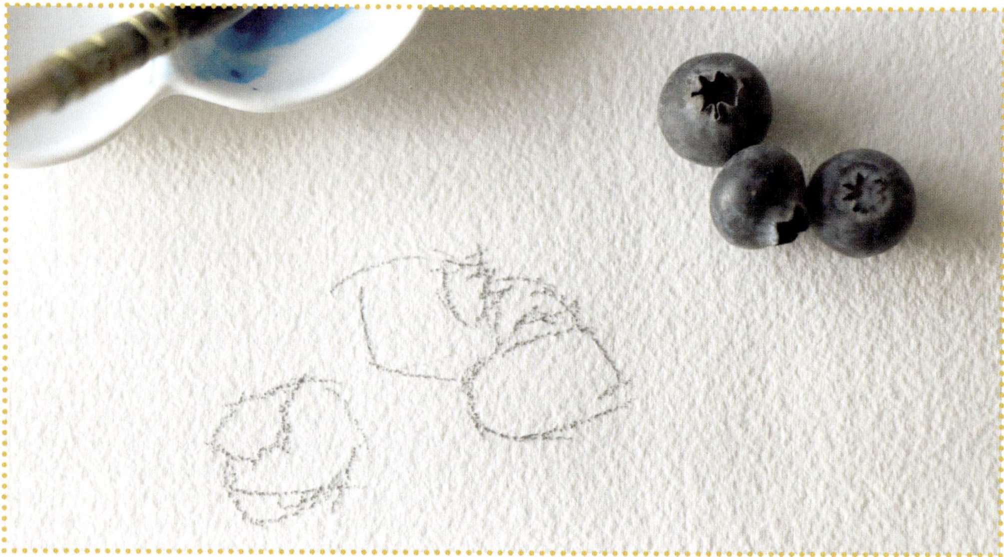

STEP 1:

Sketch out some blueberries. They are round, but slightly flat with a crown for a stem.

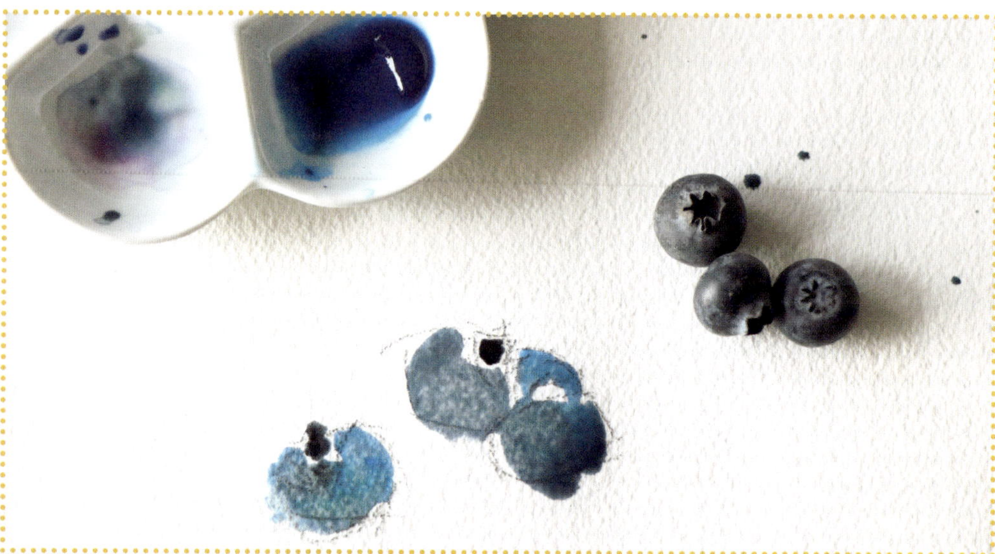

STEP 2:

Paint the blueberries with a dark blue mixture. Add some rose to the blue and a touch of burnt sienna. Add some black or blue-black to the center of the crown stems.

Use a pale watered-down blue for the lightest color of the crowned stem. It's okay if some paint goes outside the lines.

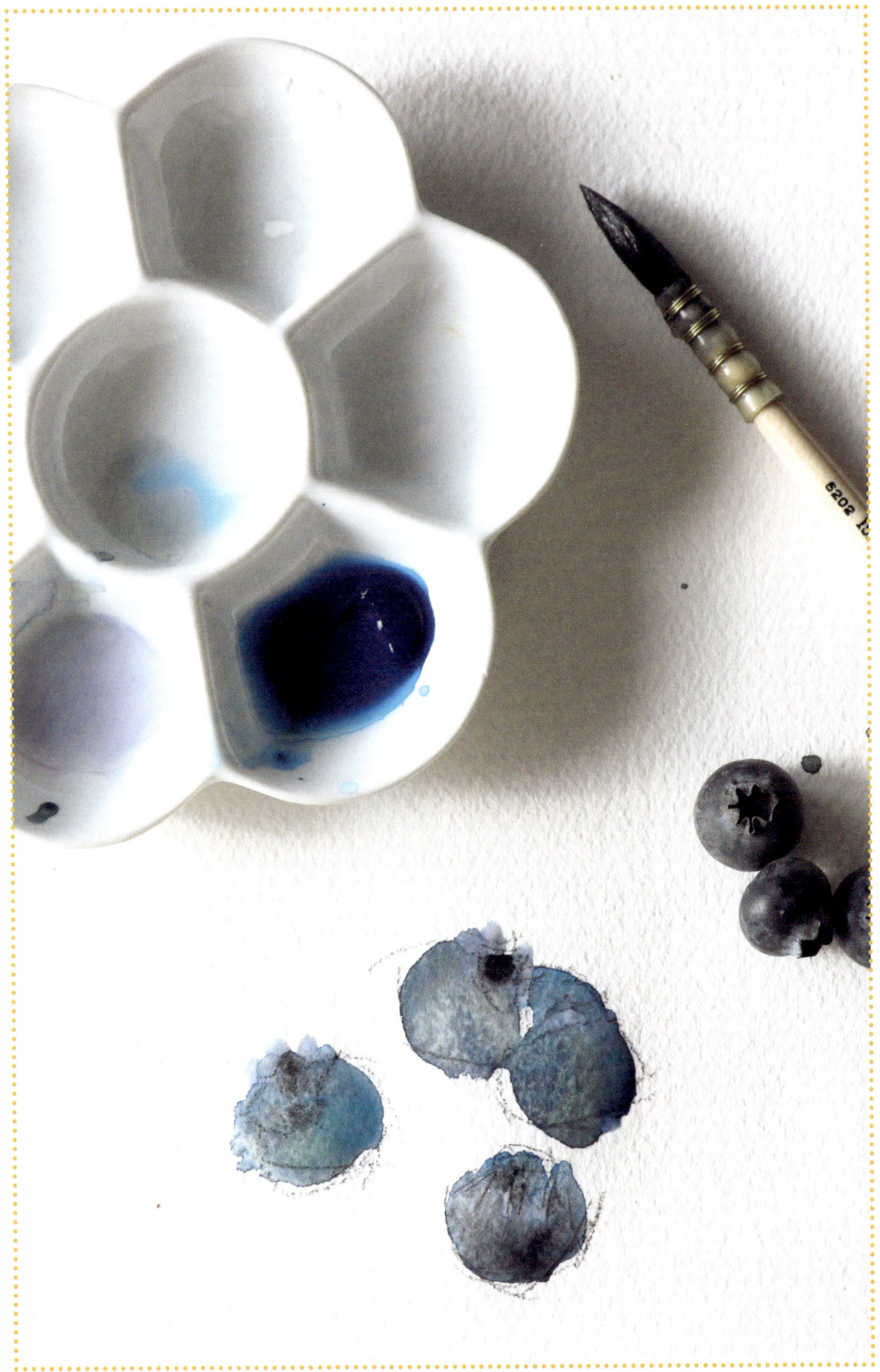

BANANA

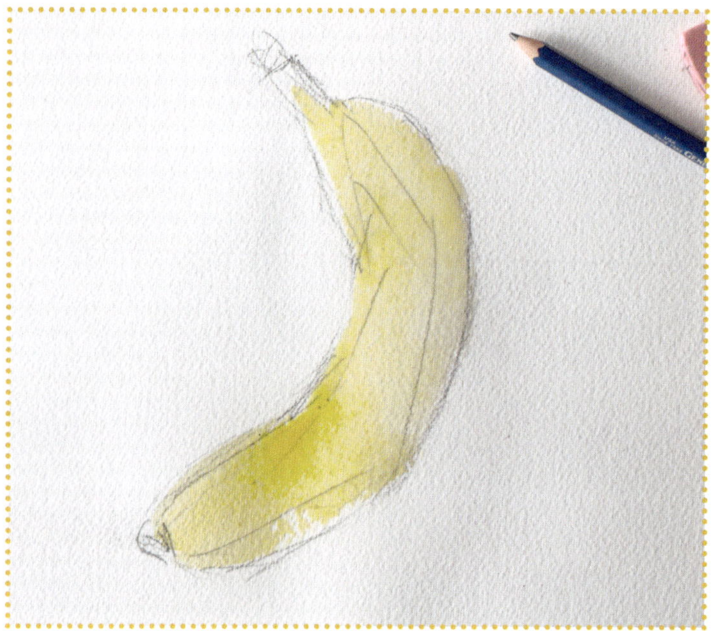

STEP 1:

Use straight yellow and a round brush for the first wash of color.

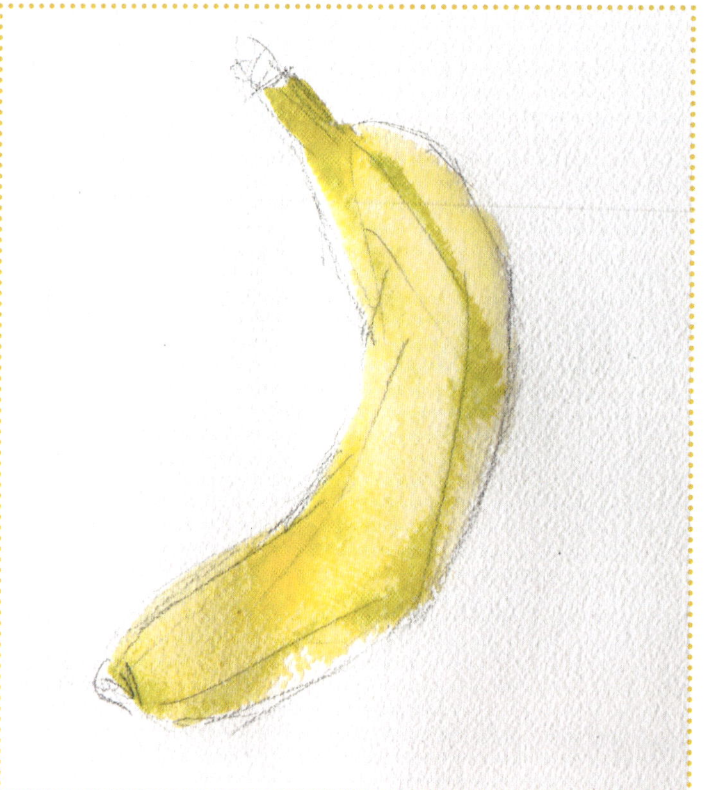

STEP 2:

Add some warm green to the stem and end of the banana. Tone the green down with burnt sienna so that it looks slightly brown. Use the tip of a round brush to paint the ribs of the banana peel wet-into-wet.

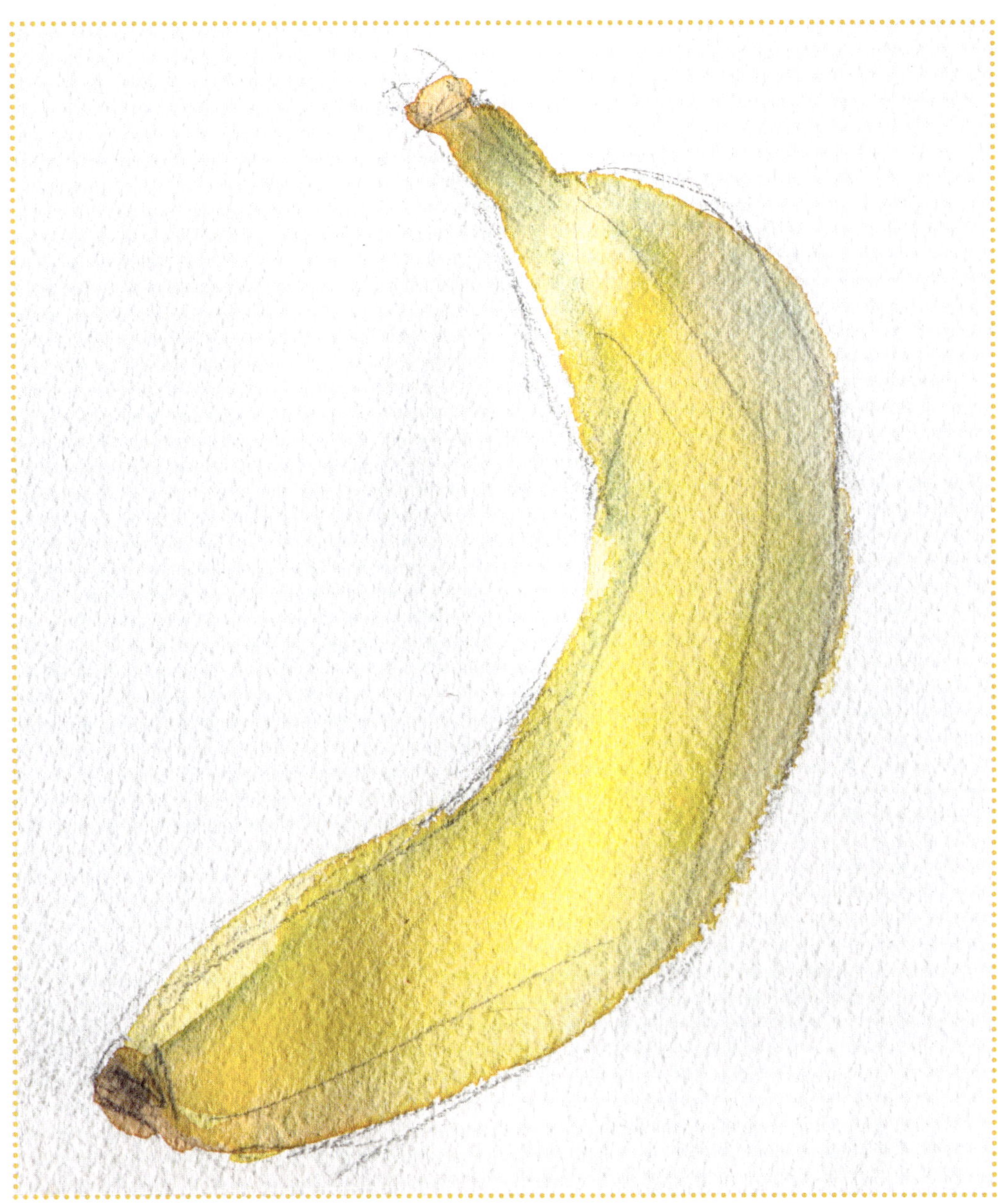

STEP 3:

Add brown paint to the stem and end of the banana. Add a touch of black to create the darkest color at the tip of the banana.

Create a violet by combining your red (or pink) and blue paint. Mix the violet into the yellow for the shaded side of the banana. Use the tip of a round brush to add more definition to the ribs of the banana peel. Add more plain saturated yellow the center of the banana.

APPLES

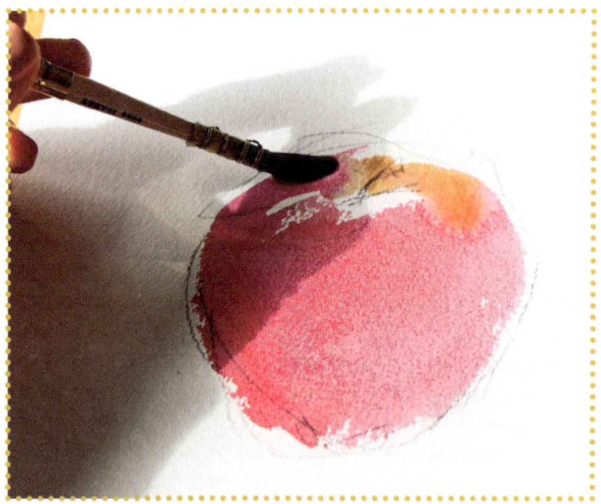

STEP 1:

Start by sketching the apple. Erase any unwanted lines. Mix a red paint for the apple. I used a rose mixed with some burnt umber and a little green.

Add some yellow to the red mixture and paint the top of the apple behind the stem, as well as the shaded side of the apple.

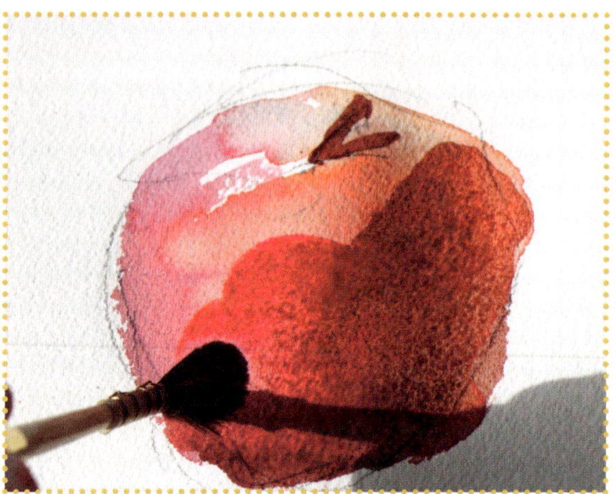

STEP 2:

Mix a dark red for the shaded side of the apple using a darker green and/or some black paint added to the red mixture. I make two different mixtures: one medium dark mixture, and one very dark mixture.

Paint the shaded side of the apple. Add some inside the stem area, if needed, to create the shadow area by the stem. Paint the center of the apple with another layer of saturated pink-red mixture. This will be the brightest part of the apple, both front and center.

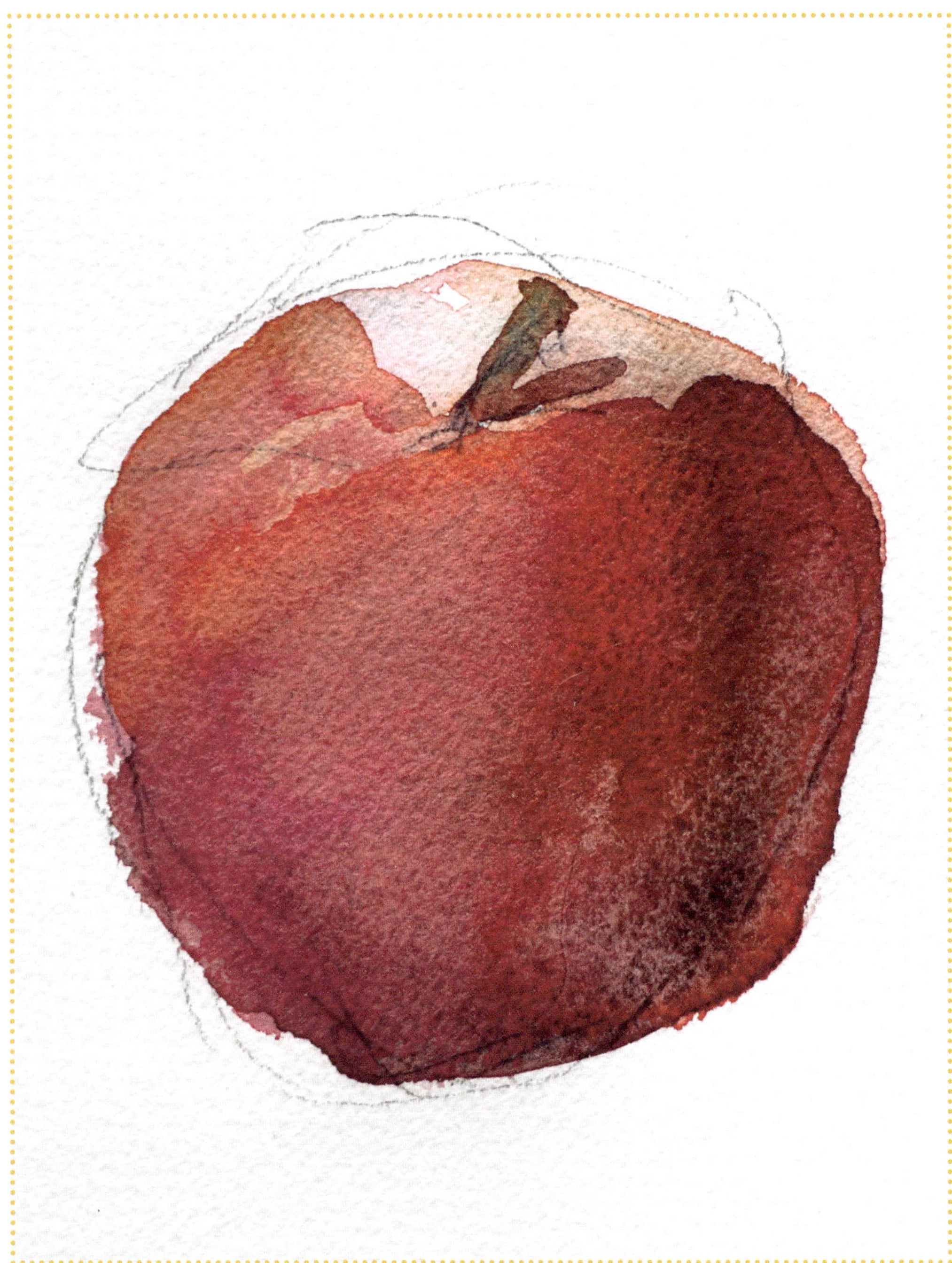

STEP 3:

Add some yellow to the saturated red mixture for the highlighted side of the apple (the side where the light hits the apple). When apple is dry, touch up the stem with more brown paint, and add a shadow of the stem onto the apple, if desired.

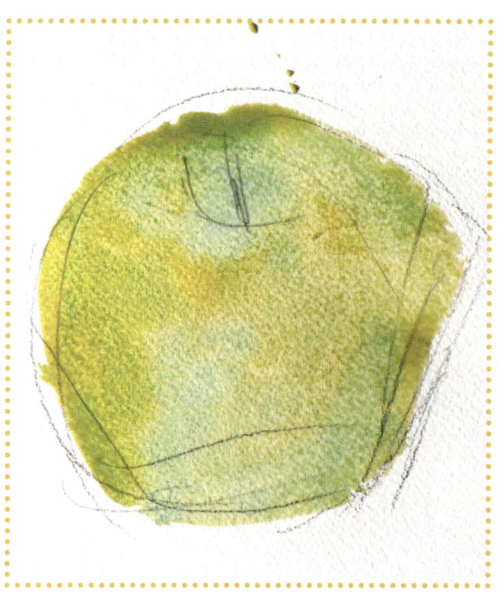

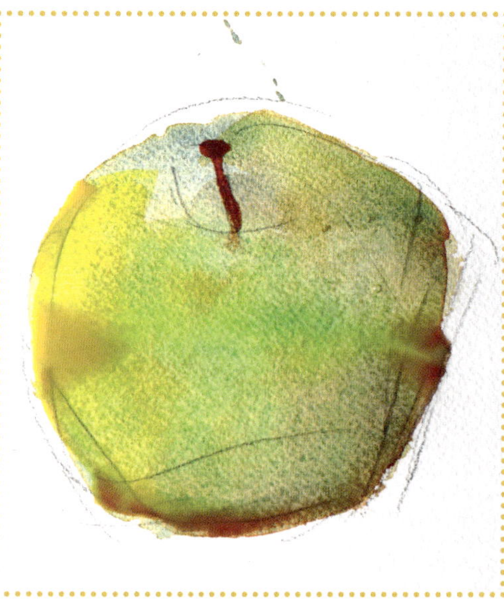

STEP 1:

Start by sketching your apple. Mix yellow, blue, and a touch of red or burnt sienna for the green. Use a round brush to paint the apple. If paint splatters or drips, simply consider it as added interest to the painting.

STEP 2:

Add more green paint to the center of the apple to make it come forward on the paper. Create dark green paint by adding red or black to the green paint. Apply to shadow side of the apple.

Quick Tip

Painting a green apple is similar to painting a red apple, but the colors are reversed. Here, green is the main color, and red is added to create the shaded side of the apple.

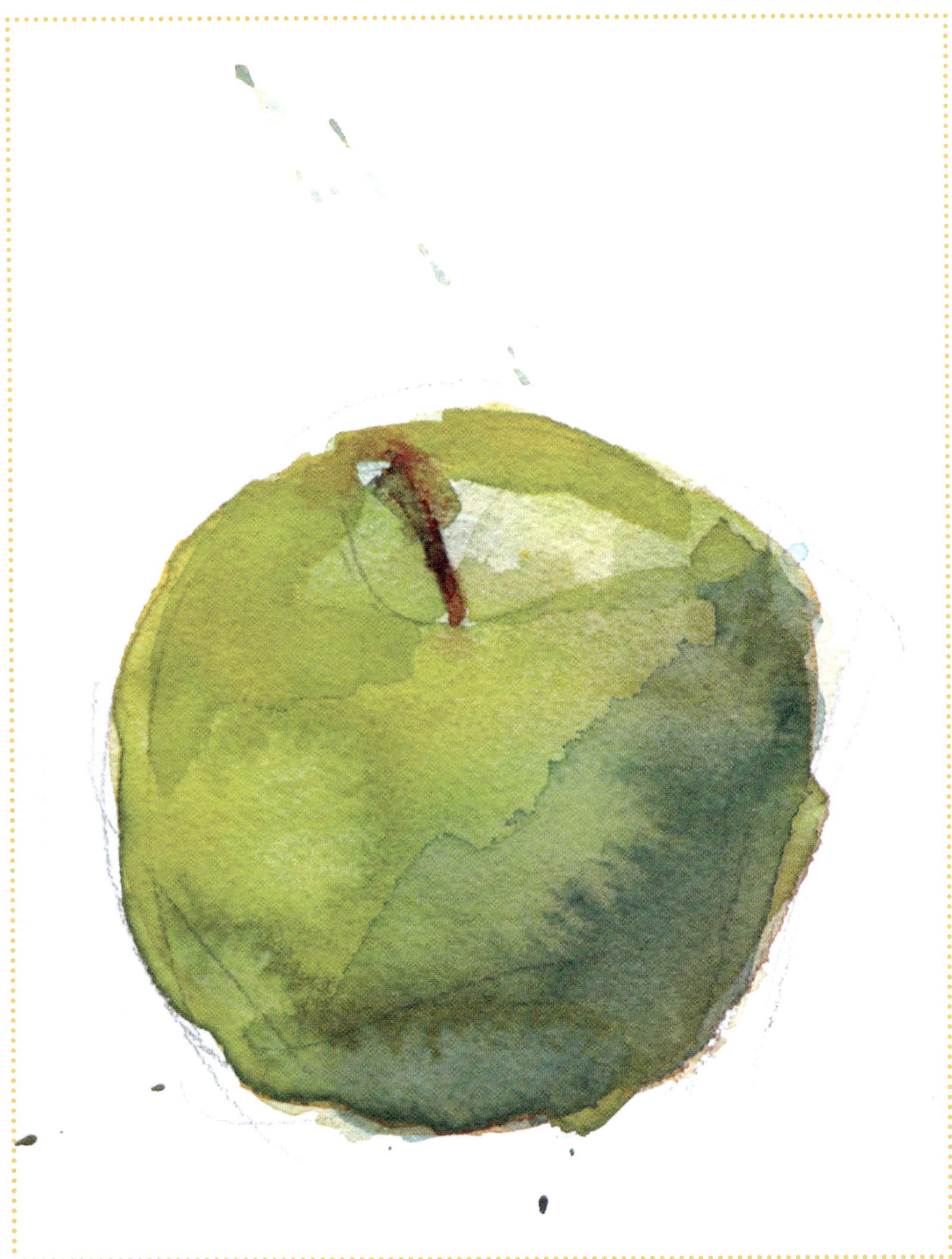

STEP 3:

To balance and soften the shadow area, add a bit brighter green paint mixture to center of the apple. When paint is dry at the top of the apple, apply brown paint to create the stem of the apple.

LEMON

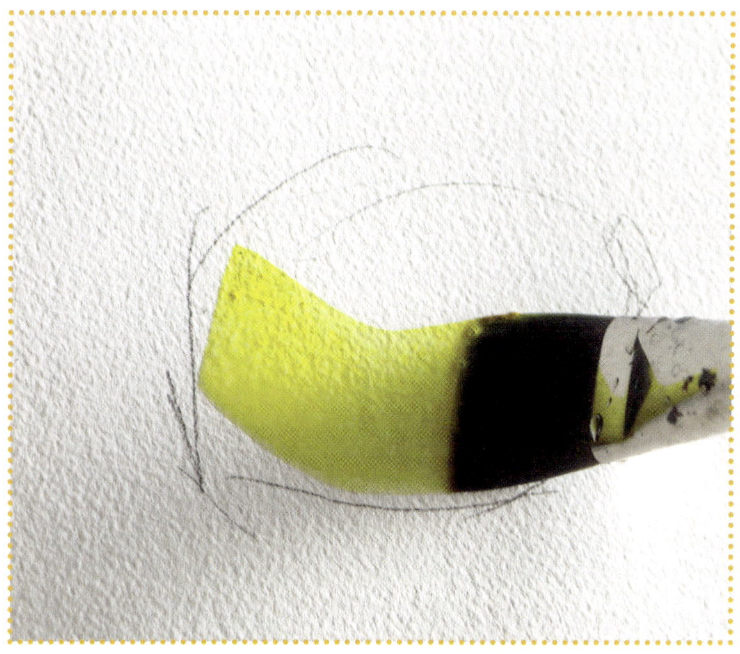

STEP 1:

Sketch the lemon shape. Use two different yellows: aureolin yellow is a little cooler than cadmium yellow. Paint the entire lemon using a flat or round brush and yellow paint.

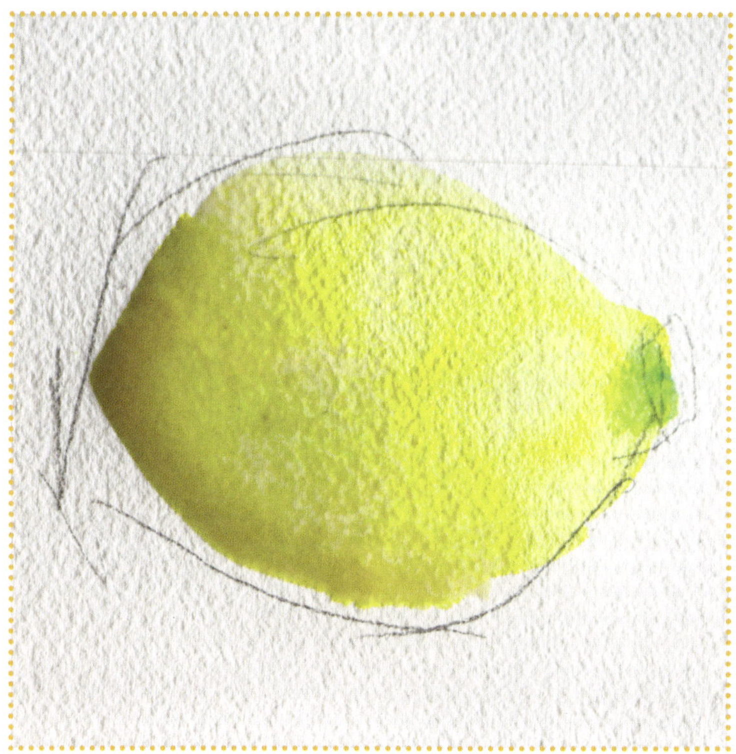

STEP 2:

For the shaded side of the lemon, add violet to the yellow mixture. Wet the paint to blend, if necessary. Add a touch of green to the stem.

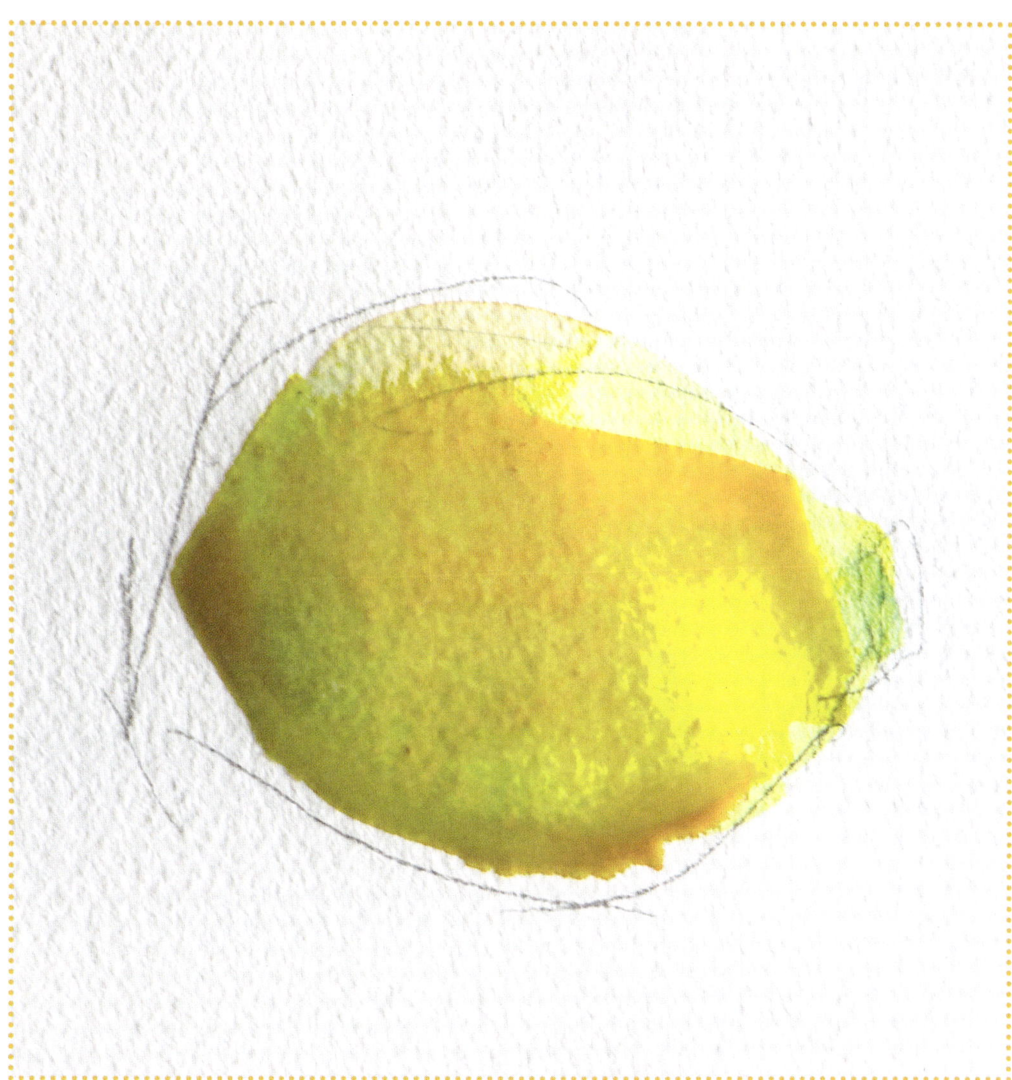

STEP 3:

Add more of the violet mix to the shaded side of the lemon, and then add cadmium yellow to the center of the lemon to add depth. Remember, watercolors are less vibrant once dry.

BOWL OF FRUIT

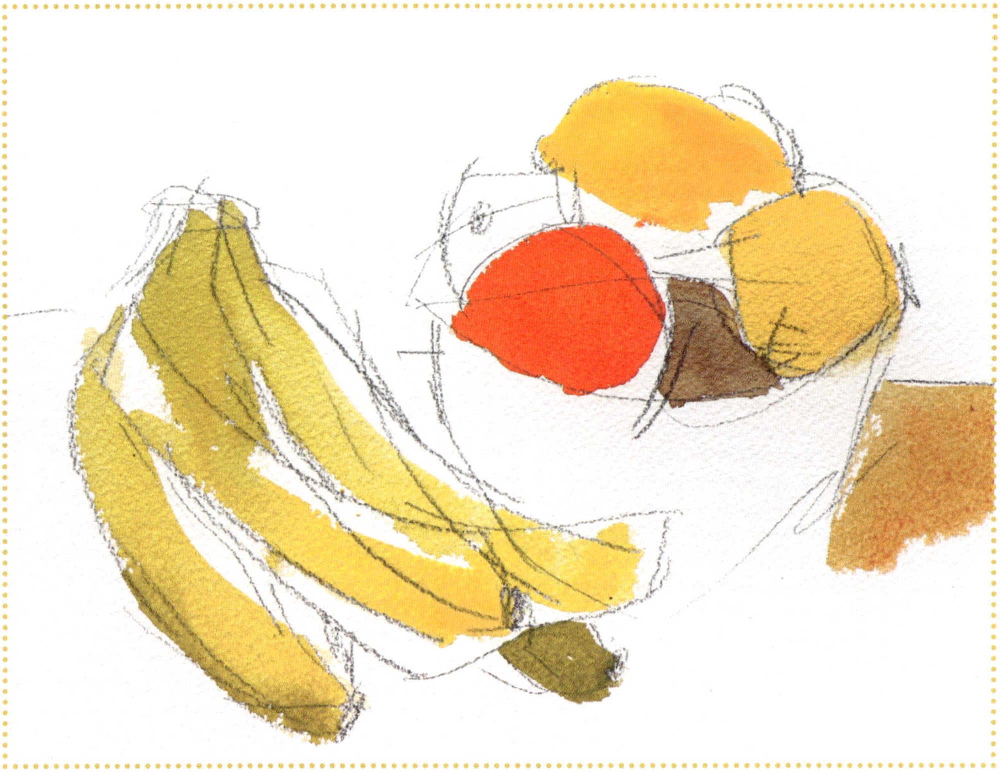

STEP 1:

Start by drawing your bowl of fruit on the table. Mix orange by combining yellow and red paint. Paint the orange if you are using oranges for your painting. Now add some blue to the orange mix to create the shaded darker side of the orange and the orange in the shadow area of bowl. Add some yellow to the lemons and bananas.

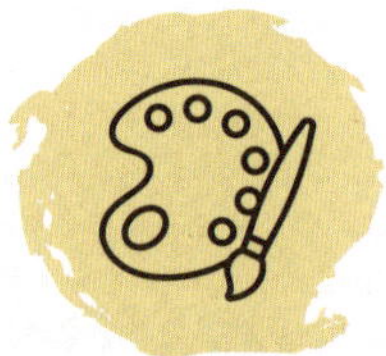

Creative Exercise: Still Life

Try sketching your own still life. You can add as many details as time permits. But don't get too caught up in the details. Just draw the basic shapes.

Quick Tip

Avoid touching and mixing colors between different colored fruits.
Make sure to rinse and dry brush between paint colors.

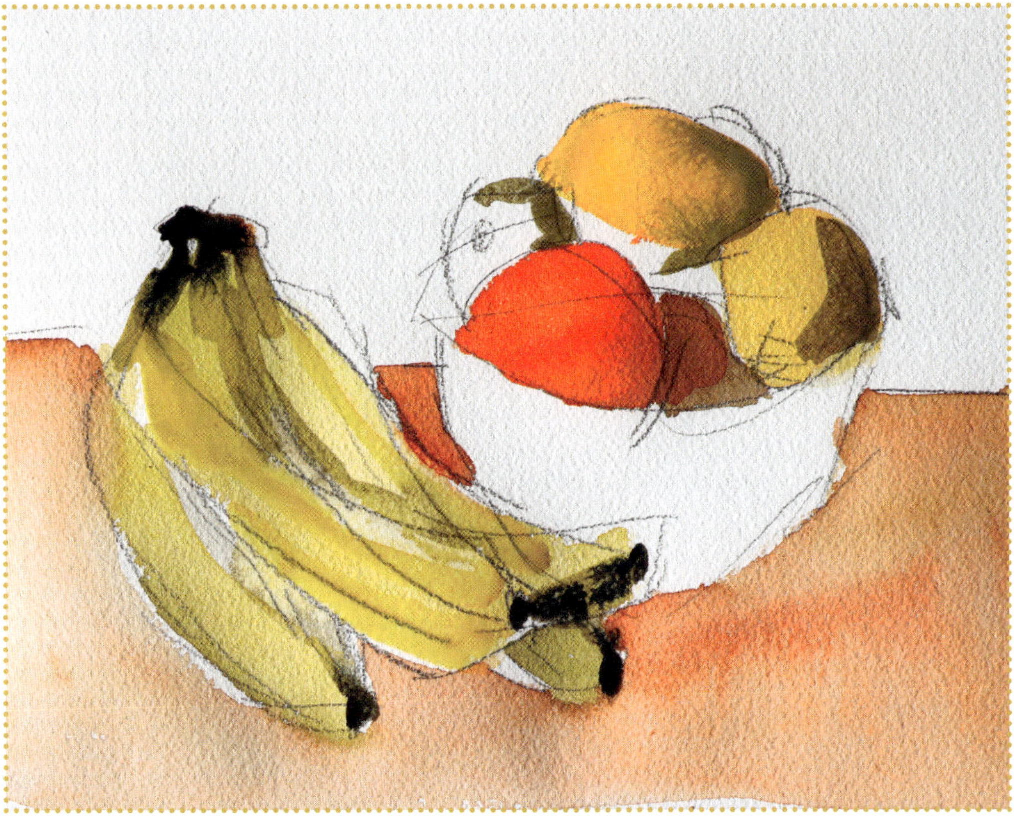

STEP 2:

Add some violet to the yellow paint on your palette. Add shaded areas to the bananas and lemons. Remember, bananas have squared sides; determine which side is bright and which side is in shadow. Mix brown and black together for the stem and ends of the bananas. It's okay if the paint runs a bit.

Paint more shadow to the lemons, using either yellow mixed with violet or yellow mixed with blue or black, and complete the table.

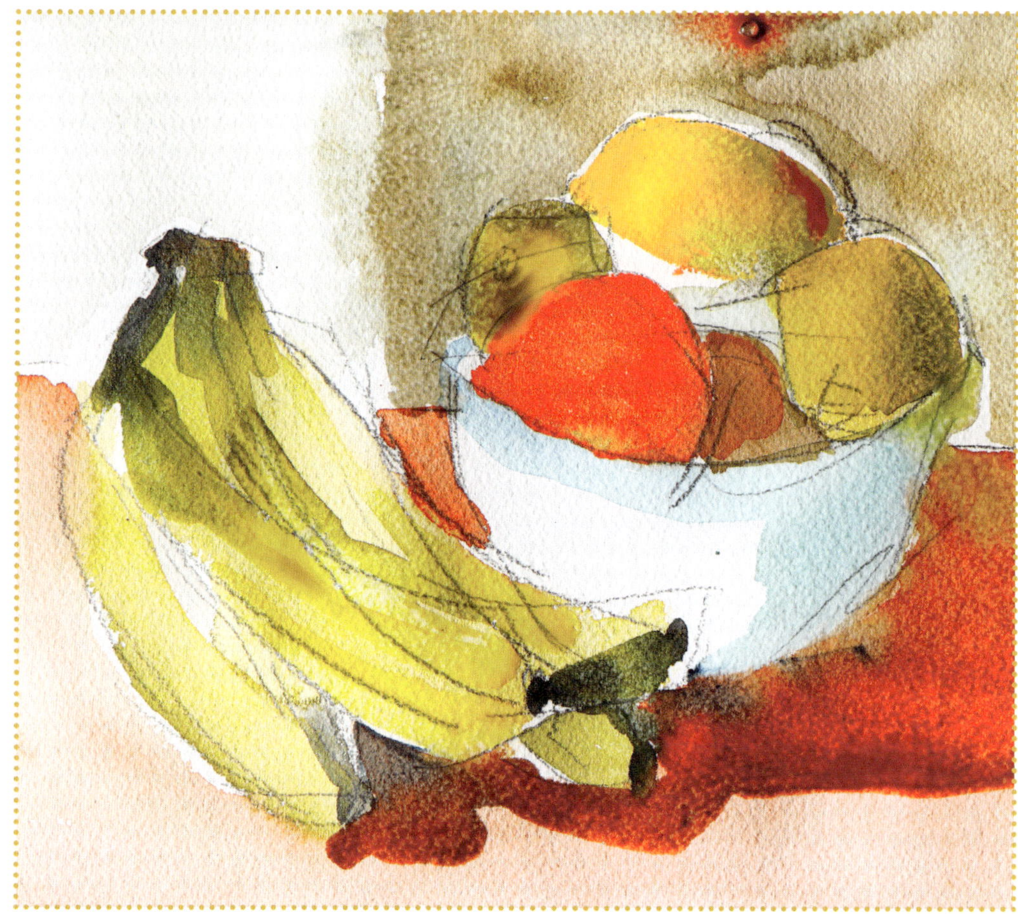

STEP 3:

Paint the background a dark brown behind the bowl of fruit and a light blue by the bananas. Using a darker color, such as transparent earth orange and blue, paint a shadow of the bowl on the table. It is late in the day, so this shadow is quite long and sharp. Also start painting the shadow side of the bowl with a toned-down blue. Tone down blue by mixing in its compliment, orange, or black or brown.

STEP 4:

When mostly dry, paint the rest of bowl with a light blue mixture. Add more saturated blue paint to middle and front of the bowl. Fill in all of the fruits with their respective colors, as needed.

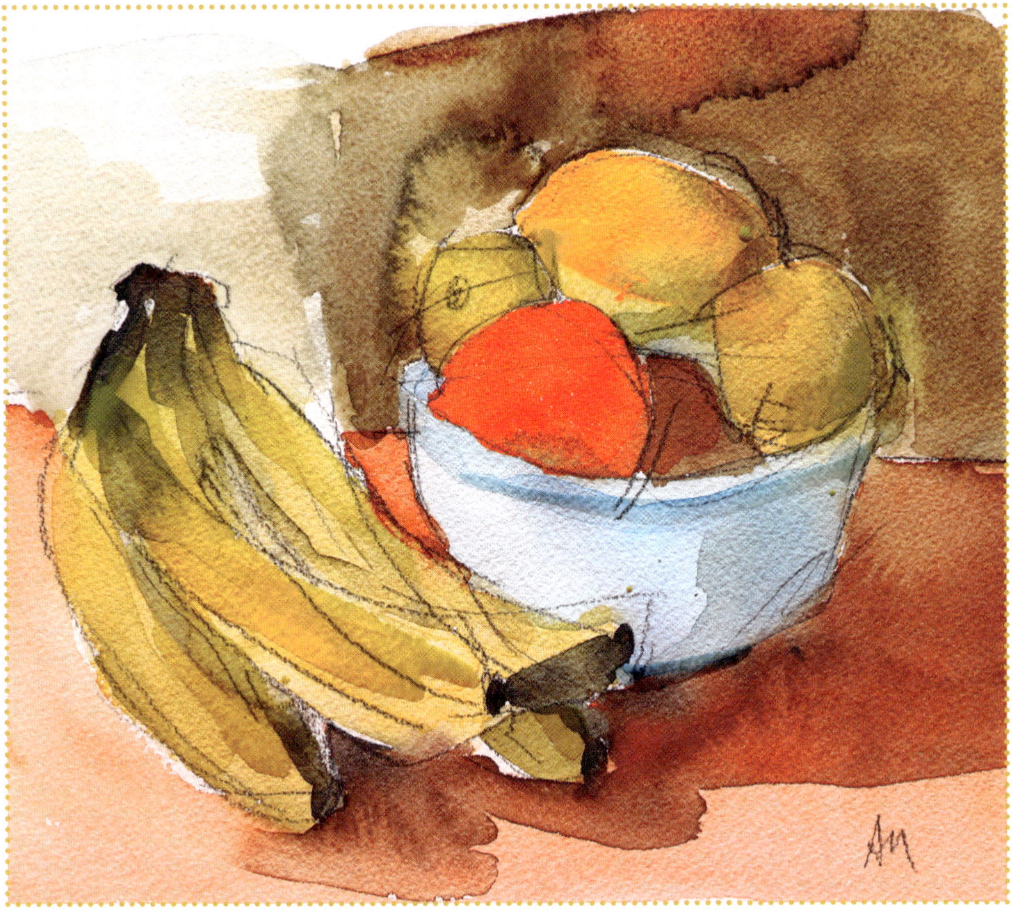

STEP 5:

Make any adjustments and add any details, as desired. I add some shaded areas to the lemons and add more dark values to the background and shadow areas.

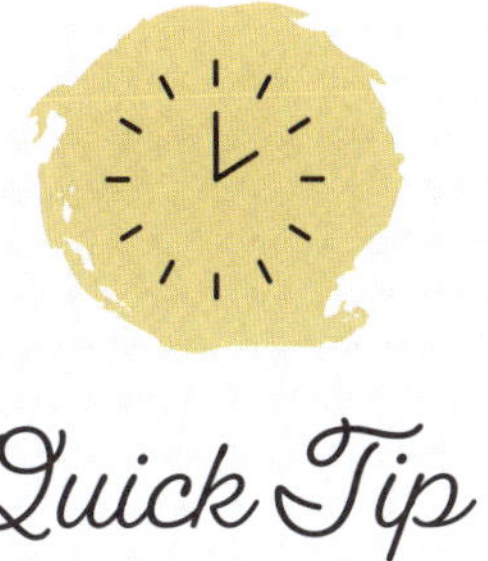

Quick Tip

If you want to paint more realistic details, just slow down and wait until each area is dry before working the next area.

Animals

Animals come in many shapes and sizes, and they provide a variety of colors to experiment with your palettes and watercolor effects.

Supplies

- Watercolor paper (block or secured on board); I prefer either 8″ x 10″ or 9″ x 12″
- Medium and small round brushes
- Small liner brush
- Watercolor paints
- Colors: red, yellow, blue, brown, and black (or Payne's gray)
- Palette for mixing paints
- Plastic or rubber palette knife or spatula (optional)
- Spray bottle (optional)
- Jar of water
- Tissue or paper towels for cleanup

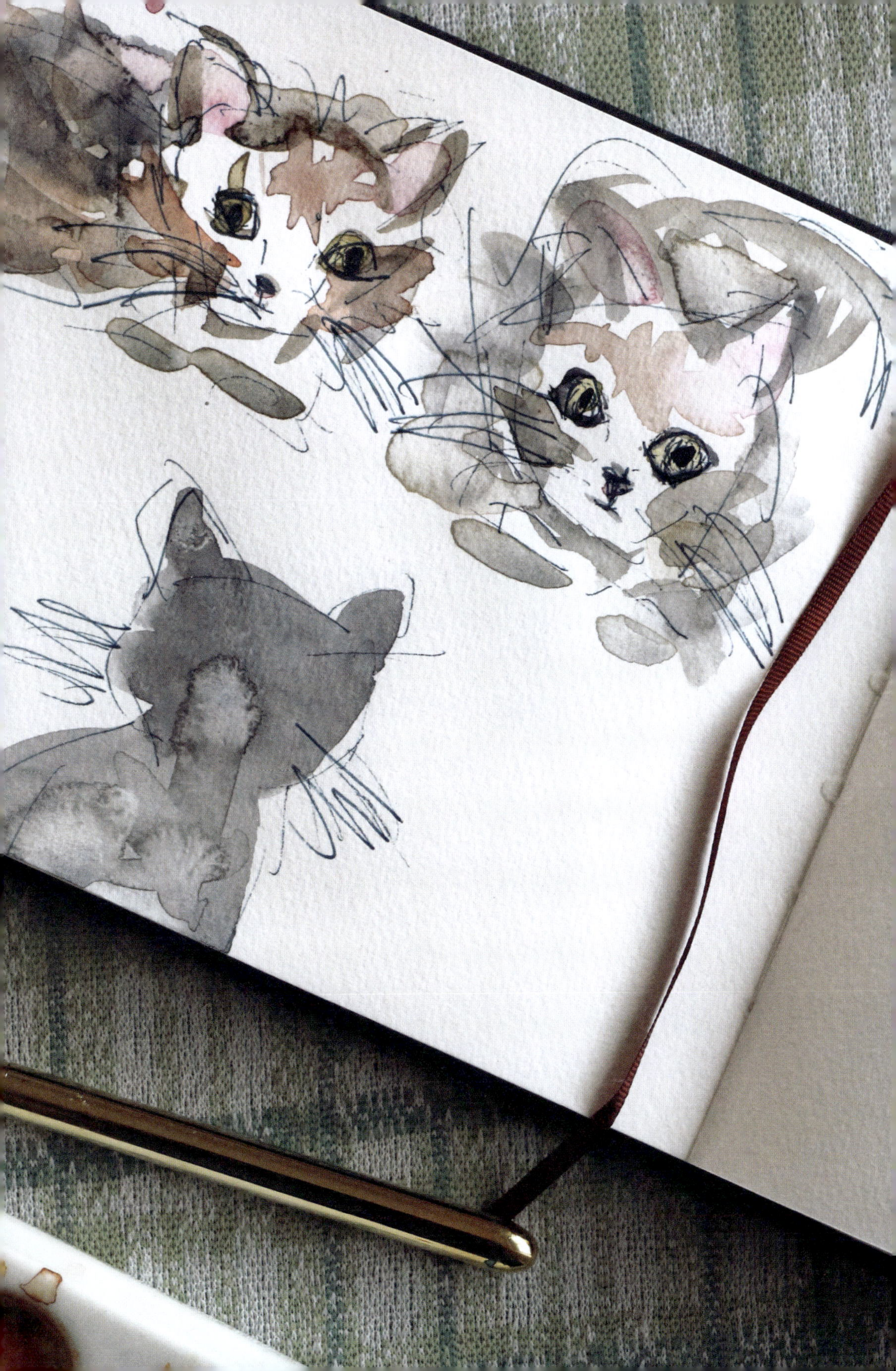

HIPPO

STEP 1:

Start by sketching the head, tail, feet, and back. Keep the sketch loose and quick. Avoid too many details.

Mix some blue-gray mixture, with phthalo or ultramarine blue and some Payne's gray. Tone it down with a touch of red for the belly.

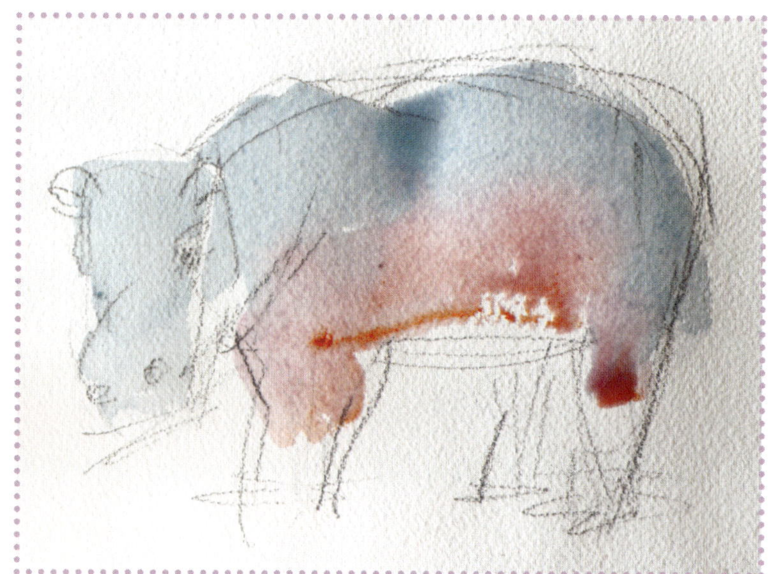

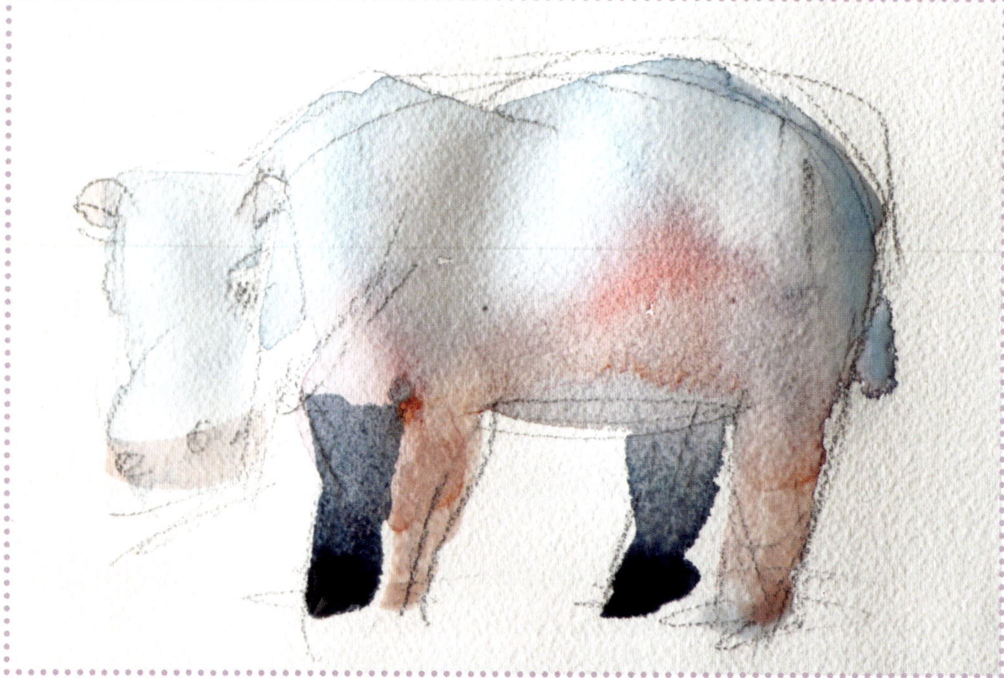

STEP 2:

Mix a warm pink color for the belly and closest legs. For the back legs, use a blue mixed with brown or black (or Payne's gray). Add a lightly shaded area (violet pink) to the snout and ears.

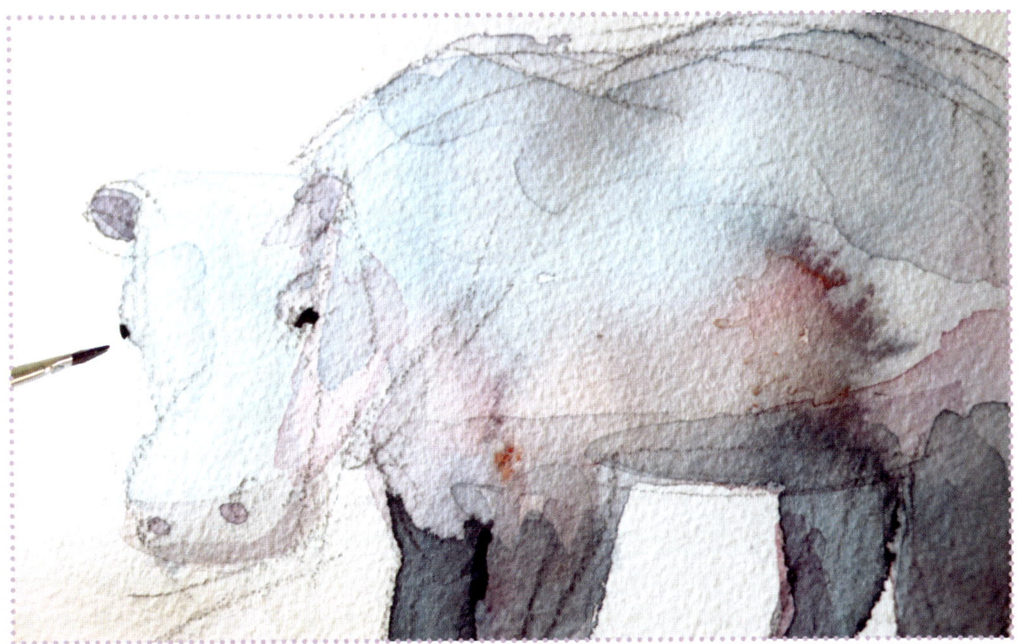

STEP 3:

Paint the eyes on the hippo, using a small round brush. Shape them to match the anatomy of the head. For the eyes and details of the hippo, use almost-straight-from-the-tube paint that is very saturated and thick. Just add enough water to thin to consistency. Add the same dark gray or black to bottom of feet to add dimension and shading.

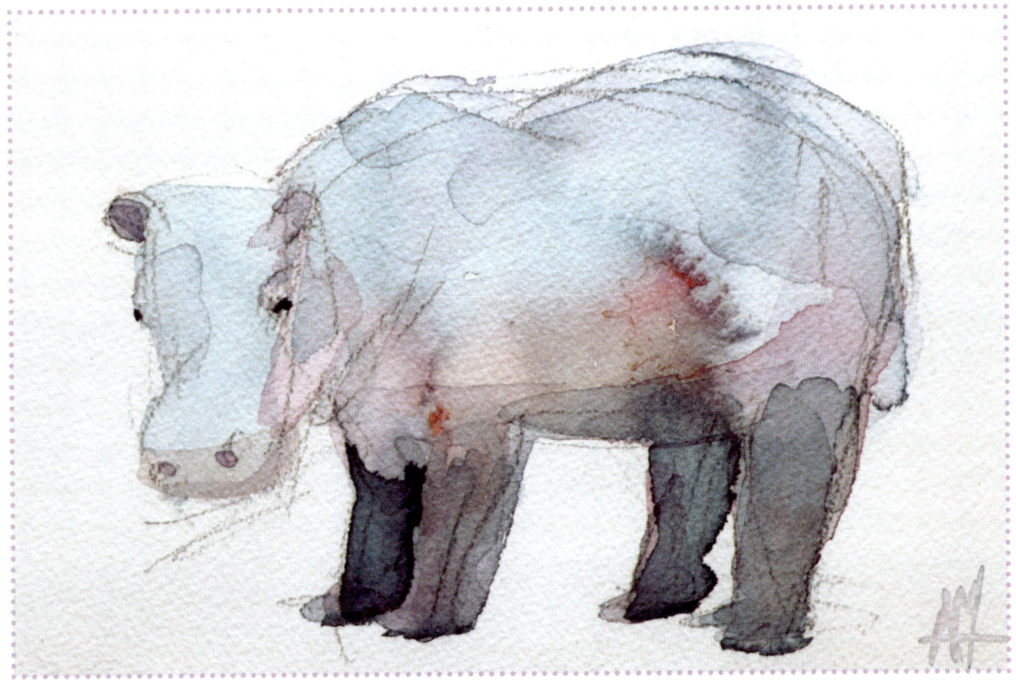

TIGER

STEP 1:

Sketch the tiger's eyes and nose, muzzle and mouth, and ears, striped head, chin, and whiskers.

Use an orange mixture with a flat brush to paint the tiger. Dab with a tissue or paper towel to remove excess paint and create a soft "fur" look. Add a pink nose, yellow eyes, and outline the ears. Once the yellow paint is dry, outline the eyes, nose, and mouth using a liner brush.

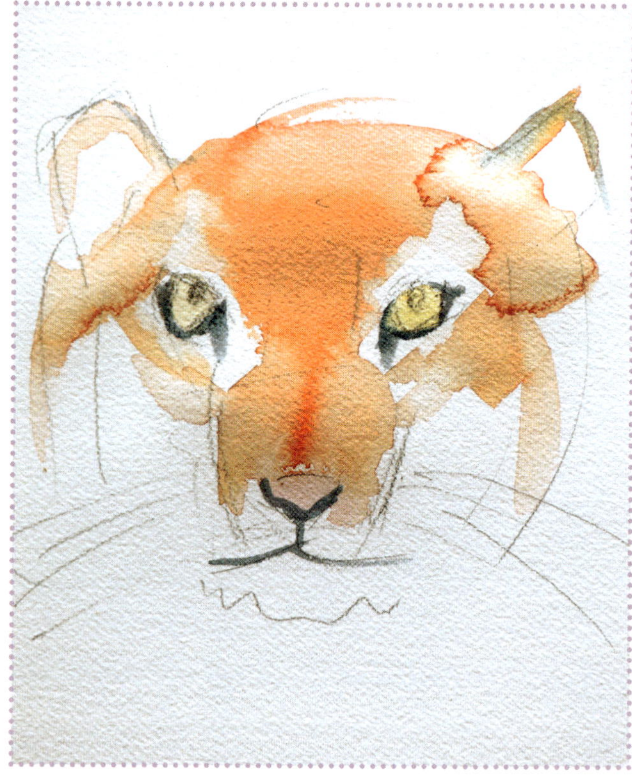

STEP 2:

Using your medium round brush, add stripes and outline the ears using curvy lines.

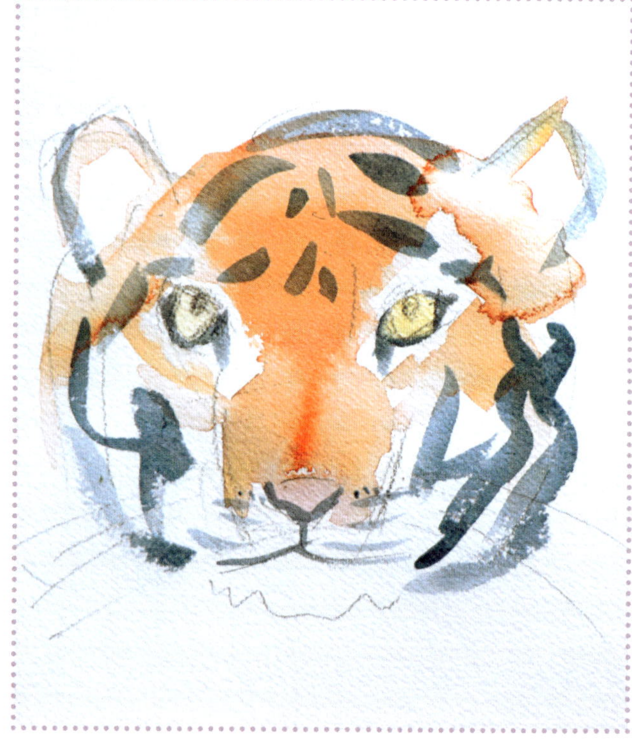

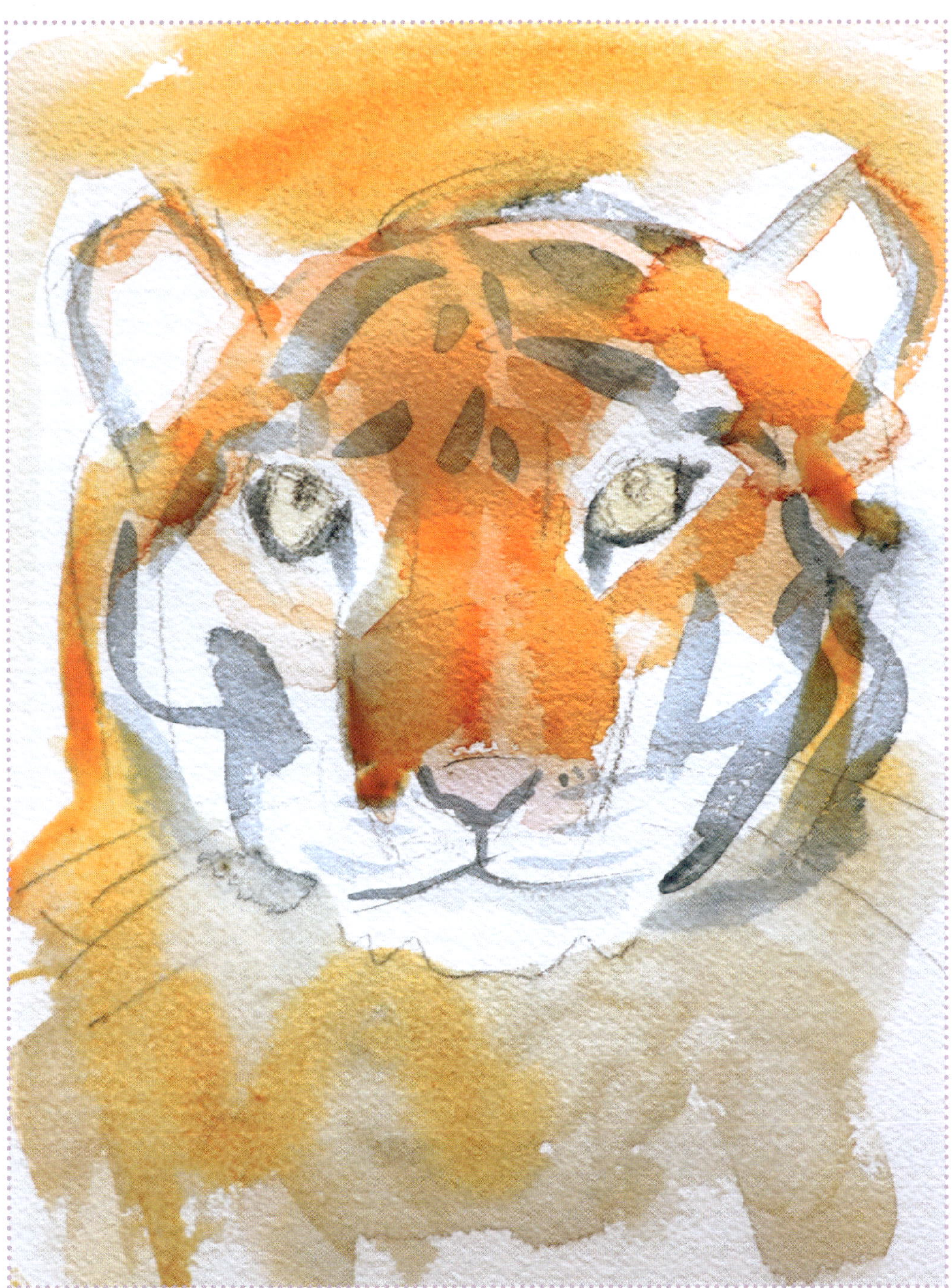

STEP 3:

I decide to paint the background a dull orange. Dull the orange by adding a touch of blue. Now add more transparent orange all over the tiger and the background to add more depth.

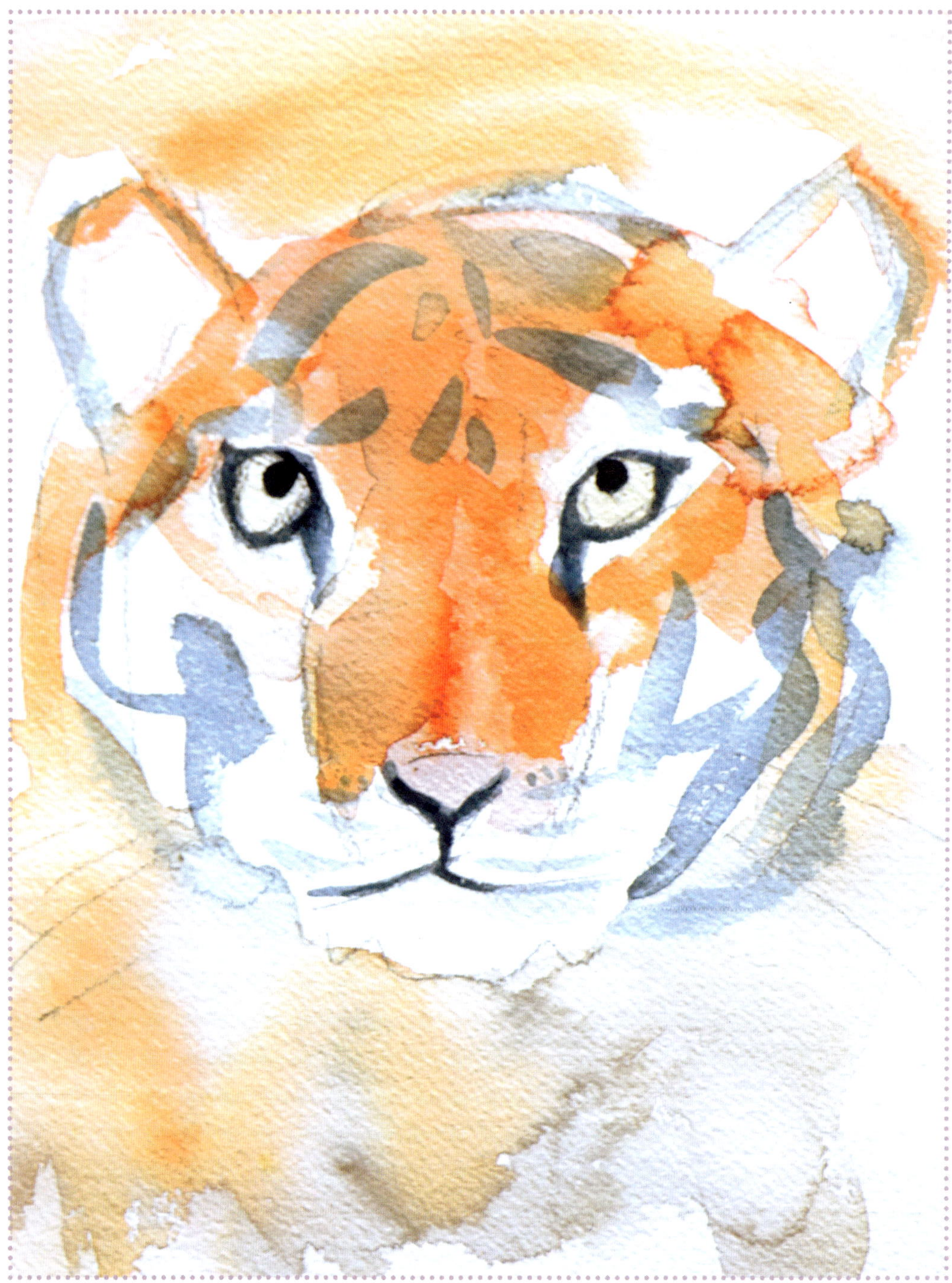

STEP 4:

Use your small round brush to paint the pupil of each eye black. Use your long liner brush to add whiskers. Use enough water that the liner brush flows smoothly across the paper.

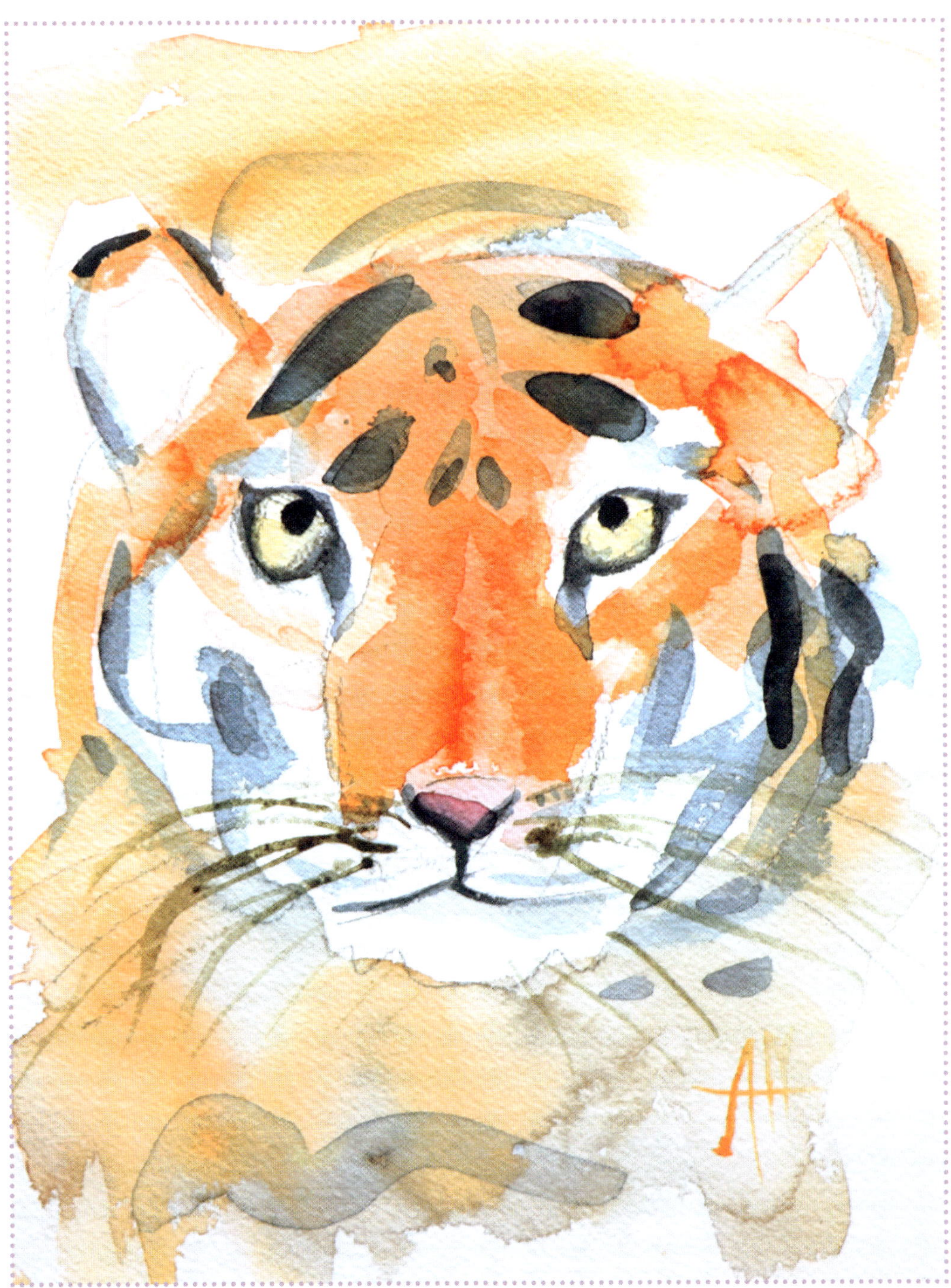

STEP 5:

Now darken any black spots that seem too light with more black or Payne's gray. You can also add a couple of stripes to the background to suggest a body.

GIRAFFE

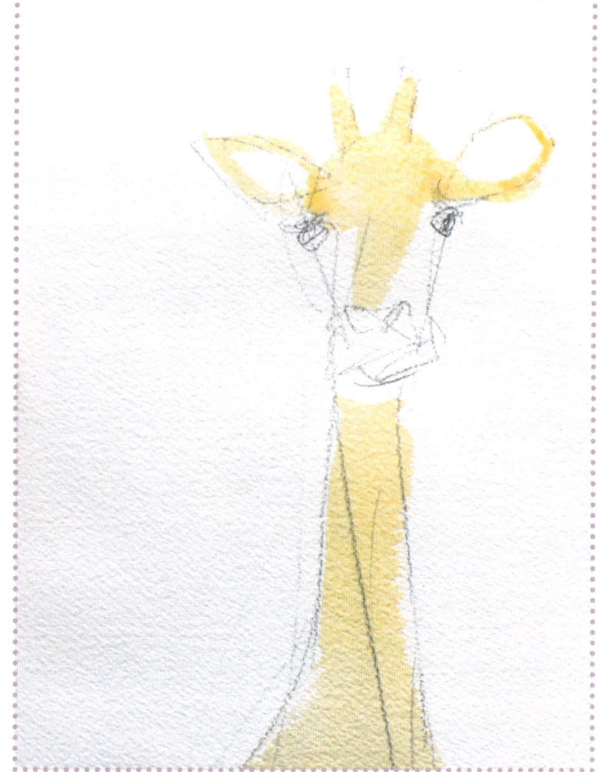

STEP 1:

Start by sketching a giraffe head and neck on your watercolor paper. Erase any unwanted lines. Paint a yellow ochre mixture on the center of the head. Next paint the neck and outline the ears.

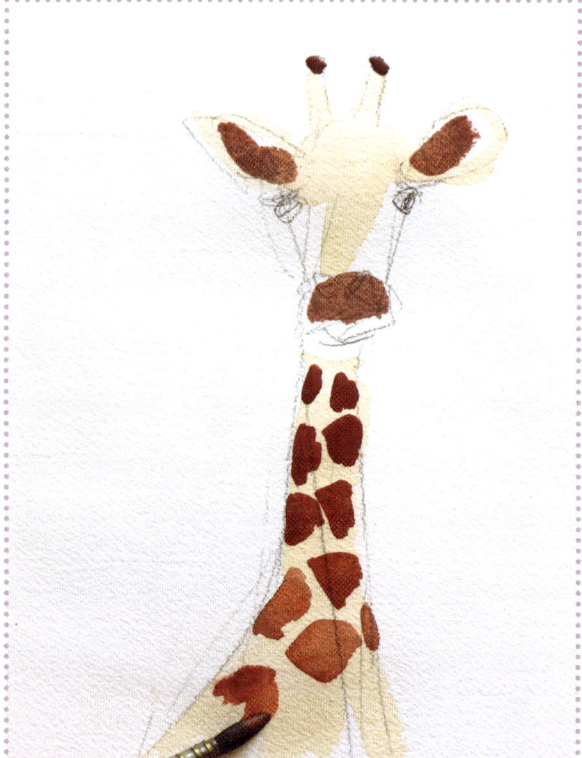

STEP 2:

Let dry, and then add brown spots to the neck and body of the giraffe. Add some of this brown to the nose, inside of the ears, and the ossicones on top of the head.

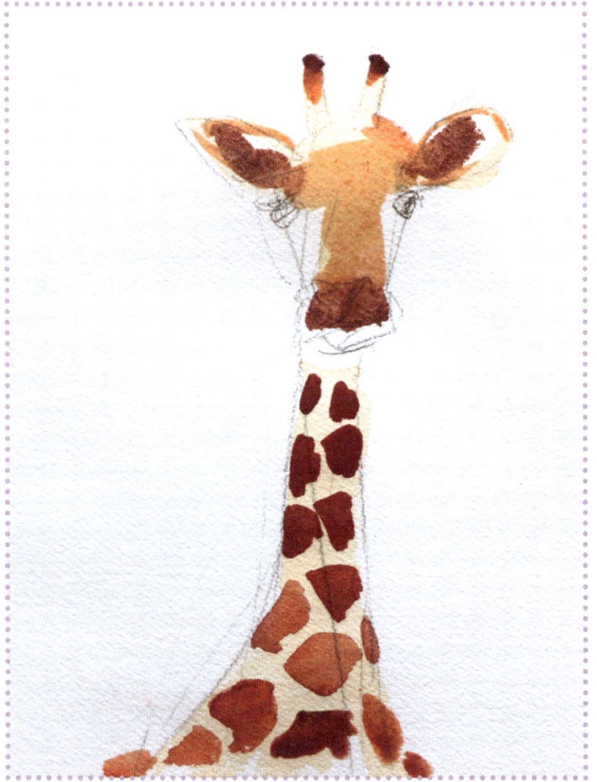

STEP 3:

Next, add some light brown to fill out the face and ears.

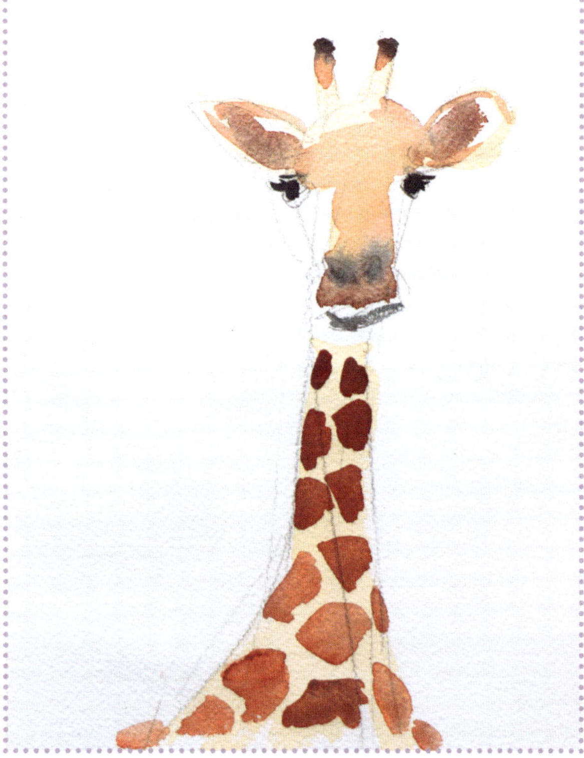

STEP 4:

Once dry, paint the eyes and eyelashes, nostrils, mouth, and top of the ossicones black.

CHAMELEON

STEP 1:

Start by sketching a chameleon with a spiral tail and a simple brown branch. Mix some blue and yellow for the green of the chameleon. If the color is too bright, add a touch of red or black to tone it down. Use a medium round or flat brush to start painting the chameleon, leaving the eye area blank.

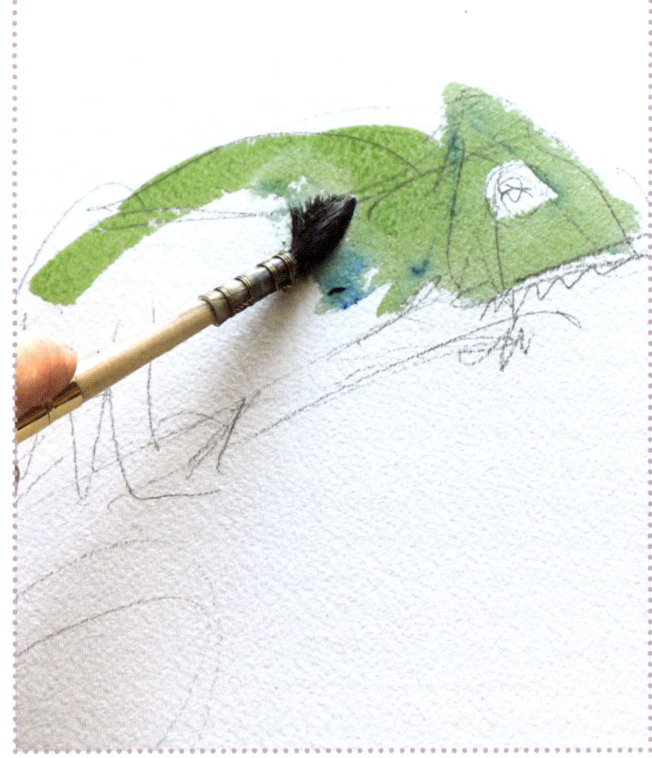

STEP 2:

Add some yellow to the green mix for the eye, arms, and legs. Add more blue to the green mixture for the tail.

Let dry a little (so it doesn't run), and then add a green or brown branch.

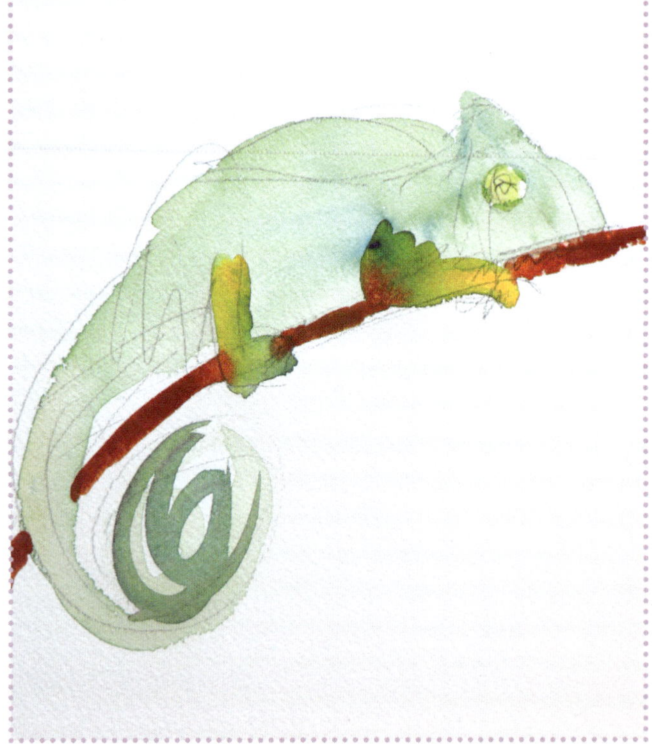

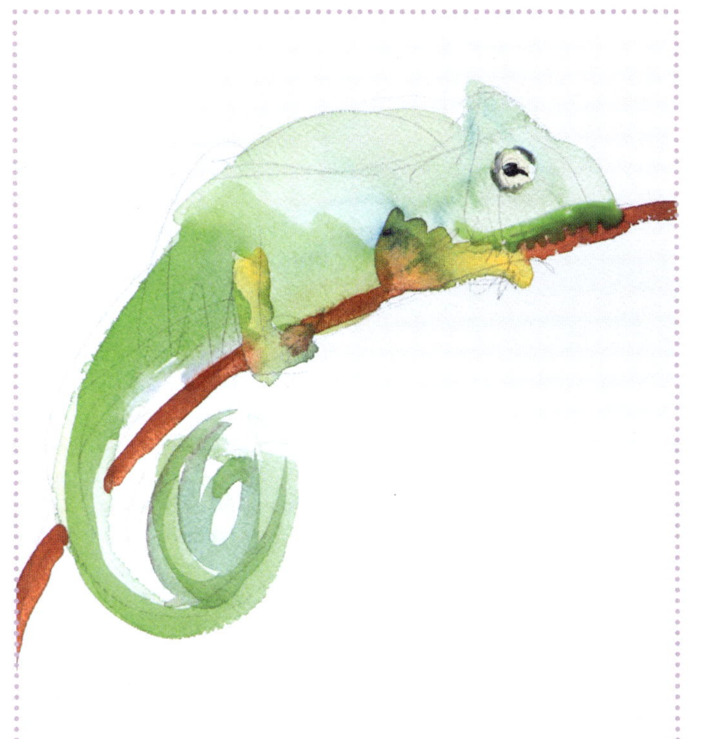

STEP 3:

Add a jagged edge to the mouth with green paint and the tip of a round brush. You can dab some brown away, if needed, to create the overhanging jaw of the mouth.

Once the head is dry, add a circle and pupil to the chameleon.

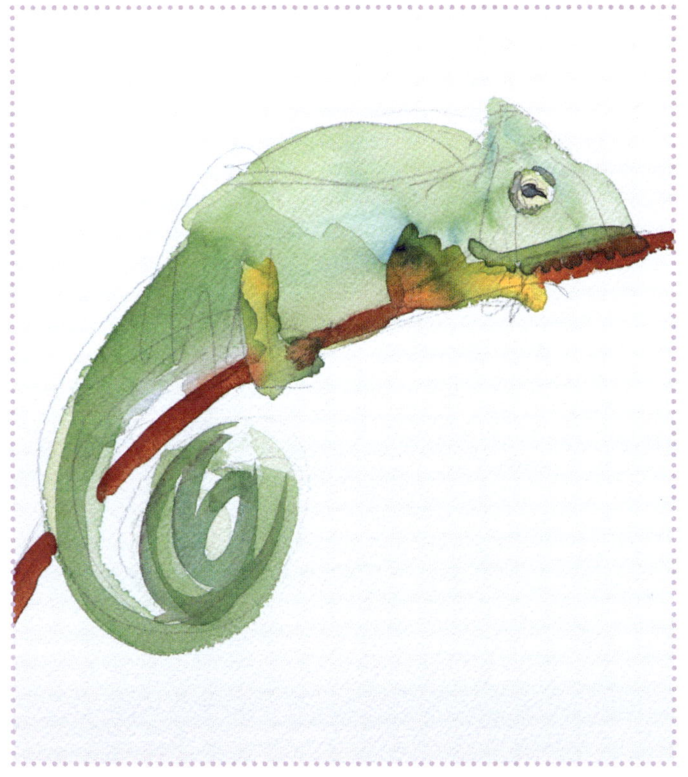

STEP 4

Let dry, and add in any last details, as desired.

Figures

Gestural movements of figures seem to jump off the page with transparent washes of watercolor paint. Hyper-realism can also be obtained with watercolor paint; but for these projects, we will focus on quick gestural sketches and touches of paint.

Supplies

- Watercolor paper (block or secured sheet on board); I used an 8" x 10" and 9" x 12" block
- Medium and small round brushes
- Medium flat brush
- Liner brush (optional)
- Watercolor paints
- Colors: earth colors, like red or yellow ochre, transparent oxide orange or red, and burnt sienna; black or Payne's gray; cerulean, cobalt, or ultramarine blue; cadmium yellow or yellow ochre; rose or quinacridone red for cool pink tones
- Palette for mixing paints
- Spray bottle (optional)
- Jar of water
- Tissue or paper towels for cleanup

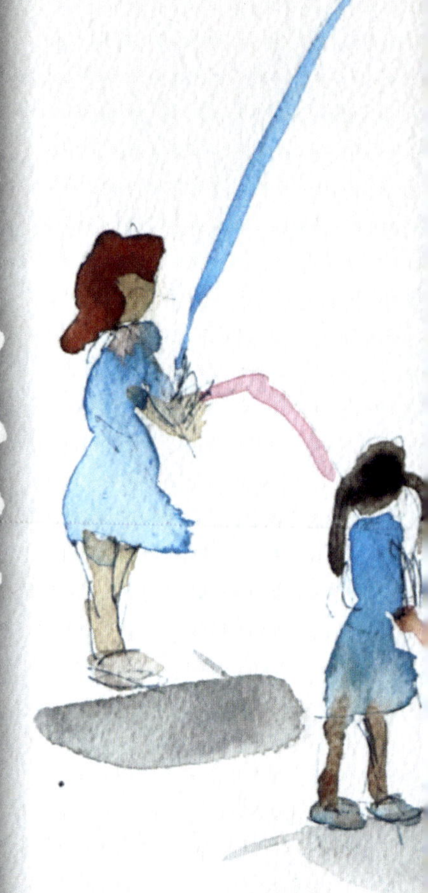

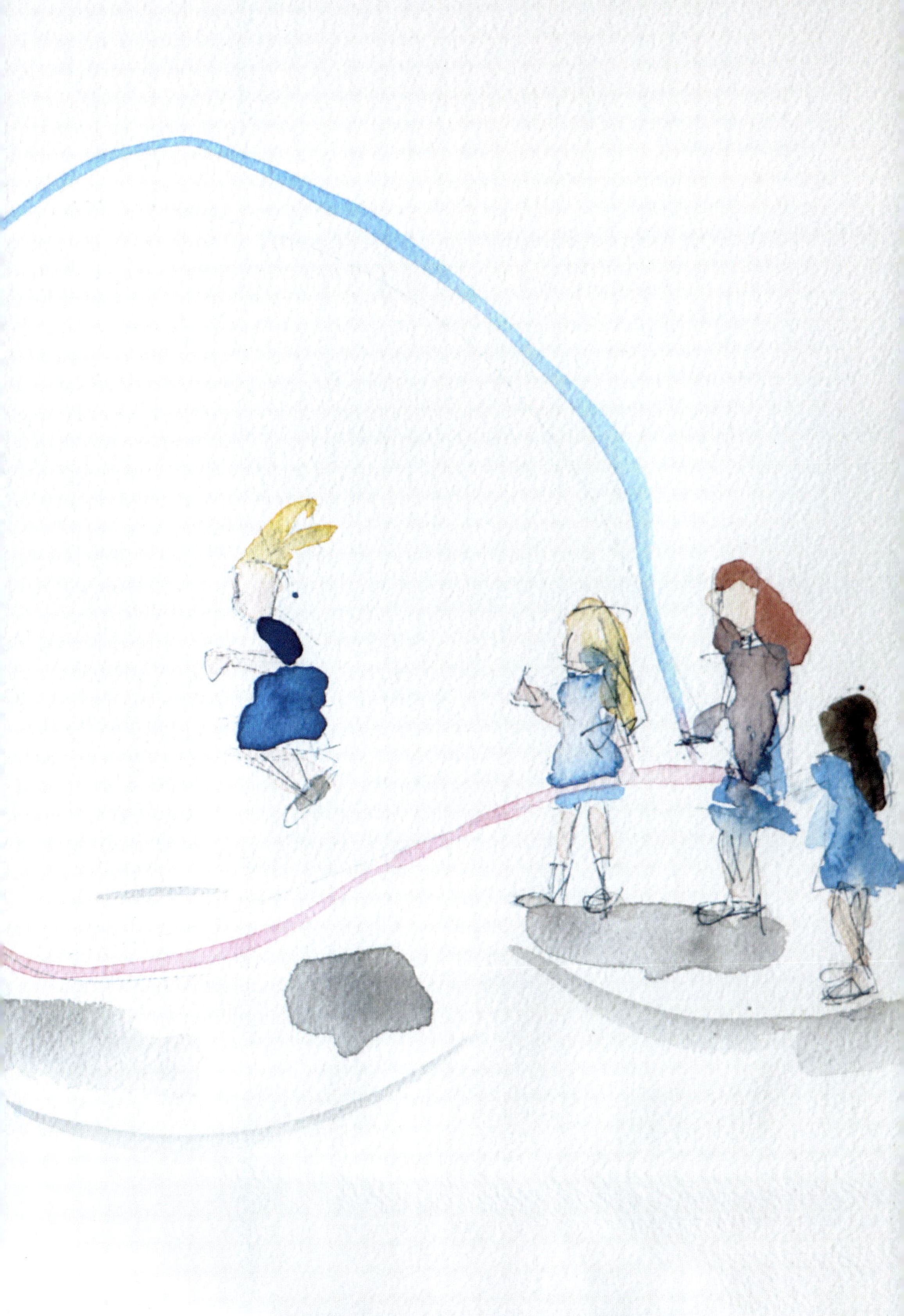

GIRL WITH BUN

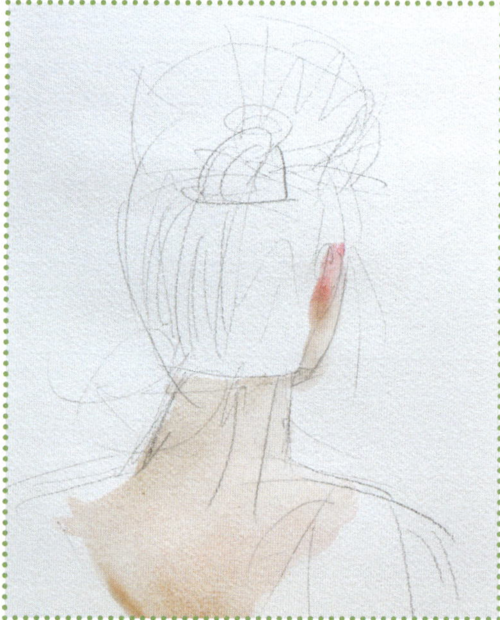

STEP 1:

Sketch the back of the neck and head with a high ponytail bun shape. Suggest a few of the hair strands and the direction they travel. Add a few wispy strands at the nape of the neck. Paint the back of the neck and shoulders.

FLESH & HAIR TONES

Flesh tones were always a mystery to me when I first started painting. Here, I break down how to come up with flesh and hair tones that work and look realistic. For the palette below, I used ochre, burnt sienna, lavender gray, opera rose, magenta, Payne's gray, and Venetian red.

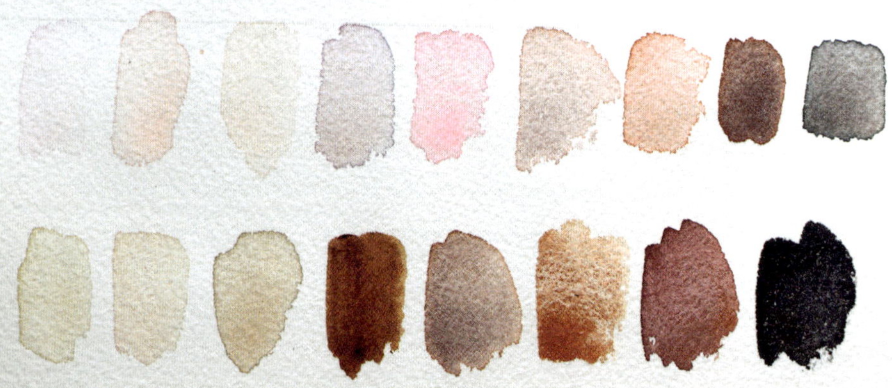

The first three colors are watered-down rose, burnt sienna, and yellow ochre. For warm tones, use mostly yellow, orange, and red earth tones like burnt sienna, earth oxides, and ochres. For cool tones, use more purple, blue, or gray. For saturated pops of bright red or pink, add more rose or red. Experiment with your own flesh tone palette and make a swatch of colors. Keep notes about each mixture to help you remember how you mixed it.

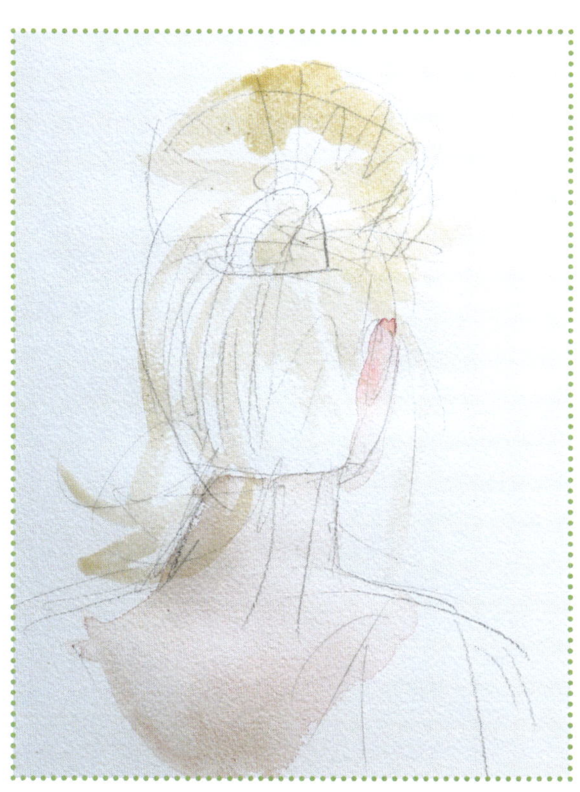

STEP 2:

For painting the bun, start with your lightest colors. In this case, the blonde highlights.

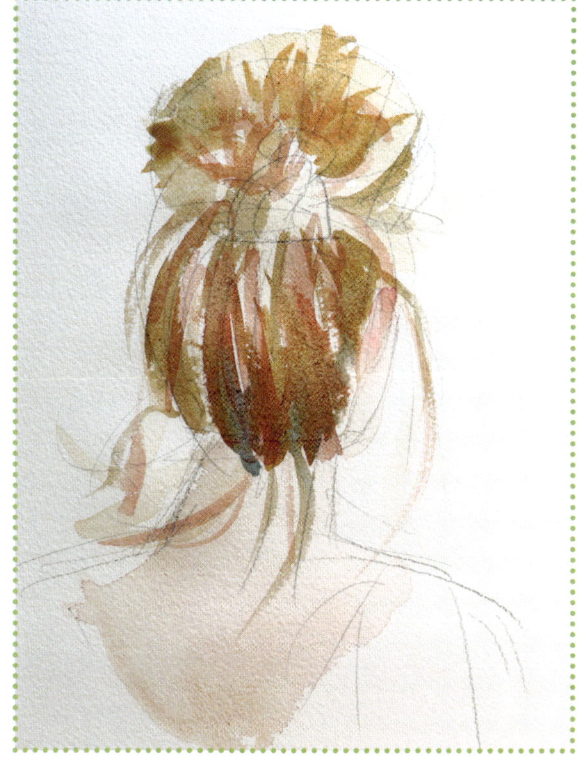

STEP 3:

Using the tip of a round brush, add some mid-tone browns and even dark gray or black to the base of the neck for the darkest areas and surrounding the ear. Add some brown wispy hairs along the nape of neck.

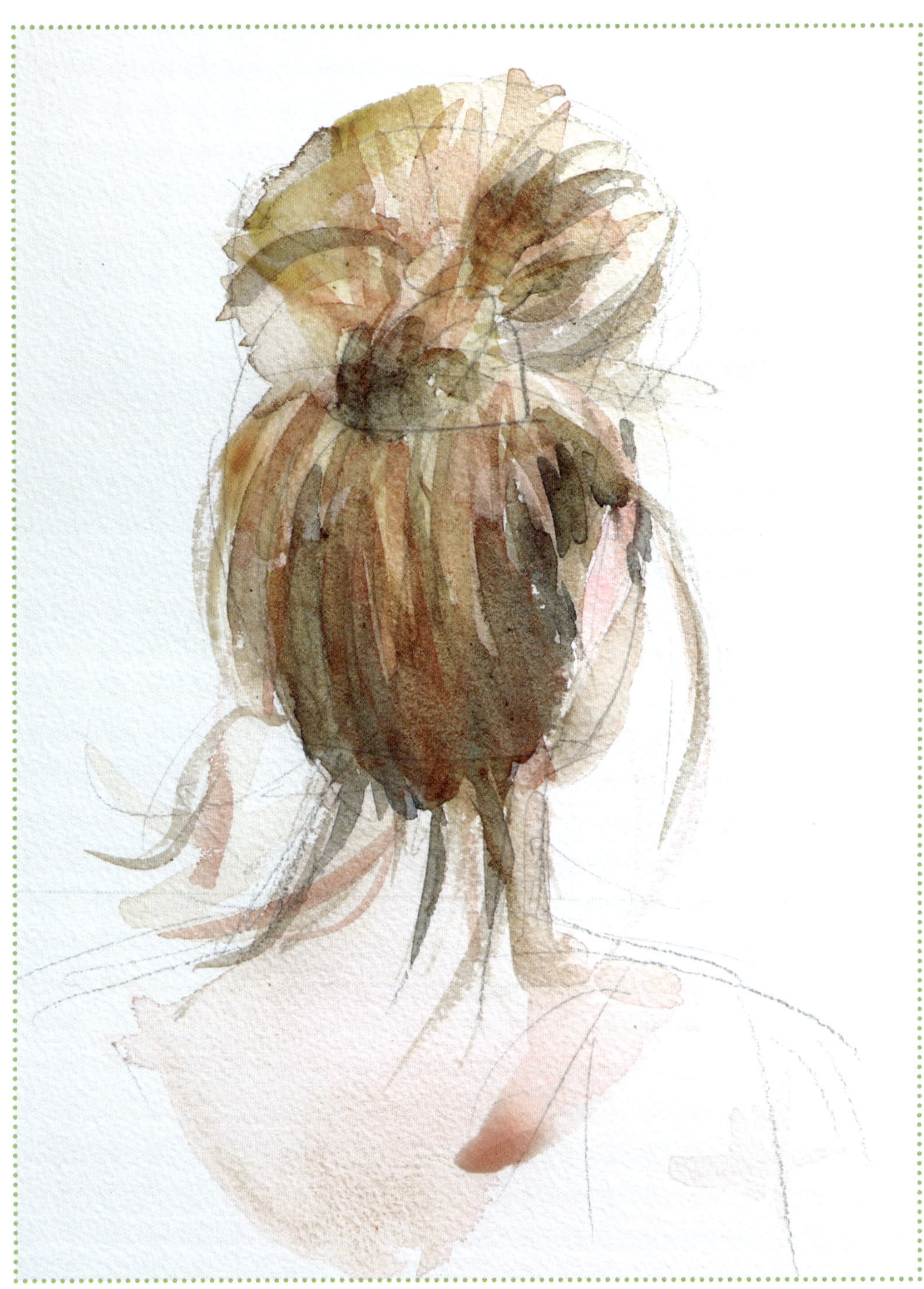

STEP 4:

Add some shaded flesh tones to right side of girl's neck and shoulder.

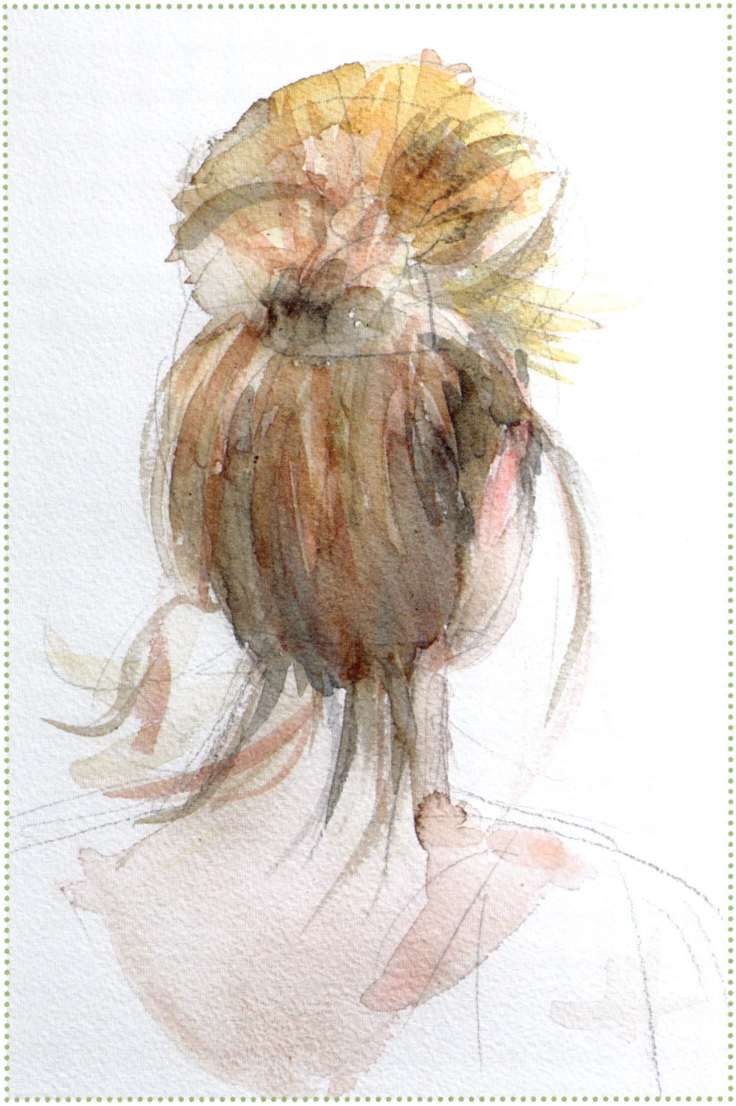

STEP 5:

Add more of the lightest shades as a wash to fill in any white space and add richness. I use golden yellow on top of the bun and the loose ends.

Use dark brown or gray to darken any areas that need increased value, especially around the ear and nape of the neck. While the paint is still wet, drag a small round brush through the paint to suggest even more strands of the hair.

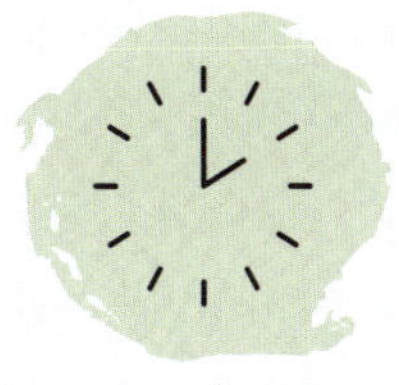

Quick Tip

Leave the clothing unpainted so the focus stays on the intricate details of the wispy hair.

MAN WITH PIGEONS

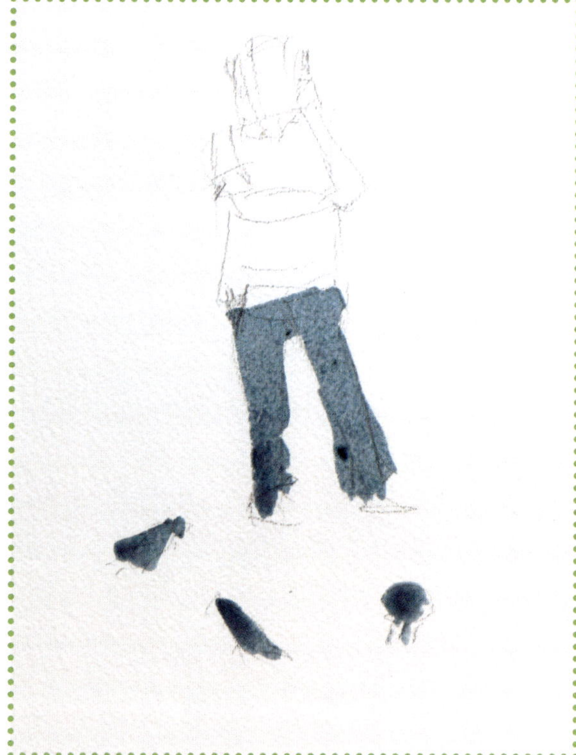

STEP 1:

Sketch a man standing with one arm across his body and the other hand near his face. Loosely sketch three pigeons on the ground in front of him.

Use Payne's gray or black paint to paint the man's pants and the bodies of the pigeons.

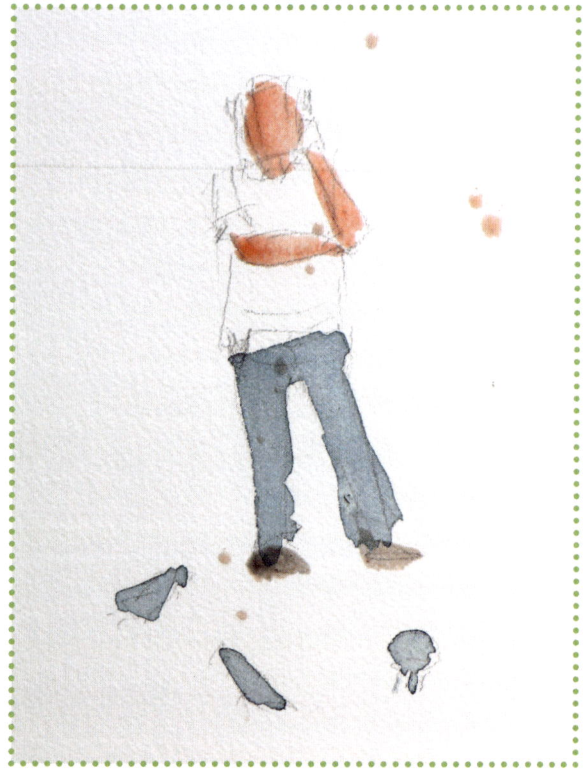

STEP 2:

Add pink pigeon legs and feet. Add the light blue shirt, and suggest hair with black or gray. Remember, keep minimal.

Add cast shadows to the man and pigeons. Add small beaks and any other details, as desired.

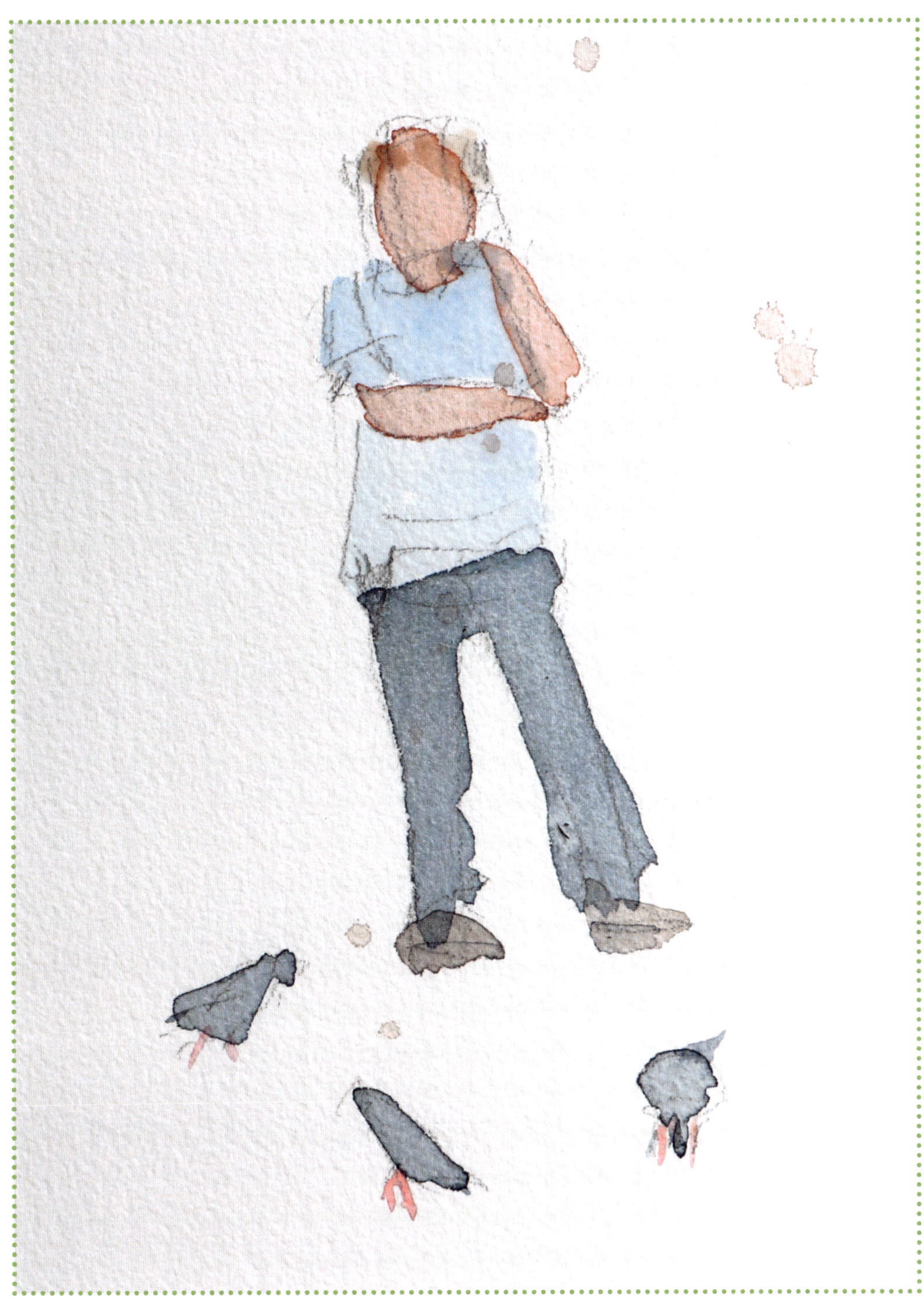

STEP 3:

Use flesh tones to paint the face, arms, and brown or gray shoes. If a few drips land on your painting, it's okay—it just adds to the effect of the watercolor.

Everyday Objects

What better way to create art than with everyday objects. Besides the personal touch, everyday objects are convenient and accessible. One can find serious, sentimental, and even whimsical objects for watercolor painting projects.

Supplies

- Watercolor paper (block or secured on board); I used an 8″ x 10″ block
- Medium round brush
- Medium flat brush
- Watercolor paints
- Colors: red, yellow, blue, transparent earth orange or oxide red lake, Payne's gray, black, white
- Palette for mixing paints
- Spray bottle (optional)
- Jar of water
- Tissue or paper towels for cleanup

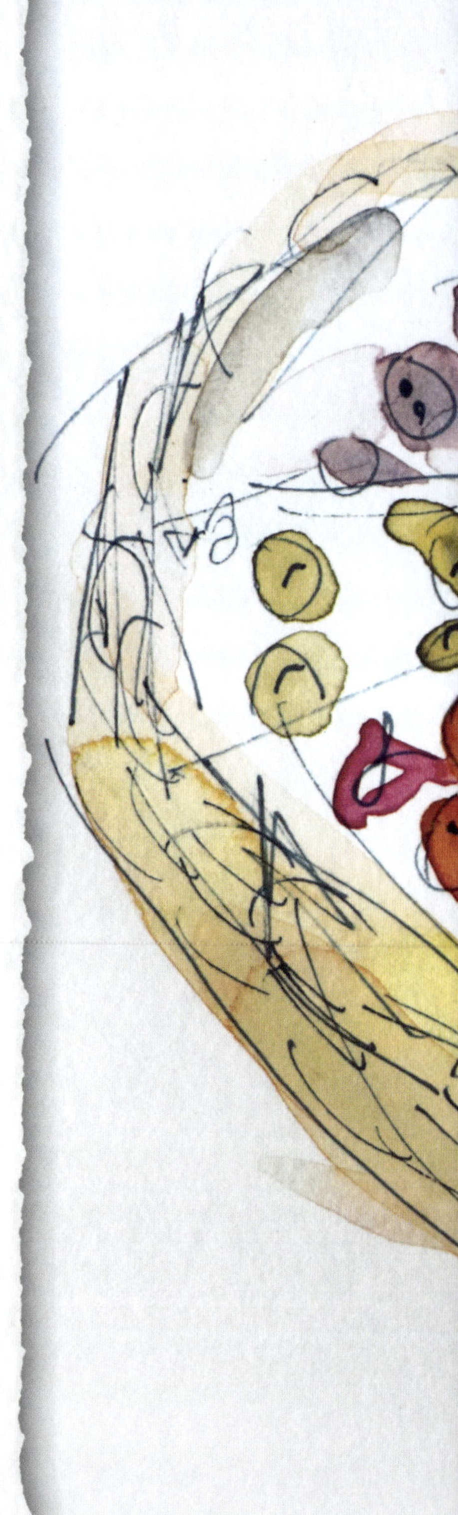

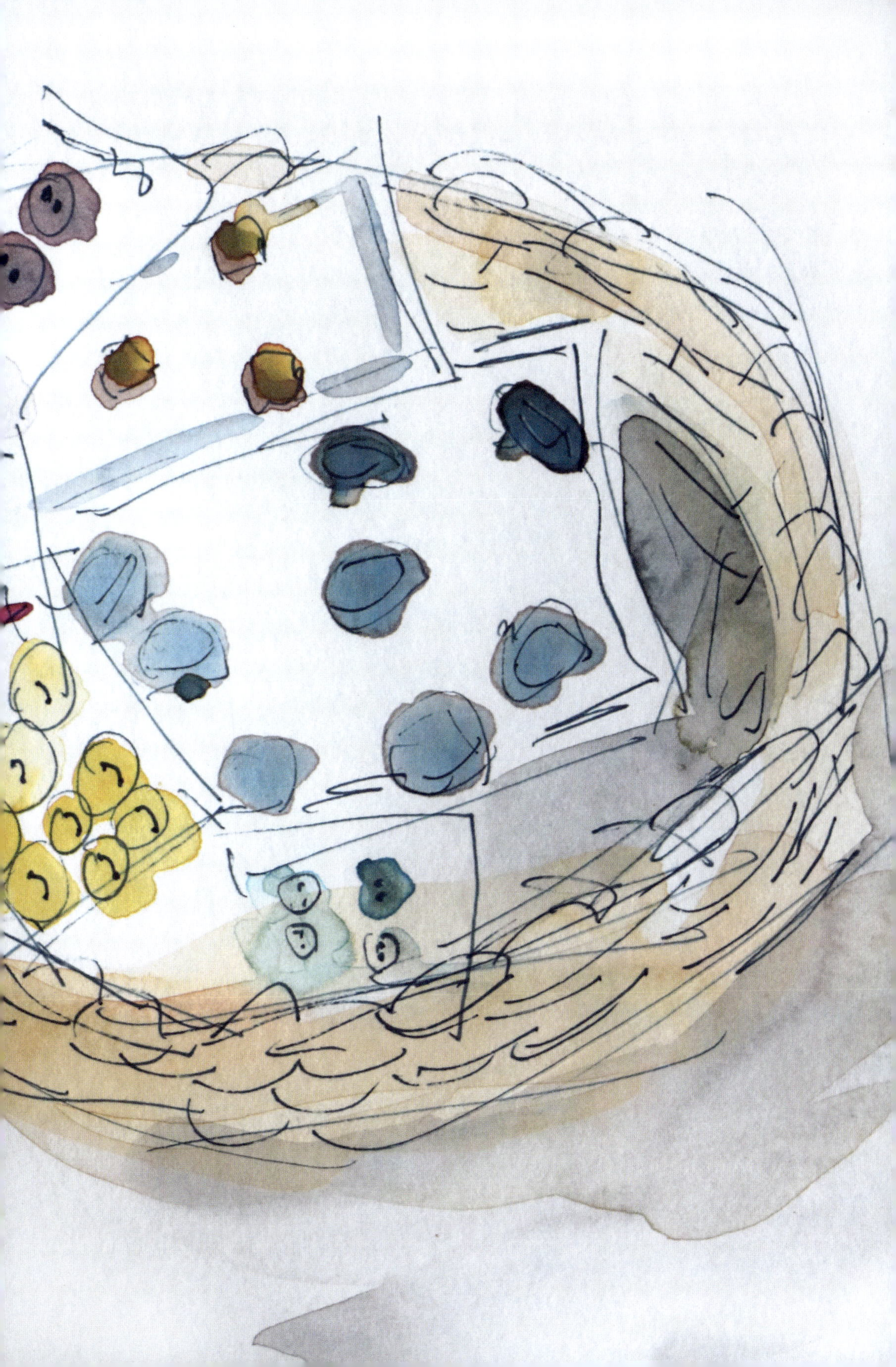

SILVERWARE

Find some old, tarnished silverware with interesting features and shapes. This project only requires two colors, Payne's gray and a transparent oxide red lake or transparent earth orange. Toward the end, I did add a bit of muted pink and yellow from my palette, but the project will work with only the two colors, if preferred.

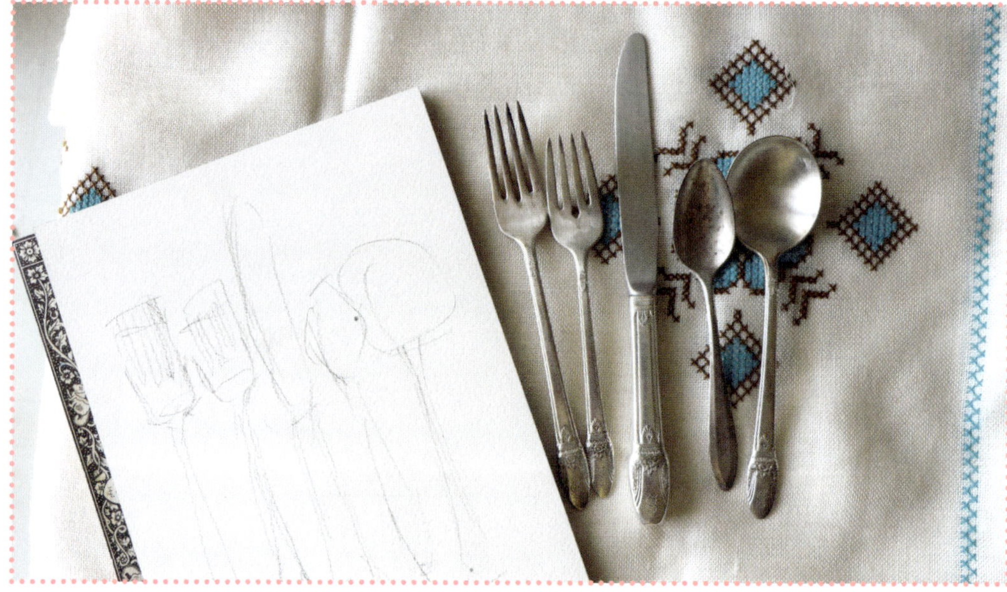

STEP 1:

Start by sketching the silverware onto your paper. I used my 8-by-10-inch watercolor paper block in portrait orientation (with the long side vertical). Place the tines and bowls of the spoons and forks first. Only sketch the basic shape and the edge of the handles. Don't worry about all the ornate details.

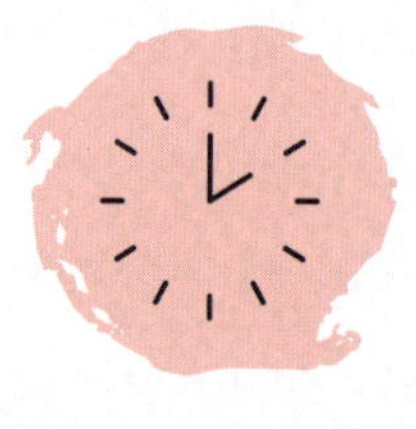

Quick Tip

It's okay if some of your lines cross inside the silverware—we are going to cover it with gray and brown paint anyway. But if there is graphite smeared outside the edges, go ahead and clean up the paper with an eraser.

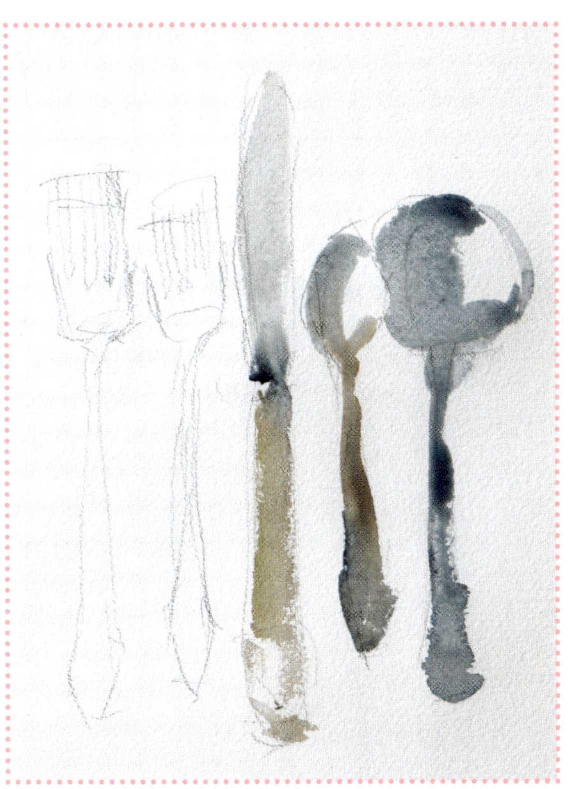

STEP 2:

Use the Payne's gray to paint the first spoon. Make sure to leave blank spots for the highlights on the shiny silverware. Add color anywhere you feel needs more detail or extra paint.

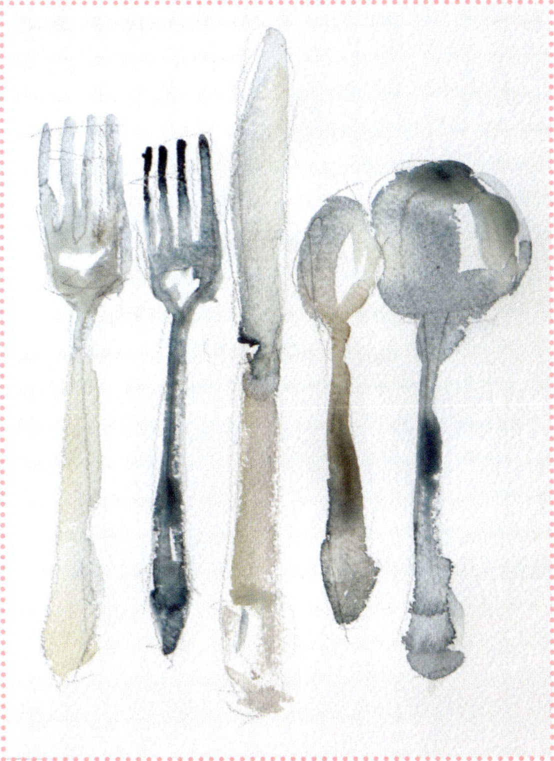

STEP 3:

Working wet-into-wet, add transparent earth orange or oxide red lake to create the tarnished parts or warmer tones of the silver.

BOTTLES

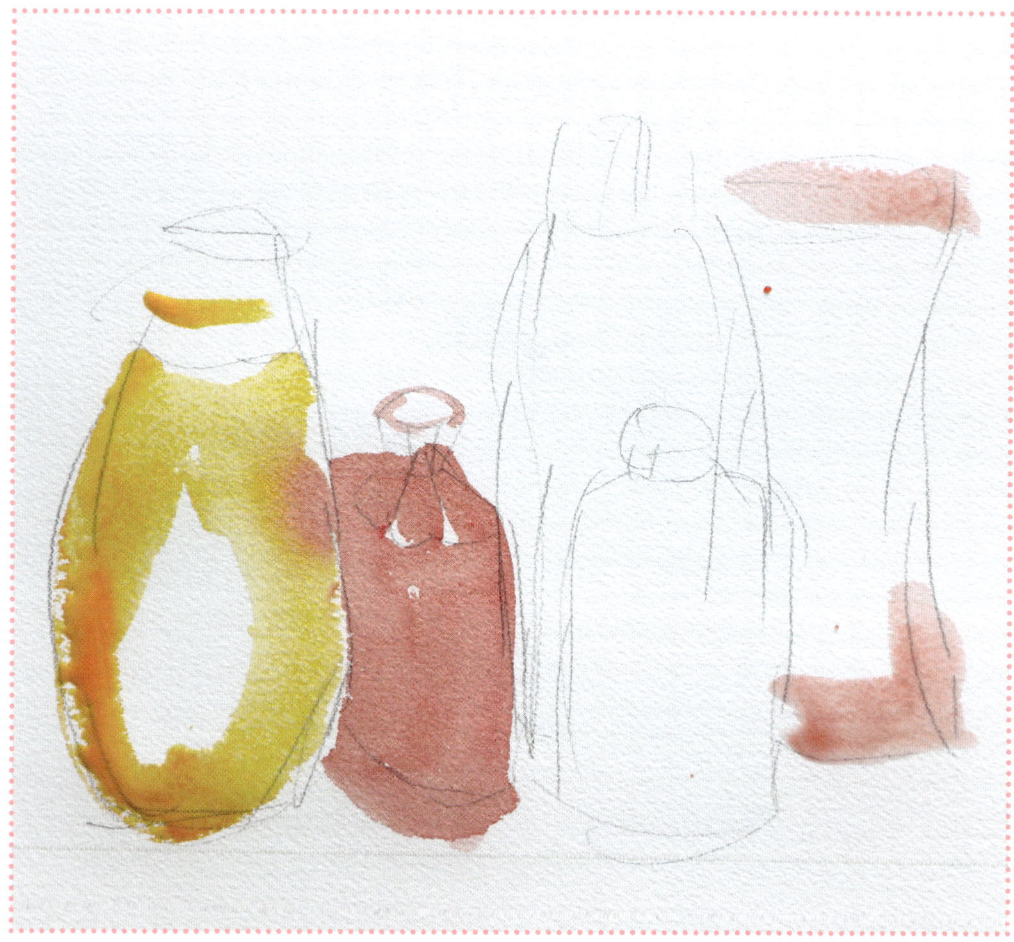

STEP 1:

Start your composition by marking on your paper where you want your bottles to be. Mark the bottoms and tops. Allow space so the composition doesn't get too close to the edges.

Use a round brush to paint the bottles of shampoo. For the first bottle, I mixed cadmium yellow and rose. I also used some warm pink for the second bottle and the shaded areas of the last tall bottle. After the paint has dried, if the bottle is clear, add a horizontal line to suggest the level of shampoo inside the bottle.

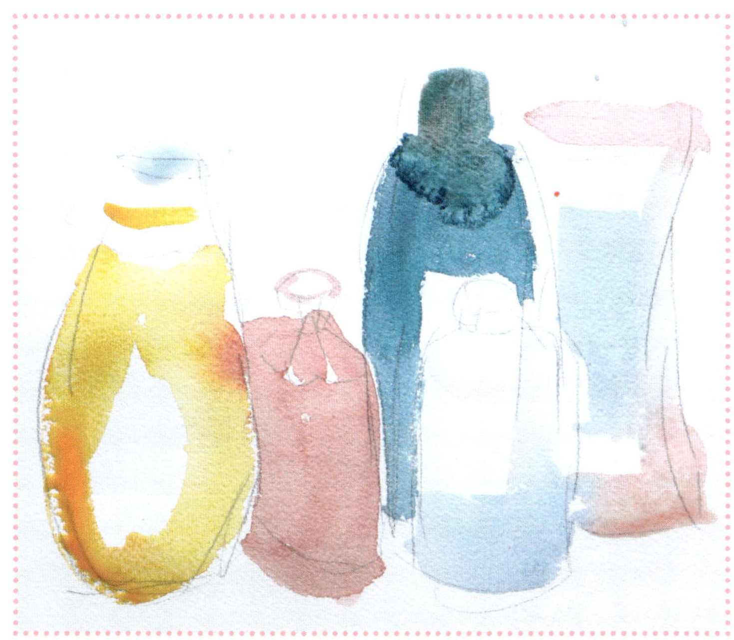

STEP 2:

I mixed a dark Berlin blue (MaimeriBlu) to paint the dark blue bottle and the label on the bottle to the right. When painting the labels, wait until the paint around the label is dry so the paint doesn't run.

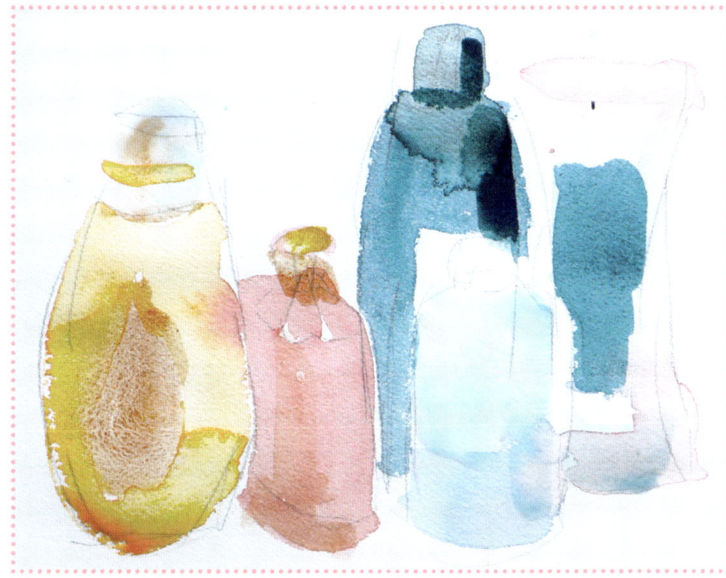

STEP 3:

Once dry, add more subtle colors for the shampoo bottle caps, labels, and shading. Just remember the colors will run together when painting wet-into-wet.

Mix some dark blue with transparent oxide red lake (or another brown) to make a dark mixture for the shadow side of the blue bottle. When most of the paint is dry, add some details to the bottles, such as the golden bottle cap on the rose bottle. Let dry.

STEP 4:

Using a mixture of the primary colors, add a gray shadow along the bottom of the bottles. Some of the wet paint from the bottles may blend into the shadow.

Add a horizon line about a third of the way down the paper to suggest the table behind the bottles. Place the horizon line either above or below the halfway point of the paper.

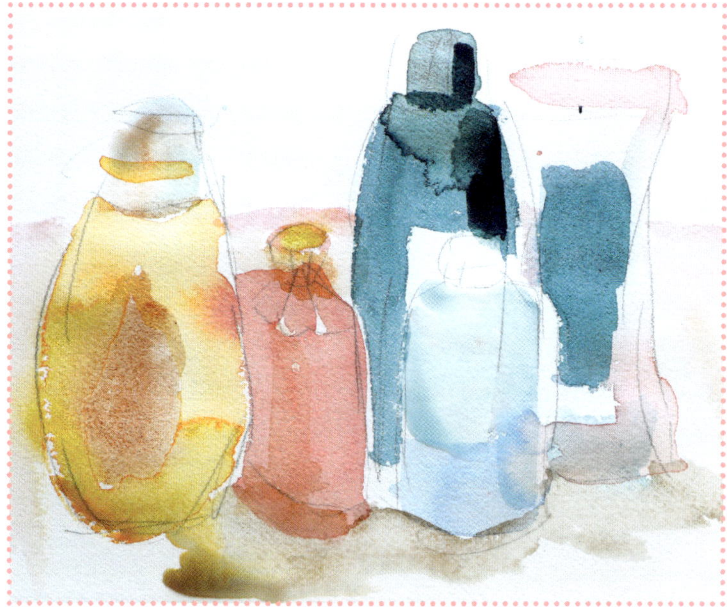

STEP 5:

Don't go overboard with the details. Suggest writing on some of the labels, which may run slightly into the wet colors for a loose and painterly effect. I also add a bit more color to the table and across the different facets of the bottles and caps. Let the painting dry completely.

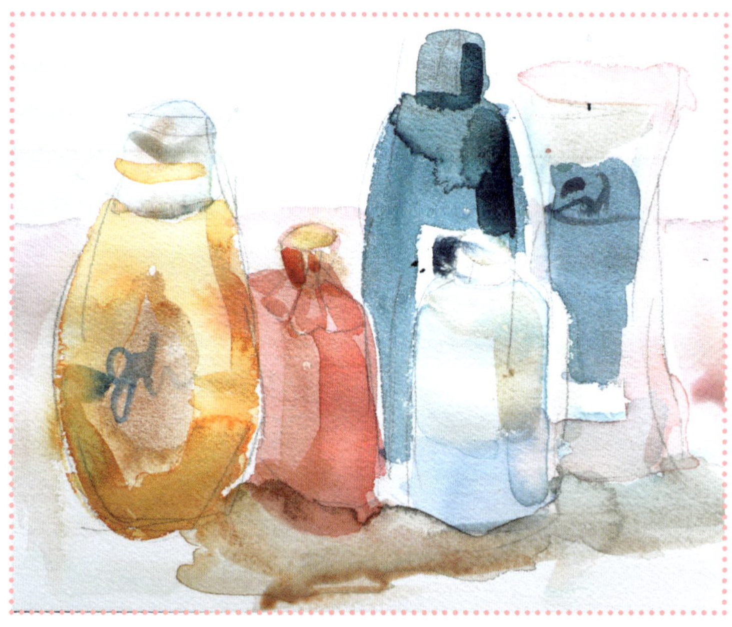

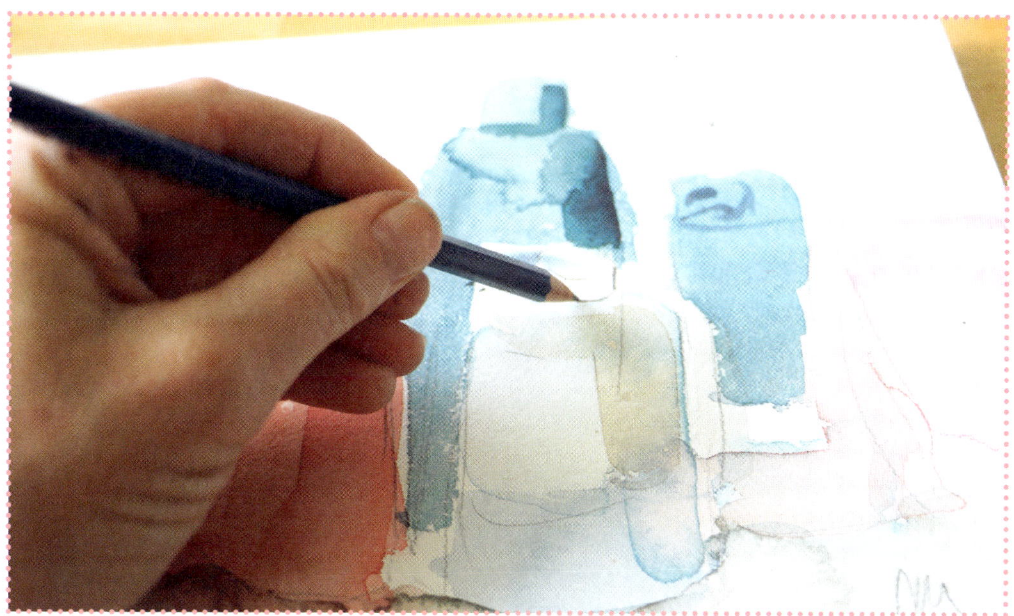

STEP 6:

Using a pencil, add any additional details and outlines. Again, avoid too many fine details to keep the painting loose. Here I outline some of the bottles' softer edges and add some details like label edges and bottle caps.

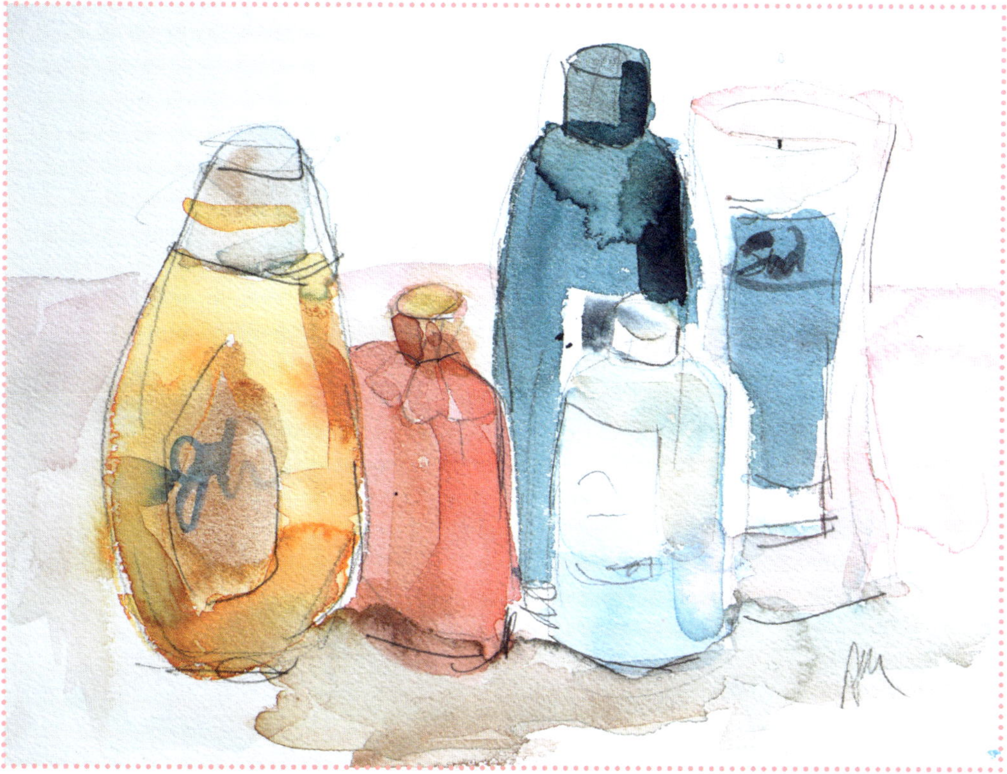

About the Author

Angela Moulton has been a full-time artist for 14 years. Self-taught, passionate, and determined, Angela learned to paint from many books, videos, and classes. From the very beginning, she was inspired by German American artist and teacher Hans Hofmann, a twentieth century abstract expressionist painter. Angela acknowledges the creative spark inside each individual that can find expression through painting.

Today, Angela has her own website and online gallery. She works with a few galleries and commercial clients in industries such as fashion, interior design, retail, and publishing. You can find her art everywhere from hotel lobbies to product packaging and greeting cards.

Angela was an art instructor at Elmhurst Art Museum. She currently hosts a YouTube channel with how-to videos for other artists. She also posts art daily on Instagram @angelamoultonart. Learn more at www.pratt-creek-art.myshopify.com and www.youtube.com/user/prattcreekart.

15 minute Painting
EFFORTLESS WATERCOLOR

Learn to paint in 15 minutes!

15-Minute Painting: Effortless Watercolor shows aspiring artists how to create accessible watercolor paintings with approachable, step-by-step projects and a few brushes and paints—perfect for the absolute beginner. After a quick overview of the basic tools and materials and an introduction to choosing and mixing colors, *Effortless Watercolor* demonstrates how to use just a few brushstrokes to create lively works of art in a simple, modern style.

Follow along step by step to create finished masterpieces, including birds, animals, still life, and more. Creative exercises and quick tips provide guidance along the way, from choosing the right brushes and paints to creating inspired works of art using easy painting techniques—in just 15 minutes!

CATEGORY: Art / Techniques / Watercolor Painting
ISBN: 978-1-60058-924-9

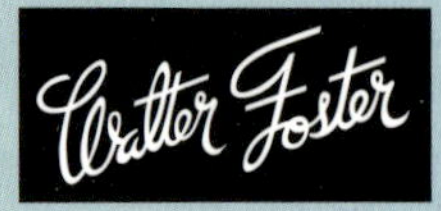

EAN 9 781600 589249 51899 MN1

$18.99 US / £14.99 UK / $25.99 CAN